WHAT YOU THOUGHT YOU KNEW ABOUT JUDAISM

341 Common Misconceptions about Jewish Life

Reuven P. Bulka

Jason Aronson Inc.
Northvale, New Jersey
London

Library of Congress Cataloging-in-Publication Data

Bulka, Reuven P.
  What you thought you knew about Judaism
by Reuven P. Bulka.
    p. cm.
  Bibliography: p.
  Includes index.
  ISBN 0-87668-867-9
  1. Judaism—Customs and practices.   I. Title.
BM700.B85   1989   89-171
296—dc19   CIP

Manufactured in the United States of America. Jason Aronson Inc. offers books and cassettes. For information and catalog write to Jason Aronson Inc., 230 Livingston Street, Northvale, New Jersey 07647.

To
Yocheved and Moshe,
our first married couple

Contents

PART V: **FOOD FOR THOUGHT—THOUGHT FOR FOOD**

PART VI: **PAST AND PRESENT**

Introduction

Every rabbi, while interacting with congregants, is occasionally called upon to correct misconceptions. Sometimes the misconception is a serious matter that involves a gross distortion of Judaism; sometimes it is of a less serious nature, but nevertheless demands correction.

Rabbis are well served by knowing how to approach these delicate situations with the utmost of tact. This means presenting the correct information in a nonthreatening, nonaccusatory, and nonjudgmental manner, with full appreciation of the congregant's background, which may explain why the congregant has made the mistaken assumption.

Having served in the rabbinate for many years, I have been faced with more than the occasional misconception. Not long ago, it struck me that this was not a unique experience at all, that in fact every rabbi goes through it. It seemed reasonable to assume that many individuals carry misconceptions with them, mistaken ideas that have not yet been addressed, primarily because they have not come to the fore. It was with the intent of addressing these individuals that I undertook to write this book, a book of the more frequent erroneous notions about Judaism, and why or how they are incorrect.

A funny thing happened on my way to writing the book. What began with excitement, even exuberance, developed into trepidation.

How does one decide what constitutes a popular misconception? Whom does one ask? Obviously, there are individuals well versed in Judaism, who already know everything in this book and even more. On the other hand, there are some glaring misconceptions that prevail within the Jewish community, not only among those with little or no Jewish education, but even among the more informed members of the community. Where does one draw the line?

Then there is the question of what constitutes a misconception. Were one to compose a treatise, filling in all the facts about Jewish history and practice that most people do not know, this would be an encyclopedia of many volumes. How does one decide what is significant enough to be discussed in this book?

Then there is the trepidation about omitting the obvious—a topic that can never really be explained in a cursory review. Indeed, as the book was developing, and one myth was set down on paper, others came to mind. Yet, the fear persisted that on the day after publication, I would think of other myths that should have been included. It was not an easy fear to manage.

Therefore, this book is presented with much hesitation— hesitation that comes more from what is not presented than from what is.

Moreover, there is also hesitation about what *is* in the book. This volume should *not* be used as a legal text. It is intended to open eyes, not to render decisions. Decisions based on issues raised here should be made in consultation with one's rabbi. This book is not intended to be the final word; it is intended only to stimulate thinking, to correct common misconceptions.

Cataloging the material was not an easy matter. Some items fit quite snugly into definite topic areas, but others either fit into two or more topic areas, or into none at all. I hope the reader will forgive the unavoidable arbitrariness of some placements.

The book is divided into six sections, and each section is further divided into two chapters. A quick look at the contents pages gives the picture quite clearly.

In order to maintain easy readability, the sources for the

text and for the quotations appear in a separate section at the back of the book. Also, only basic and readily available sources are cited, pointing the way to further explanation.

I am most grateful to Arthur Kurzweil, whose excitement about the book actually energized me to tackle it with more vigor and dispatch. The equal excitement and vigor of my secretary, Blanche Osterer, brought this work into manuscript form.

Special thanks and appreciation go to my dear wife, Naomi. Although occupied with countless responsibilities, she still found the time to wield her skillful editorial scalpel to make the work more coherent.

Reuven P. Bulka
Ottawa, Ontario
Canada

Part I

SPECIAL EVENTS AND SPECIAL DAYS

1

Special Events

Birth and Brit
Redemption
Bar Mitzvah and Bat Mitzvah
Conversion

Misconception: In Jewish tradition, a child is named only after someone who is deceased.

This statement reflects Ashkenazic tradition. However, within the Sephardic community, this is not the case. In the Sephardic community, children are often given the name of a grandparent who is still alive.

Custom is very important in the development of community. Custom does not deal with matters of right and wrong, but with prevailing practice within a community. What is acceptable for the Sephardic community may not be customary in the Ashkenazic community. Each can and should maintain its own customs, while respecting the practices of the other.

Misconception: Every Jewish child should have both a Hebrew name and a name for everyday use.

Jewish people outside of Israel are unique in giving their children two names. In previous generations, when being Jewish was dangerous, the idea of having a Hebrew or Yiddish name, to be used within the Jewish community, and another name, to be used for one's involvements outside the Jewish world, was an understandable necessity.

Today, however, especially in North American society, this is hardly the case. One is not compelled to hide one's Jewish identity, and being Jewish is rarely an impediment to gaining employment or advancing in the business world.

There is simply no reason to give any child two names.

At home now in a society that places few restrictions on one's identity affirmation, it seems slightly absurd that Jews should attempt to hide that identity. Thanks to the State of Israel, the world at large has already become familiar with modern Hebrew names as well as the ancient ones. They know Hayyim, Simha, Menahem, Moshe, Geula, Golda, Hannah, Shulamit, and have no problems with such names. Neither should we.

Misconception: The circumcision of a child always takes place on the eighth day.

Usually, the *brit milah* of a newborn male takes place on the eighth day following birth. Thus, a child born during the day on Wednesday, would be circumcised the following Wednesday.

However, this is not always the case. There are occasions when the circumcision cannot take place on the eighth day.

When the child is premature or has health problems which would make it potentially dangerous, circumcision is postponed until the child is of sufficient weight and healthy.

If a child is born during twilight on Friday afternoon, the circumcision cannot take place on the eighth day. Since twilight is a period of doubt, the doubt being whether the twilight belongs to the previous day or to the following day, we do not know if the child is considered to have been born on Friday or on Saturday.

Because of this, the circumcision cannot take place on Friday, since the possibility exists that twilight belongs to Saturday; this would mean that the circumcision is taking place on the seventh day, which is prohibited. On the other hand, the circumcision may not take place on *Shabbat*, since the twilight might possibly belong to Friday, in which case *Shabbat* is not the eighth day, but the ninth day. Circumcision can be performed on *Shabbat* only when it is definitely the eighth day.

What is done in such circumstances? The circumcision is delayed until Sunday, which may be the ninth or the tenth day, but it is still the earliest possible time that it can take place.

Misconception: If a child is born on *Shabbat*, then the *brit milah* of that child always takes place on *Shabbat*.

The statement is generally (but not always) true. Barring any mitigating circumstances, the circumcision of a Jewish child born on *Shabbat* would take place on *Shabbat* itself.

But there are mitigating circumstances. For example, if the child is not born by natural childbirth, but is delivered instead via Caesarean section, then the child's *brit* (circumcision) will not take place on *Shabbat*. Instead it will be held on the following Sunday. The reason for this is that the biblical requirement for actually permitting the circumcision on the *Shabbat* is predicated on a natural childbirth, so that *Shabbat* is truly the child's eighth day.

There are some authorities who suggest that even a child born on *Shabbat* after labor was induced, should not be circumcised on *Shabbat*, since we do not know if the child would actually have been born on *Shabbat* with non-induced labor.

In other words, when there is an intervention that compromises the natural aspect of the birth process, it also disallows the *brit milah* from being held on *Shabbat*.

Misconception: The ideal time for circumcision is at noon.

Many families schedule the circumcision of their child for noon of the eighth day (or the day circumcision actually takes place). However, this is not done as a fulfillment of a legal requirement; it is more a matter of convenience.

In actuality, circumcision on the eighth day (or any day subsequent to the eighth day) can take place anytime from the morning until just before evening.

However, the best time for circumcision, indeed, the best time for fulfilling all religious obligations, is as early in the day as possible. It is one of the hallmarks of our exercise of responsibility that we avoid procrastination, fulfilling our obligations at the earliest opportunity. Thus, beginning the day with the morning prayers, and following immediately with the circumcision is most consistent with the principles of Judaism.

Misconception: Having a professional *mohel* perform the *brit milah* is altogether proper.

This statement is based on the assumption that since circumcision is an intricate procedure demanding expertise, it is better that one who is experienced in doing circumcisions actually perform the *brit milah*.

This is part of an ongoing trend concerning many areas of Jewish life that have fallen into the hands of professionals, areas that are the province of parents.

In reality, the obligation of circumcision rests with the child's father. It is the father who must circumcise the child, as much as he is obligated to raise the child, educate the child, and even provide the educational training needed to make a living.

The *ideal* would be if the father *actually* performed the circumcision. However, since many fathers are not able to perform this delicate procedure, they ask a professional, called a *mohel*, to do the job for them. But, prior to the circumcision, it is *imperative* that the father *appoint* the *mohel* to act in his stead, to do that which the father ought to do.

Misconception: Godparents are a basic component of a circumcision.

At the circumcision, the ceremony that launches the child into the covenantal community, there are a number of important players. In addition to the child and his parents, they include the couple who bring the baby into the room, the one who actually performs the circumcision (the *mohel*), and the one who holds the baby during the circumcision.

In contemporary times, many families have seen fit to add godparents to the roster. But the very term "godparents" is a questionable appellation. Using "god" as a prefix for any human being's title is arrogant, to say the least, and quite possibly, even sacrilegious.

Aside from that, honoring individuals with this title, and the attendant responsibility to raise the child (should anything happen to the parents) is a dubious action: (1) it is very rare that those who have been named as the godparents, or more precisely, the potential parental surrogates, actually assume this role later on; (2) if, God forbid, a tragedy should occur within a family, necessitating a restructuring of family responsibilities, this is a responsibility that no one may evade, but is usually taken over by the closest relatives. Ironically, the closest relatives are not always the ones chosen to be the godparents.

The custom of naming godparents is essentially a foreign intrusion onto the Jewish scene. It adds very little and actually detracts from the circumcision ceremony.

Misconception: A newborn son of Jewish parents who has not been circumcised is not Jewish.

At a *brit milah* the comment is often heard that now, because circumcision has taken place, the child has entered the Jewish fold.

There is something to the remark, but not precisely what may be intended. The circumcision formally brings the child into the Covenant of Abraham with God. This is not related to the individual's status as a Jew.

Whether the child is Jewish or not depends on whether the mother is Jewish. If the mother is Jewish, the child is Jewish. A child of a Jewish mother who has not yet been circumcised has not formally entered into the Covenant of Abraham, but he is still Jewish.

Misconception: All first-born sons are required to have a *pidyon haben.*

The general assumption is that any son who is the first-born child of his parents must be redeemed at the age of thirty days. Although this is the general rule, there are many exceptions.

1. A child who is born by Caesarean section is not required to have the *pidyon haben* (redemption ceremony).
2. A child whose father is a *Kohen* or *Levi* does not require a *pidyon haben.*
3. If the child's mother is the daughter of either a Priest or a Levite, her child as well is not required to have a *pidyon haben.*

Very often, when surprised parents are told that they are exempt and not required to redeem their son, they lament the fact that they are deprived of a good reason for a party.

This exemption is intended not as the denial of a reason to celebrate, but as a "tax break" for the parents. Not being required to have a *pidyon haben* means that the parents need not spend the sum involved in redeeming the child from the *Kohen.* The Priest cannot demand the redemption money, and this is an advantage to the parents who are excused from this financial obligation.

There is always much reason to celebrate the birth of a child, male or female, but the exemption from *pidyon haben* was never intended to be a denial of a *simhah* (joy). Rather, it was the removal of a potentially onerous financial responsibility.

Misconception: For redemption of the first-born son, five coins should be used.

This assumption is based on the biblical statement that the redemption of a first-born son is achieved through the giving of five shekels. Naturally, one could easily jump to the conclusion that what was then five shekels is today five silver dollars.

However, this is not necessarily the case. The five shekels were less a matter of currency, and more a matter of silver weight. The five silver shekels added up to a specific weight. The problem—what was that weight, and how do we relate that weight to the contemporary context?

By various calculations, it appears that approximately 110 grams is equivalent to the five shekels of biblical times. This means that for the redemption ceremony, the parent must transfer a weight equivalent to five shekels, or 110 grams of silver, to the *Kohen*. Often, the silver dollar of a country may be only partly silver, or not silver at all.

It would, therefore, be important to know the weight of the coin, and how much of that weight is actual silver weight. Having calculated this, it is possible to know how many coins must be used for the redemption. Often, it is at least six coins that are needed, rather than the traditionally assumed five.

Misconception: Redemption of the first-born son is a once-in-a-lifetime experience.

Inasmuch as a family can have only one first-born child, it would seem that at the very most, one can experience redeeming one's first-born son only once in a lifetime.

However, this is not necessarily the case. If the first marriage terminates, and the husband remarries and has a child by his second wife, and the child is the first-born son of the second wife, that child too must be redeemed. All depends upon whether the child "opens the womb" of the mother, and is the *mother's first son*. A child born by Caesarean section does not open the womb; a child born subsequent to a Caesarean section, which does open the womb, is not the first-born son. Thus, it is only the first son who is also a womb-opening child, who must be redeemed.

A man who marries more than once, and in each instance is blessed with a first-born son, experiences more than one redemption of the first-born son.

Misconception: All first-born sons receive a double portion of inheritance.

Although it is generally the case that the first-born son receives a double share of the inheritance, this does not apply to a child who is first-born by Caesarean section. A child born naturally, after another born through Caesarean section, would likewise not be considered first-born. Even though such a child is the first naturally born, it is not the first.

Likewise, a first-born son who is born after the death of his father, does not claim a double portion.

First born for inheritance purposes suggests there was another child. How is this possible if the first born comes into the world after the father's death?

It is possible if the mother gave birth to twins. Had the father been alive, the first-born son of the twins could claim a double portion, but if the father passed away before the birth of the twins, that child does not have such claim.

In order to claim a double portion, which is a monetary claim, circumstances must satisfy specific parameters delineated in the *Torah*.

Misconception: A boy attains the status of *Bar Mitzvah* at the age of thirteen.

A child becomes a *Bar Mitzvah*, one who is required to fulfill religious obligations, after reaching the age of 13 and having entered into the fourteenth year. It is specifically the entry into the fourteenth year, 13 years plus one day, that signals the child's becoming a *Bar Mitzvah*.

Misconception: A girl attains the status of *Bat Mitzvah* at the age of 12.

Again, as with the case of a *Bar Mitzvah*, it is not being 12 that is the key factor; instead it is the entry into the thirteenth year that is the decisive consideration, assuming that the extent of biological maturation is appropriate to the age.

For boys and girls, the precise time a child attains the status of an adult is upon entry into the fourteenth or thirteenth year, respectively. Regardless of what time the child was born, the day of birth counts as a complete day. Subsequently, 13 or 12 years later, with entry into the first day of the next year, one becomes responsible to fulfill religious duties as an adult.

It is also important to note that the girl's age of maturation is not the same as a boy's. Girls generally mature earlier, and thus they reach their age of responsibility one year earlier than boys.

Although this may seem to be a legal fiction with no practical implications, this is not the case. For example, based on the fact that only an adult can lead the congregation in services, with some liturgical exceptions, it is important to pinpoint precisely when the child becomes an adult. More importantly, the matter of when the child graduates from "learning about" to "being obligated" to is the key issue.

In fact, the age for *Bar Mitzvah* and *Bat Mitzvah* should really be more dependent on the child's maturational level on attaining the stage of puberty, rather than on the more arbitrary age of 13 or 12. However, the more personal and subjective criterion for maturity is fraught with difficulties and potential embarrassment for those who reach puberty either very early or very late. Stipulating a specific age for religious responsibility becomes a communal norm, and everyone is, therefore, more comfortable.

Misconception: A child born in the month of February would become *Bar Mitzvah* or *Bat Mitzvah* in the month of February.

The child's secular birthday is irrelevant in terms of calculating when the child becomes obligated to fulfill the precepts. The age of *Bar Mitzvah* or *Bat Mitzvah* is calculated as either 13 years plus a day or 12 years plus a day, respectively, from the Hebrew date of birth. At times, the date might come close to the secular birthday, but it is entirely possible that a child born in February could become *Bar Mitzvah* in January or March. Discrepancies of more than just a few days are entirely possible, especially when the *Bar Mitzvah* year is in a Hebrew leap year and the year of birth was not, or vice versa.

Misconception: The *Bar Mitzvah* ceremony must take place on *Shabbat*.

Bar Mitzvah, the ceremony signifying a boy's entry into Jewish adulthood, involves his reciting a blessing over the *Torah*. This signifies his new status as an adult member of the community, by virtue of doing that which only an adult can do.

This call to the *Torah* can take place on any day when the *Torah* is read. It could be on a Monday or a Thursday, on a *Rosh Hodesh* (New Moon), a festival, even on the Day of Atonement.

Yes, it may take place on *Shabbat*, but that is not mandatory.

Misconception: The reading of the *Haftorah* is an appropriate choice for a *Bar Mitzvah*.

The most logical choice to indicate that an individual has reached a specific stage is an expression that could not be evoked in the previous stage. It would be appropriate for the *Bar Mitzvah* to recite something on the day that he reaches maturity that he could not recite previously.

The irony of all this is that one need not be a *Bar Mitzvah* in order to recite a *Haftorah*, the prophetic reading which follows the *Shabbat* or festival *Torah* reading. A child of seven years old who is able to properly recite the *Haftorah* may be called for that purpose, and he may also recite the blessings for reading of the last part of the *Torah*.

Bar Mitzvah boys usually choose the *Haftorah* as their *Bar Mitzvah* trump card. Reading the *Torah*, leading the congregation as the *hazzan* (cantor), or having an *aliyah* (being among the basic seven who are called to the *Torah*) are more significant indications that the youth is actually entering into responsible religious adulthood.

The choice of *Haftorah* is not without its own logic. Thirteen is the basic age of responsibility, but some children have not matured biologically by that age. Rather than create problems associated with dubious maturity, the choice of a significant, yet problem-free, reading has become the norm.

Misconception: A child who is not a *Bar Mitzvah* or a *Bat Mitzvah* cannot assume representative adult responsibility.

Bar Mitzvah or *Bat Mitzvah* is not an initiation rite, as it is commonly understood. A child becomes responsible as an adult upon attaining the age of responsibility, the fourteenth year for a boy or the thirteenth year for a girl. The ceremony is merely a public declaration of this status, but the status itself is independent of the public experience. One is not pronounced a *Bar Mitzvah* or a *Bat Mitzvah*; one automatically becomes obligated to fulfill the precepts.

Misconception: The present rate of assimilation is unprecedented in Jewish history.

What is unprecedented in Jewish history is the scope of freedom and opportunity that is available to Jews who reside in a democratic society, especially in North America. With greater opportunity also comes the greater likelihood that assimilation will occur. This does not mean that assimilation must occur, but obviously the chances are greater.

Those who are imbued with a strong sense of the vitality of Jewish values will repel the assimilationist tendency, and instead will integrate these values into their life-style.

The intermarriage rate today is much higher than it has been in previous generations, primarily because the opportunity is there. However, many generations ago, the problem of assimilation was more pronounced. One such instance was in the time of Ezra, and a more pointed example was in the period of the Maccabean revolt, the revolt which gave birth to the festival of *Hanukah*, in the second century B.C.E. The Hasmonean uprising began with only a handful of Jews, because the majority of the population had already become assimilated and saw no reason to fight for their religious autonomy. The miracle of *Hanukah* was such a vital moment in Jewish history, not only because the Jews returned to the *Bet Hamikdash* (the Temple), but also because the Jews returned to their roots.

Misconception: Conversion is discouraged, because Judaism does not welcome converts.

It is the general procedure for a rabbi meeting a prospective convert to use various means of discouraging the convert.

Generations ago, the conversion process did not take more than an hour or so; it was condensed into a short period of time. Because it was condensed, the "discouraging" was less than subtle.

In the contemporary situation, the conversion procedure takes significantly longer, and one need not discourage the convert three times at the first meeting.

Additionally, the reason for discouraging the convert must be more fully appreciated. Judaism does not discourage converts, but it also does not seek to find them. Judaism has never espoused the belief that righteous individuals who are not Jewish are therefore denied a claim to eternal life. No one is condemned for not being Jewish.

Therefore, there is no desire to force individuals to accept Judaism, as if that is the only way to salvation. The Judaic accent is on universal righteousness.

However, if one sincerely wants to join the ranks of the Jewish community, then the Jewish community's reaction should be one of delight at the prospect, assuming that the reason for joining is not suspect. For the conversion to be meaningful, the convert must be apprised of all the dangers and pitfalls associated with being Jewish. A convert who is simply ushered along in a facile manner without being made aware of the potential problems of converting, enters the Jewish fold with blinders on, and may be heading for a rude awakening later on.

Rather than subjecting the would-be convert to this possibly devastating experience, we insist on discouraging the convert. This discouragement forces the convert to take a more sober look at the situation. If, in spite of the discouragement, the convert still pushes forward, we can at least be more confident that the convert is making this significant change fully aware of its implications.

Jews must stand in awe and admiration of individuals who make an obviously overwhelming gesture to embrace Judaism. As excited as the community may be about the prospect, it cannot be so eager for this boost to its ego, that it is oblivious to the ultimate welfare of the prospective convert. If, through discouragement, the convert actually rethinks the matter and has a change of heart, then the discouragement has done exactly what it was intended to do—to screen out those whose understanding of the implications of the conversion is minimal.

Misconception: If a prospective convert approaches a rabbi because of the desire to marry a Jewish person, that applicant is automatically rejected.

The idea of conversion for the purpose of marriage is alien to the Jewish community. Acceptance is predicated on the convert's desire to embrace Judaism for its own sake and on its own terms.

In previous generations, when conversion was a brief process, if the purpose of conversion was related to marriage, then the convert would have been rejected.

Even today, if the convert seeks to embrace Judaism for an ulterior motive (most often, for the purpose of marrying a Jew), then the conversion itself is suspect. It does not augur well for the prospective convert, or for the marriage, if a significant change has been undertaken with less than wholehearted dedication. This makes a mockery of the process and sets the stage for future recrimination.

However, there is now a significant span of time between the prospective convert's first meeting and the completion of the conversion process.

Therefore, the original motive is not as crucial as it might have been in previous generations. There is still enough time to discern and separate the original reason for coming from the final motivation for converting.

When the convert is ready to make a decision, if the underlying reason for conversion is the marriage, then a problem remains. However, if, after extensive study, the convert is genuinely ready to accept Judaism, independent of extraneous factors, then there is no reason why the conversion should not proceed smoothly.

Misconception: When a Jew marries a non-Jew who converts, it is an intermarriage.

Sociologists who measure the rate of assimilation among the Jewish population usually label the marriage of a Jew to a non-Jew who converts as an intermarriage. Some do make the distinction between types of intermarriage. They may refer to mixed marriage (without conversion) and intermarriage, or to conversionary marriage and intermarriage.

However, from the perspective of Jewish thinking, a non-Jew who converts to Judaism is a Jew, plain and simple. After legitimate conversion, it is a case of one Jew marrying another Jew, and it is not an intermarriage.

Misconception: Conversion is made by a rabbinic tribunal.

The rabbinic tribunal that holds court to decide whether to allow a conversion must gauge the sincerity and commitment of the prospective convert.

If the convert is sincere, and expresses a strong, uncompromising desire to become attached to the Jewish community and affirm Jewish values, then the rabbinical court supervises the procedure, including acceptance of commitment (*kabbalat hamitzvot*), circumcision (in the case of male converts), and ritual immersion in a body of water known as a *mikvah*.

It is the convert who converts. The rabbis do not pronounce; they supervise and give finality and communal acceptance to the affirmative act of the convert.

Misconception: A Jew who is baptized ceases to be Jewish.

An individual born of a Jewish mother, or an individual who undergoes a legitimate conversion, is Jewish forever.

From the perspective of Jewish law, there is nothing that the individual can do to change that. Even one who renounces Judaism or joins another faith is always considered a Jew.

This is not to suggest that the act of renunciation is considered insignificant. It is significant, it is serious, and there are wide-ranging repercussions of such an act, including the denial of basic privileges that are granted only to members of the Jewish community, such as being given an honor in the synagogue, or burial rights.

One who renounces Judaism, and then wishes to reconsider, cannot gain automatic entry back into the Jewish community.

Once an individual has adopted another faith, reentry would require an act of reaffirmation of one's Jewish identity and a symbolic ritual immersion to signify spiritual renewal.

Misconception: The convert is not the same as a born Jew.

Once a person joins the ranks of the Jewish community, that person is fully Jewish. One is not allowed to pejoratively remind the individual of his or her non-Jewish roots.

The legal status of a convert is the same as that of a born Jew. Were this not the case, we would have difficulty thinking of King David as belonging to our ancestral tradition, nor could we readily accept luminaries such as Onkelos, Rabbi Akiva, and Rabbi Meir, among others.

Obviously this is an absurdity, because these individuals figure prominently in the unfolding of Jewish destiny. One hardly remembers their original roots, if, indeed, one thinks about it at all.

If that process of integration and acceptance was possible in previous generations, it certainly is possible today. More than just being possible, it is desirable.

Misconception: Those who are born Jews have no obligations to converts.

There is a specific biblical obligation that makes every Jew obligated to welcome and love the stranger. Having lived through historical periods when we were strangers in foreign lands, we should be able to empathize with those who may feel that same sense of being unwelcome.

Additionally, there is a prohibition against reminding converts of their background. One is not allowed to ridicule a convert who has made the difficult and emotionally overwhelming leap to embrace Judaism. Simply speaking, this is unconscionable behavior.

2

Special Days

Shabbat
Rosh Hashanah
Yom Kippur
Sukkot
Hanukah
Purim
Pesah
Fast Days

Misconception: For each child, one must add one more candle for kindling the *Shabbat* lights.

It is not rare that one finds families who light candles according to family size. In a family with seven children, nine candles are lit, and in a family with three children, five are lit, and so forth. There are those who do add one candle for each child, beginning, upon marriage (without children), with the two required candles.

However, there is no obligation to add a candle for each child. The practice of adding one candle for each child may be related to another law. If one should forget to light candles on any given *Shabbat*, then one is obliged to add a candle permanently from then on.

After childbirth, it is possible that the mother would spend a *Shabbat* in the hospital. She might forget to light the *Shabbat* candles that week, thus necessitating the compensation of one extra candle from then on.

Although it is not obligatory to add a candle for each child, there certainly is nothing wrong with such practice. There is much significance to adding a candle for each child. After all, each child adds a measure of brightness to the home!

Misconception: If there is no wine, one cannot recite the *kiddush*.

The *kiddush* is the sanctification prayer and blessing recited in the evening to usher in the *Shabbat* or festival, and in the morning to reaffirm the sanctification of the *Shabbat* or festival.

Normally, the *kiddush* is recited over a full cup of wine. A cup full of wine symbolizes joy. *Shabbat* and *Yom Tov* (festival) are days in which we express our sense of spiritual fullness.

However, if there is no wine available, one may recite the *kiddush* over the *hallah*, the loaves of bread that are required for the *Shabbat* or *Yom Tov* meal.

In such an instance, the substance blessing recited in the *kiddush* is not the blessing over wine; it is the blessing over bread.

Misconception: *Shabbat* is a day of rest.

If *Shabbat* is a day of rest, rabbis are in deep trouble. They work harder on the *Shabbat* than on any other day of the week, so that they who preach about the *Shabbat* are some of the worst offenders. This is only so if one assumes that *Shabbat* is a day of rest. In fact, this is not precisely true.

Shabbat is more precisely linked to cessation. On this day, one ceases from being involved in material creativity. Instead, the major thrust of our energies is directed toward human fulfillment. Nothing is cooked, nothing is baked, nothing is sewn, nothing is built. Only human interaction and direct human experience are the order of the day.

Shabbat is different, *Shabbat* is a change, but it is not intended to be a rest. It is intended to be an invigorating experience. The rabbi or cantor who works hard on *Shabbat* works in the context of pedagogical, inspirational activity. This is work, this is sweat; this is not rest, but this is an appropriate endeavor for *Shabbat*.

Misconception: *Shabbat* is merely a host of restrictions.

Many activities are proscribed on *Shabbat*. There are main categories of work (cooking, building, weaving, and so forth) that are prohibited, as well as derivations of these categories that are likewise prohibited.

In addition, there are rabbinic fences to protect the *Shabbat*, adding to the already imposing list of restrictions. One who approaches the *Shabbat* by looking at the list of prohibitions may become overwhelmed by the list, but has approached this observance in the wrong way. The restrictions are in place to create a framework for the positive fulfillment and contentment afforded by this unique period of cessation from material creativity.

By renouncing all attempts to materially change the world, by focusing on inner space, on introspection, on enjoyment of family, on study and dialogue, one creates a uniquely spiritual and human day in which the individual comes in touch with the self. Once compromises are initiated, once even a minor activity is allowed as *the* "exception," whether it be mowing the lawn or using the telephone, then the spirit of complete immersion in spiritual and human concerns is immediately neutralized.

Shabbat is not restriction for restriction's sake; it is restriction for fulfillment.

Misconception: The work that is prohibited on *Shabbat* is hard labor.

Some of the categories of work that are prohibited on *Shabbat* can be strenuous. Construction work is one example.

But many work prohibitions do not involve taxing effort. Baking, sewing, or carrying even a light object from the private to the public domain are certainly not intensive labor—but they are prohibited.

The work that is proscribed on *Shabbat* relates more to the issue of material creativity, interfering with any component of nature. On *Shabbat*, we are asked to experience the world as it is. For six days, we can work and enhance the world. On *Shabbat*, we move from material creativity to the world of human spiritual experience. The cutoff from intervention in the natural order is dramatic and radical, but only in this way is the complete, blissful *Shabbat* experience possible.

Misconception: The *Shabbat* sermon is a basic Jewish institution.

In the nineteenth century, the idea of a *Shabbat* sermon given by the rabbi in the course of services was considered an intrusion upon the sanctity of the Jewish way, an emulation of other religions, unwelcome within the sanctuary.

However, history sometimes takes funny bounces, and with regard to the sermon, this is indeed the case. There are some houses of prayer where there is no sermon at all on *Shabbat* morning, especially in Israel. This is also likely to be the case in a *shtiebel*, or in a smaller *minyan* gathering.

However, in larger congregations, the original aversion to the rabbi's speaking on the *Shabbat* has dissipated. At least, the aversion for religious reasons has dissipated; there are still some who would, for other reasons, prefer the rabbi not to speak.

In some congregations, the rabbi may not sermonize but will instead deliver a *dvar Torah*, a relatively short explanation of a biblical verse or an insight into an appropriate theme. Whatever the style, the contentious objection to the delivery of sermons as a matter of principle is, for all intents and purposes, a thing of the past.

Misconception: Jewish communities the world over share the reading of the same *Torah* portion every specific *Shabbat*.

Under normal circumstances, the *Torah* readings for *Shabbat*, based on the annual cycle of reading, start with the first *Shabbat* immediately following *Simhat Torah* (festival when the *Torah* cycle is concluded and begun), and conclude with the final *Torah* reading on *Simhat Torah* itself.

It would be expected, inasmuch as all communities adhere to the same formula, that they should read the same *Torah* portion, the specific portion read on any given *Shabbat*.

However, it does not always work out that way. Take, for example, the situation when Passover begins on a Friday night. In such a circumstance, the Passover outside Israel would last for an eight-day period, literally from one *Shabbat* to the next, or from Friday night of one week to Saturday night of the following week.

During that time, the *Torah* readings are of Passover-related themes. The regular cycle, going from the beginning to the end of the *Torah*, is interrupted. For the eight-day period of Passover, when Passover includes two *Shabbat* days, there would be two occasions when the regular cycle is interrupted.

However, in Israel, where Passover is observed for only a seven-day period, the second *Shabbat*, which is the eighth day in countries outside Israel, is in fact an ordinary *Shabbat*, and the *Torah* reading for that week would not be on a Passover-related theme. Israelis resume the normal cycle, usually with the reading of *Sidrah Shmini*. In other words, in Israel one portion would be read and in countries outside Israel, another would be read.

Does this discrepancy continue for the balance of the year? Thankfully, no. There are a number of biblical readings for the *Shabbat* that, on occasion, can be joined to other readings, to form a "double-header" reading. Eventually, a double reading outside of Israel will be spread out over two *Shabbat* days in Israel, so that Israel and the rest of the world will be back on track, fully synchronized.

Misconception: There is nothing wrong with playing indoor sports on *Shabbat*.

There are two components to the *Shabbat*. One is the prohibitive side, the other is the fulfillment side. The host of prohibitions makes possible the atmosphere for spiritual renewal.

Indoor activities pose less of a problem than outdoor games, insofar as transgression' is concerned. Inside the house, the problem of carrying is avoided because the restriction applies only to carrying outdoors, or from the indoors to the outdoors.

However, even though there may be no legal injunction against such activity, the real question is not whether it is prohibited, but whether it is consistent with the spirit of *Shabbat*. Does one who spends the entire *Shabbat* afternoon playing Ping-Pong actually glean the spiritual uplift that the *Shabbat* can offer?

The real challenge on *Shabbat* is not to avoid doing what is wrong; the challenge is to affirm and actualize what is right.

Misconception: It is permissible to use the services of a non-Jew on the *Shabbat*.

The idea of a *Shabbat goy*, a non-Jew who acts on behalf of a Jew for things that the Jew is forbidden to do on the *Shabbat*, is alien to Jewish tradition.

True, there have been instances in the past and there probably still are instances in the present, when a *Shabbat goy* is employed—but this does not make it correct.

There are times when the services of a *Shabbat goy* are permitted, such as in times of danger. If a house becomes cold, and this poses a danger to its inhabitants who may suffer from the effects of bitter cold, the services of a non-Jew may be employed to bring heat to the house. In such a situation, one may employ the services of a *Shabbat goy*. Even then, one must be extremely careful not to directly ask the non-Jew to do the task.

However, under normal circumstances, it is wrong to ask a non-Jew to cook, bake, sew, or build for you on the *Shabbat*. Not only must we not engage in material creativity on *Shabbat*, we also must not ask others to act on our behalf and for our benefit on the *Shabbat*.

Misconception: The *havdalah* (separation) ceremony at the conclusion of *Shabbat* is unrelated to *kiddush* (sanctification) recited at the onset of *Shabbat*.

The *kiddush* blessing serves to usher in the *Shabbat*, with its attendant sanctity. With the *kiddush*, we remember the *Shabbat* to sanctify it.

However, the connotation of sanctity, the idea of the sacred, is bounded on both ends. *Shabbat* is a day apart, a distinct and unique experience. That uniqueness must be projected not only at the beginning of *Shabbat* but also at the conclusion.

After all, if something is special, its special character does not automatically evaporate. There must be some distinctive action that delineates the uniqueness of the day even in its passing.

For this reason, the *havdalah* ceremony at the end of the *Shabbat* is a form of *kiddush*. In *kiddush* we sanctify what is about to begin. In *havdalah*, we sanctify what has just ended. What was ushered in with dignity, must likewise be ushered out with equal dignity. The *havdalah* culminates what the *kiddush* initiated.

Misconception: *Rosh Hashanah* is the birthday of the world.

Even though, in some of the prayer liturgy of *Rosh Hashanah*, we refer to this day as the birthday of the world, it is more accurately the birthday of humankind. *Rosh Hashanah*, the day on which we take stock and investigate our actions of the past year, is actually the universal birthday of humankind, and thus an appropriate day for such introspection.

In a sense, the world did not become a true habitat until the culminating act of Creation—the human being—appeared on the scene. With the creation of the human being, the world came into its own; it was born into its full purpose.

Misconception: The naturally appropriate time for blowing the *shofar*, is after the reading of the *Torah* and just before *Musaf* (additional service).

One of the principles in the fulfillment of one's religious obligations is that "the eager get up early to fulfill the commandments."

"The earlier, the better" is the general rule of thumb. This should apply to the sounding of the *shofar*, because it is a commandment, a *mitzvah*, and should be performed as early as possible.

Centuries ago, as reported in the Talmud, a problem arose when, indeed, this was the practice. It was interpreted by the occupying powers as a call to war, with sometimes tragic consequences.

In order to allay the fears of the Romans who thought that the Jews were sounding the *shofar* in order to launch an offensive, the time for sounding the *shofar* was moved to later in the day. A *shofar* blown later in the day did not convey military intentions. The new time placement alleviated the fears of the Romans, and thus eliminated a source of potential tragedy for the Jews.

We maintain the later time placement for sounding the *shofar* today as a continual reminder of the dangers we faced in the past for simply fulfilling our obligations. Hearing the sounds of the *shofar* awakens us to our responsibility and to our good fortune—being able to sound the *shofar* in freedom. It should also alert us to the plight of our brethren who are not so fortunate, who may not even sound the *shofar* at midday.

Misconception: The *shofar* is sounded only on *Rosh Hashanah*.

The *shofar* is the classical instrument used for the process of awakening. It is blown on *Rosh Hashanah,* but it is also sounded for the thirty-day period prior to *Rosh Hashanah.* This is obviously a warm-up, alerting the population to the impending introspection, and getting a head start in the process. The *shofar* is not sounded on the day prior to *Rosh Hashanah,* in order to intervene between the optional sounding of the month prior to *Rosh Hashanah* and the mandatory sounding on *Rosh Hashanah* itself.

Centuries ago the *shofar* was also sounded on *Yom Kippur* at the beginning of the Jubilee Year. This signalled the moment when individuals returned to their own land, which might have changed hands during the period subsequent to the previous Jubilee. Slaves gained their freedom at this time.

Additionally, the shofar-like sounds of a trumpet were heard as a rallying call in peacetime and as a supplicative prayer to God in wartime, in the hope that God would help in attempts to ward off the enemy.

Thus, there is much more to the *shofar* than meets the ear.

Misconception: At *Tashlikh*, one throws one's sins into the river.

On *Rosh Hashanah*, one experiences the relationship to God as magisterial, with God as Ruler of the universe. The text of prayer is adjusted for the ten-day period from *Rosh Hashanah* to *Yom Kippur*. From the beginning of the year to the Day of Atonement, we refer to God as our Holy Ruler.

Significantly, kings were anointed by the side of a river, a symbolic expression of the hope that the king's reign would flow smoothly, without interruption, like the river. The *Tashlikh* prayer thus recalls this magisterial ceremony. We pray to God as Ruler, by the side of a river. We hope that God's reign will likewise be smooth and everlasting, and that we will directly experience that smoothness and everlastingness for as long as possible.

There are those who fill their pockets with crumbs, in order to be able to unload their "sins" into the river following the *Tashlikh* ceremony. However, this is a gross misconception. Symbolically, we may empty our pockets in order to project the idea of freshness, to show that we are not carrying any excess and harmful baggage from one year into the next. This is a purely symbolic gesture, and even if there are no crumbs, not even a speck of dust coming out of the pockets, there is no problem. It is the idea of symbolic emptying that is crucial, not the polluting of a river.

Misconception: The *Tashlikh* prayer must be recited on *Rosh Hashanah*.

Rosh Hashanah, the holy day signaling the beginning of the year, is the traditional time when the community goes to a river to recite appropriate prayers.

However, not every community is blessed with a river within walking distance. For them, the recitation of the *Tashlikh* on *Rosh Hashanah* is verily an impossibility. This prayer, although better recited as early as possible, can be recited as late as *Hoshanah Rabbah* (Great Salvation), which occurs on the seventh day of the Tabernacle festival (*Sukkot*).

Additionally, there are those who question the tendency to socialize during the *Tashlikh* service on *Rosh Hashanah*. People gather together on *Rosh Hashanah* afternoon, recite the prayer, and then often get into irrelevant, trivial conversation, or worse still, conversation of the gossipy type. Such conversation is an utter contradiction to the spirit of repentence and meticulousness about one's behavior that should prevail on *Rosh Hashanah*, and, indeed, during one's entire life.

It is recommended that instead of large groups gathering together for these prayers, they should be recited individually, in a way and at a time that is more conducive to meditation and less likely to intrude on the sensitive spirit that *Rosh Hashanah* should engender.

Misconception: *Yom Kippur* is the holiest day in the Jewish calendar.

The fact that *Yom Kippur* occurs only once a year has given it a singular place of significance. That which occurs on a more regular basis is not as intriguing and exciting as that which occurs on a once-a-year basis.

It may come as a surprise to learn that the weekly *Shabbat* is, indeed, the holiest day of the year. This is not to say that the Day of Atonement is not holy; rather, in comparison, the *Shabbat* ranks higher. But how can this assertion be justified? Can an entire community be wrong in its assumption?

One may wonder how a hierarchy of importance can ever be established, inasmuch as the Bible does not explicitly state that one commandment is more or less important than another. However, there are indications of a hierarchy that come from a most unlikely source. That unlikely source is the punitive measures that are linked with breach of commandment.

That a breach of a particular commandment brings with it a capital punishment projects the severity of such a breach. If the punishment is less severe, then one can assume that the breach is not as serious.

Within the domain of breaches that are considered of capital import, there is another gauge to assess relative importance. If the capital punishment is to be administered by a lower court, that is, a court on this earth, then the breach is more serious than if punishment is left to the heavenly court.

The biblically required punishment for the breach of *Shabbat* is stoning, administered by a lower court, while the punishment for transgressing the prohibition of *Yom Kippur* is the death penalty, administered by the higher court, God's court. The lower court does not administer the death penalty for the transgression of *Yom Kippur*.

This contrast in penalty assessment indicates that the sanctity of the *Shabbat* is, in fact, greater than that of *Yom Kippur*. This notion is reinforced by comparing the number of people called to the *Torah* on *Shabbat* and *Yom Kippur*. On an ordinary day, the Monday or Thursday reading, three are called. On a festival, five are called. On *Yom Kippur*, six are called, and on *Shabbat* at least seven are called. The holier the day, the more people are called to the Torah reading.

Misconception: A sick person must fast on *Yom Kippur* or any other fast day.

If a person is sick to the extent that fasting may create potential hazards to life, that person is not merely denied the option of fasting; it is actually forbidden for that person to fast. No religious observance of a positive nature is allowed to interfere with life itself.

Thus, an individual with diabetes, whose fasting may have serious, if not devastating impact, is simply prohibited from fasting, even on *Yom Kippur*.

Misconception: A 7-year-old child who feels up to it may fast if he or she so desires.

It is generally assumed that fasting by young children is dangerous. Therefore, even if the child insists that fasting is no problem, the child is told that adults know better. There is no allowance for very young children to fast and deny their bodies the necessary sustenance for proper development. Even fasting for a little while must be done with extreme caution. Not until the child is 11 should fasting be permitted, even on *Yom Kippur*.

Misconception: The only distinguishing mark of *Yom Kippur* is the fast.

Fasting is the main focus of repentance on *Yom Kippur,* but fasting is not an end in itself, it is a means. By fasting, one totally removes one's self from material concerns and immerses the self in the spiritual. This makes possible the immersion in introspection, and the repentance and resolve that is fundamental to the Day of Atonement.

In keeping with this idea of being removed from material and bodily concerns, the observance of *Yom Kippur* extends to other areas. Thus, washing, bathing, conjugal relations, and the wearing of ordinary leather shoes are prohibited on this day. *Yom Kippur* is totally removed from the material world, and is an exercise in the world of the spirit. It only occurs once a year, but when it does occur, we do not go half way. The accent on the spiritual is total and uncompromising.

Misconception: It is ridiculous to enter a sanctuary on the holy day of *Yom Kippur* in running shoes.

One may agree that coming into a very sacred public gathering dressed in one's best clothing, combined with running shoes, is unconventional. However, *Yom Kippur* is not merely a fast day. It is a day in which there are other operative norms. One of them requires us to wear leather-free shoes on that day. In the explanation of Maimonides, we should be able to feel the earth's pebbles and rocks as we walk. Obviously, this will be a reminder that it is a special day, a day for total introspection.

The norm regarding leather-free shoes is one of the basic regulations of *Yom Kippur*, such that entry into the house of prayer thusly attired is totally consistent with the dictates of the day.

Misconception: It is inconsistent with the spirit of *Yom Kippur* to conduct charity appeals in the sanctuary.

Some congregations have voted to eliminate appeals to their congregants on the Day of Atonement primarily for this reason. They claim that the appeal demeans the sacred spirit of the day and compromises the dignity of the *Yom Kippur* service.

However, Judaism affirms the significance of charity, a significance that is emphasized in the prayers of *Yom Kippur*. The giving of charity is a meritorious act that reflects well upon those who give charity.

Much lip service is given on *Yom Kippur* to the process of repentance and introspection, but all this is of little value if there is no action attached to the contemplation. There is hardly an action that is more noble and indicative of proper priorities than the giving of charity. It shows a sense of caring, sharing, and empathizing with others, a humane spirit that must be the order of the day on *Yom Kippur*, and hopefully, afterward.

Not only is the appeal for charity on *Yom Kippur* consistent with the themes of the day, it may even be said that the refusal to make such appeal is totally inconsistent with the spirit of *Yom Kippur*.

Misconception: If we pray on *Yom Kippur*, all will be forgiven.

Yom Kippur is the Day of Atonement, when we hope that we will be forgiven for all that we have done wrong or failed to do right. Mouthing words on *Yom Kippur* does not amount to much. Praying for forgiveness on *Yom Kippur* must be an authentic expression of remorse, coupled with a sincere resolve for the future.

In matters between individuals, one may pray for the entire day, but it could be a futile exercise. If, for example, one has insulted a neighbor and then begs God's forgiveness for this intrusion on another's dignity, it is useless. One must actually seek the forgiveness of the aggrieved party. It is absurd to go straight to God for forgiveness, when one has failed to show genuine remorse by correcting the wrong directly. In matters between a human being and God, a direct, immediate approach to God is the proper procedure. In matters between human beings, the first step is to correct matters on a human level. Only then can the heavenly atonement process for the iniquity be initiated.

Misconception: There is only one day of atonement each year.

Yom Kippur, a twenty-five hour day of total removal from any material concerns, as well as from any direct experience of pleasure, comes only once a year. However, there are many other days of atonement throughout the Jewish year.

Prior to the first day of each month, *Yom Kippur Katan* (small *Yom Kippur*) is observed. Individuals assess their spiritual inventory and try to make improvements for the month at hand.

In addition, there is another day of atonement for the bride and groom who are about to marry. The day of their marriage is somewhat of a *Yom Kippur*, in that they are starting a new life together, with a clean slate and no debts. It is for this reason that the groom, underneath the *hupah*, traditionally wears a white garment called a *kitel* to symbolize a new beginning. Bride and groom actually fast on their wedding day to acknowledge that this day is of supreme importance and significance to them. The liturgy of the *Yom Kippur* confessional is added to their pre-wedding prayers.

The theme of atonement, therefore, is much more prevalent than one would ordinarily imagine.

Misconception: The stricter observance concerning *Sukkot* involves eating, not sleeping.

The seven-day period of *Sukkot* (eight days outside Israel) is a time when the *sukkah* becomes one's domicile.

Eating in the *sukkah* is a way in which the domicile factor is affirmed. However, even when one lives in a house, there are occasions when one will grab a snack outside the house. It is the regular meals that one is most likely to eat at home. Therefore, it is permitted to have a snack outside the confines of the *sukkah* during the festival.

However, sleeping is also a manifestation of domicile, and one does not catch a nap in the afternoon in another house or in a hotel. One's normal sleep, and one's catnaps, are in the home. If the *sukkah* is to be one's domicile for the seven days, then even a catnap must take place in the *sukkah*.

One has much less flexibility concerning sleeping in the *sukkah* than one has with regard to eating. The only reason why sleeping in a *sukkah* has not become a primary feature of *Sukkot* observance in North America is because of weather conditions. It is usually cold, and sleeping in a *sukkah* is, therefore, potentially hazardous and, at the very least, uncomfortable. Thus, most people do not sleep in the *sukkah*. However, in theory, sleeping in the *sukkah* is an essential component of the *mitzvah*.

Misconception: *Hol Hamoed,* the intermediate days between the first and last days of *Pesah,* and the days buffering *Sukkot* and *Shmini Atzeret,* are ordinary days.

Hol Hamoed is actually not as intense as the festival preceding it, but is certainly not ordinary. Although they may be treated by many as ordinary, these days are special. In the prayer service, there is a *Torah* reading, and an additional prayer also called *Musaf.*

The obligation to be joyous on the festival applies to *Hol Hamoed.* One should dress in a festive manner and minimize work. Only work which is absolutely necessary, or would involve significant loss if not done, should be contemplated for these intermediate days.

Other than that, these should be happy days when one incorporates the ambience of the festival into one's activities.

Misconception: *Simhat Torah* is a biblically ordained celebration.

One may mistakenly reach this conclusion since *Simhat Torah* follows on the heels of the Tabernacle festival (*Sukkot*), and the subsequent celebration of *Shmini Atzeret*.

In Israel, *Simhat Torah* is superimposed upon this Eighth Day of Assembly. Outside Israel, we tend to mistakenly refer to the ninth day of the *Sukkot-Shmini Atzeret* festival as *Simhat Torah*. Actually, that day is also *Shmini Atzeret*, the additional day of *Shmini Atzeret* observed in the Diaspora. *Simhat Torah* is superimposed on this last day as an additional celebration.

The name of the day is *Shmini Atzeret*, but we celebrate this day by concluding the cycle of *Torah* reading, and launching the new cycle from Genesis.

Simhat Torah is, in a way, a response to a call. The Eighth Day of Solemn Assembly is traditionally viewed as a heavenly request not to rush home, but to stay one day longer. The Jewish community's response is to not merely linger, but to infuse the day with a meaningful expression. That meaningful expression is the joy of completing the *Torah* reading cycle, as well as the joy of launching the new cycle.

Simhat Torah is thus, in reality, *Shmini Atzeret* plus — plus whatever the Jewish community has spontaneously injected into the *Shmini Atzeret* festival.

Misconception: *Hanukah* is a major Jewish festival.

Hanukah's arrival onto the scene as a major Judaic observance comes mainly as the result of its proximity to another celebration observed by millions around that time of year.

Hanukah, when compared with other Jewish festivals, is a minor festival. The major festivals are those that are legislated in the Bible, including *Rosh Hashanah, Yom Kippur, Pesah, Shavuot* (Pentecost), *Sukkot,* and *Shmini Atzeret.*

The postbiblical holidays, *Hanukah* and *Purim* (Feast of Lots), do not have the same legal parameters attached to them. The wide-ranging work restrictions that apply to the biblically ordained festivals do not apply to *Hanukah* and *Purim.* Certainly, *Hanukah* and *Purim* are not ordinary days, but they are not as extraordinary in their observance pattern as are the major festivals.

Misconception: *Hanukah* is a celebration of the military victory of the Maccabees.

The original revolt of the Maccabees was to protest the religious persecution and denial of religious freedom by the Syrian Greeks. It was a protest against the introduction of pagan religion into the land of Israel, including the Temple itself.

Unfortunately, the only way to regain religious autonomy was through military means, and finally, after a long uphill struggle, the Maccabees were able to march to Jerusalem, cleanse the Temple, and rededicate it. Thus, the name *Hanukah* is derived from the word for "dedication." The rededication was expressed most saliently by the kindling of the *Ner Tamid*. It is not the military victory itself that is celebrated; instead it is the reestablishment of the *Bet Hamikdash* as the theological center of the Jewish community.

As a rule, we never celebrate military victory. We only celebrate the ensuing peace and tranquility.

Misconception: The obligation to kindle the *Hanukah menorah* is one light on the first day, two on the second day, three on the third day, and so forth.

The basic practice of *Hanukah*, the lighting of the *menorah*, is quite well known. We are to kindle one light on the first day, two on the second, three on third day, all the way up to eight on the final day of *Hanukah*.

This has become such an ingrained practice that we think this is the fundamental, basic *Hanukah* obligation.

However, this is not precisely the case. The fundamental obligation with regard to *Hanukah* fulfillment is to kindle one light every day for the eight days. We recall the great events of the *Hanukah* period, when our ancestors had only enough oil to last for one day. It was only one light that was kindled, and that is all we should do.

However, the Talmud indicates that those who want to go out of their way to adorn and beautify the commandments add an extra candle for every day. It is a tribute to the Jewish community the world over that they have adopted the extra measure and have incorporated it as a norm rather than as an extra.

It is important to be aware of this, especially in circumstances when, for whatever reason, one is unable to obtain more than eight measures of oil or eight candles for *Hanukah*. Some, who may be used to the one, then two, then three pattern, would light them on the first, second, and third day, and be left with nothing for the balance of *Hanukah*.

The fundamental fulfillment is one per day; if one has only a total of eight, the proper thing to do is to just light one every day. It is better to do the basics every day, than to do the extra for a few days and nothing after that.

Misconception: *Hanukah* is gift-giving time.

This is one of those practices that has crept into many Jewish homes through the back door, through the assimilative process of imitation. There is nothing wrong with people giving gifts at any time, as a show of affection. However, to hallow the process of gift-giving as indigenous to *Hanukah* is a distortion. *Hanukah* is an important time in the Jewish calendar, but it is not the Jewish counterpart of a holiday observed by many others among the population. It is a festival of its own, with a particular and unique meaning.

There are some unique observances connected with *Hanukah*, such as the playing of *dreidel* (spin toy), to recall the time Jews played with the *dreidel* as a camouflage when they were forbidden to study Torah. *Hanukah gelt* (money) is traditionally given to the children, but the obligation to give gifts is nonexistent.

If anything, this flies in the face of what *Hanukah* is all about. If *Hanukah* is a victory against the Hellenizing forces of assimilation, it is crudely ironic that today so many have chosen to celebrate *Hanukah* through the assimilative process of imitating practices of another faith for this uniquely Jewish event and observance.

Misconception: *Purim* celebrates the military defeat of the enemy.

The festival of *Purim* was preceded by a confrontation between the Jews and those who desired to annihilate them. That confrontation took place on the day prior to what is now celebrated as *Purim*.

The day of military victory, the day when we escaped unscathed from the confrontation, is not a day of celebration. In fact, it is a day of fasting. We do not gloat in military victories. Our joy is only at the consequence of the military victory, namely, being able to live in peace. It is not the death of enemies that is a cause of celebration. As a matter of fact, the death of enemies is cause for upset. We are happy not with war, but only with peace.

Misconception: Esther fasted on the day before *Purim*.

The Fast of Esther, referred to in the *Megillah* read on *Purim*, took place on three days in the month of Nisan, with the last day of the three-day fast actually being on *Pesah*. Esther fasted at the first opportunity, almost immediately after she found out about the decree threatening the Jewish people.

The Fast of Esther, now observed on the day before *Purim*, is the day of the confrontation with those who would have annihilated the Jews. It is assumed that the Jews fasted on that day because of their anxiety and in the hope that God would help them. It is named the Fast of Esther to honor the heroine of the *Purim* redemption.

Misconception: All Jews celebrate *Purim* on the same day.

In the story of *Purim* as it is related in the *Megillah*, the Jews of the Persian capital Suza (Shushan) needed an extra day to counter the enemy attack. They did not rest from the danger until the 14th of Adar, so their celebration of being able to live in peace did not commence until the 15th of Adar. In all other communities this celebration took place on the 14th.

To this day, the differential of a day between Shushan and other Jewish communities is maintained. All cities that were walled from the time of Joshua follow the Shushan pattern and celebrate *Purim* on the 15th of Adar, while other cities celebrate *Purim* on the 14th.

In Israel, Tel Aviv celebrates *Purim* on the 14th of Adar; Jerusalem celebrates it on the 15th. The difference of dates only applies to specific cities within Israel but does not pertain to communities outside Israel, all of which celebrate *Purim* on the 14th of Adar.

Misconception: The evening *Megillah* reading on *Purim* is the main reading.

If one were to gauge the importance of the *Megillah* readings based on attendance alone, this would certainly seem to be the case. It is the general rule that more people attend the evening reading of the *Megillah* than attend the morning reading.

However, attendance notwithstanding, the major reading of the *Megillah*, the essential *Megillah* fulfillment, is the morning reading. The evening reading is more a matter of establishing a thematic consistency to the day of *Purim*, so that one recalls the miracle even on the evening prior to the day of *Purim* itself.

Misconception: The drowning out of Haman's name during synagogue services for *Purim* is altogether proper.

During the reading of *Megillat Esther* on *Purim*, it is customary to make noise at each mention of Haman's name. This is a derisive reaction to an individual who would have eliminated the Jewish people from the face of the earth. However, it is a controlled reaction. We do not go out and deface houses or utter profanities.

Yet, too much of even a good thing can cause problems. In the case of the noisemaking, too many have seen this as the primary expression of the *Purim* celebration. The most important part of the *Megillah* reading is the reading of the story, the understanding of the circumstances, and the ensuing combination of appreciation and joy for deliverance.

All too often the noise becomes an end in itself, and even interferes with one's ability to hear the actual reading of the *Megillah*. Such a trade-off is pointless.

Misconception: *Hamantashen*, which we traditionally eat on *Purim*, were really named for that "wicked, wicked man."

Everyone knows that the tri-cornered pastry with various types of fillings that we all eat on *Purim* is called a *hamantash*. The question, however, is: Is this really an appropriate name for the pastry.

Haman was the arch villain of the *Purim* story, the Hitler of his day, who wanted to decimate the entire Jewish people. He was a descendant of the Amalekites, the people whose memory we are obliged to obliterate because their ethos was wanton hatred and murder.

It therefore seems incongruous that we should honor Haman by naming a food after him. In a modern perspective, it would be unthinkable to name a candy or a tasty dish after Hitler and eat it on the day set aside to remember the Holocaust, *Yom Hashoa*.

It is also reasonable to assume that *hamantash* may not have been its original name. One of the more popular fillings for this three-cornered cookie was *mohn* (poppy seed). *Tash* is the Yiddish word for pocket, and the pastry was a pocket with *mohn* in it. Possibly the original name was *mohntash*, not *hamantash*, but through the ages it became distorted and evolved into *hamantash*.

It would be appropriate to call this delicacy by its rightful name, either a mohntash, a lekvar tash, a peanut butter tash, or whatever tash.

Misconception: It is obligatory to get drunk on *Purim*.

There is an obligation to become intoxicated on *Purim* to the extent that one cannot differentiate between "blessed is Mordechai and cursed is Haman." The precise meaning of this is unclear, but the fact that we must be joyous on *Purim* is to reenact the presumed joy of the Jewish community who survived the threat of extinction and celebrated their deliverance. When life is threatened, it is inappropriate and almost psychologically impossible to celebrate. But once the threat is removed, the natural instinct is to celebrate.

Celebrating *Purim* until one cannot differentiate between "blessed is Mordechai and cursed is Haman," at first blush seems to be quite an advanced state of drunkeness. However, it may just suggest that we should be so happy that the issue of Haman's machinations becomes irrelevant. The focus is on the present mood, not on the past crisis. Even falling asleep from one too many may fulfill this obligation. Certainly, there is no justification for becoming so drunk as to be irresponsible and a potential danger to others.

Wine and intoxicants are effective instruments for making one happy. However, beyond a certain point, one is not happy; one is not even in the real world. Such is not the design for the *Purim* celebration.

Misconception: The last festival days of *Pesah* celebrate the drowning of the Egyptians.

The obligation to celebrate the seventh day was transmitted to the Israelites in Egypt, even before the Exodus. The Israelites knew that the seventh day after the Exodus was to be a celebrative day. Having been told this prior to their departure, it was clear to them that what happened to the Egyptians on the seventh day would be irrelevant to the celebration.

The two stages of *Pesah* indicate the two stages of freedom. In the first stage, the Israelites left Egypt. In the second stage, Egypt left the Israelites. It was unfortunate that the Egyptians insisted on pursuing the Israelites, even after the Israelites had fled, with the intent of bringing them back to subjugation. Their blind determination in this regard was an unfortunate indication that the only force that would stop them was death itself, but their drowning was no cause for celebration.

To this day, the entire *Hallel* (song of joyous thanksgiving) is recited only on the first (or first two days). For the balance of the festival, we shorten the *Hallel* recitation, because any joy we experienced at attaining complete freedom came at the expense of suffering to the Egyptians. We lament the fact that our freedom came at such a price, even though the Egyptians left the Israelites no choice in the matter.

Additionally, the custom of flicking out a drop of wine at the mention of each of the plagues is to further impress upon us that our cup cannot be full when our freedom must be gained through the suffering of others. We may be happy, and legitimately so, because freedom is so important; but at the same time, we must temper that joy because of the related suffering. The Egyptians may have had only themselves to blame for their intransigence and ultimate suffering; but we must be sensitive even to that.

The biblical command to be kind to the stranger is linked to our having been strangers in a strange land. Even though later enslaved in Egypt, we had gone there to escape a famine.

For allowing us to live, albeit not as free men and women, some gratitude is due to Egypt. Therefore, we must have some measure of gratitude to the host country, all the suffering imposed upon us notwithstanding.

Misconception: The search for *hametz* is a hide-and-seek exercise.

The evening before *Pesah*, one must search the entire house for any leaven.

There is a custom in many places to spread ten pieces of bread throughout the house. Part of the reason for this is the fear that one may not find any leaven whatsoever, thus rendering the blessing said at the beginning of the search as unnecessary and, therefore, a "taking of God's name in vain."

If one reduces the search to a hide-and-seek exercise, just to find the ten pieces that have been hidden, *this* would make the blessing a vain blessing. Instead of attempting to assure that the house has been properly prepared for Passover, all one is interested in is finding the pieces that were hidden. This is not a search for *hametz*; this is merely a game.

The object of the exercise is not to find leavened products; the object of the exercise is to search for it. If one has done such a good job of cleaning the house that there is nothing left, so much the better. The additional pieces of bread cannot harm, as long as one concentrates on looking for *hametz* wherever it may be.

Misconception: Prior to *Pesah*, people sell their *hametz* to
the rabbi, who in turns sells it to a non-Jew.

The Rabbi does indeed sell the *hametz* to a non-Jew. However,
he does not buy that *hametz* from the members of his congregation or others who employ his services. Instead, they delegate the
rabbi to act as their agent to sell *hametz*.

In simple terms, they give the rabbi the power of attorney to
act on their behalf in selling the *hametz* before *Pesah*.

Misconception: The sale of *hametz* is not a legally binding transaction.

Many people engage the services of their rabbi to effect the sale of their leaven products prior to *Pesah*, to fulfill the prohibition against having any leaven products in their possession during the Passover period. It is taken for granted that the rabbi will sell the *hametz* before *Pesah* and buy it back from the non-Jew immediately after *Pesah*.

It is also presumed that the non-Jew who buys the *hametz* will, of necessity, sell the *hametz* back after *Pesah*. But the sale is not a formality at all; it is a legally binding sale, and the non-Jew is under no obligation to sell the *hametz* back after Passover.

The fact that it is a legally binding sale also obliges those who are a party to it to refrain from using the leaven products from the time that the transaction goes into effect. Such use is not only a contravention of *Pesah* regulations, but also a breach of contract. The sale is not to be taken lightly, and rabbis who engage in this procedure do it with the utmost seriousness.

Misconception: *Matzah* symbolizes freedom.

Matzah is often referred to as the bread of affliction. On the other hand, we associate *matzah* with our freedom. Which is the correct impression?

The answer is that both are correct. *Matzah* is essentially the bread of affliction, the wafer-like staple that the Israelites were forced to eat in Egypt, because the oppression was so intense that they did not have the luxury of time to bake bread. Had they spent the time baking the bread, they would not have met their quotas and would have been severely beaten or killed.

The only bread-like substance the Israelites had time to bake was the *matzah*, which was made relatively quickly by mixing flour and water and then baking this in intense heat.

When it became clear that the Israelites would be gaining their freedom, they did not rush to taste the bread that had been denied them for so long. On the night of the Passover *seder* in Egypt, the people still ate *matzah*. They affirmed that in their freedom, they would not squander the precious moments they finally had for themselves on baking bread. They used this time for reconnecting with their families and with themselves. They showed that freedom means not only being free from enslavement and oppression by others; freedom also means not being a slave to one's intense desires.

Matzah, the bread of affliction, evolved into the bread of freedom.

Misconception: Any *matzah* is fit for Passover use.

A mixture of flour and water that takes more than 18 minutes to bake is assumed to have become leavened, because the baking process was prolonged. Therefore, it is considered to be *hametz* (leaven), or a product that is unfit for Passover use.

The *matzah* for Passover is prepared under exacting conditions, to assure that the flour and water mixture is processed in less than 18 minutes.

One should not assume that all *matzah* is prepared under such conditions. Unless the package that contains the *matzah* specifically states that it is *kosher* for Passover, it is not fit for Passover use.

Additionally, there are problems attached to the use of egg *matzah* on Passover. There are some views that the extra ingredients placed into the mixture in order to make egg *matzah* actually precipitate a leavening process, so that egg *matzah* is by definition unfit for Passover use. It is generally accepted that only in extenuating circumstances (for sick people who cannot digest regular *matzah*), may egg *matzah* be eaten on Passover.

Misconception: Moshe Rabbenu (our teacher Moses) is not mentioned in the *Haggadah*.

The *Haggadah* is the classic text that is used on the nights of the Passover *seder* to recount the story of the Exodus from Egypt.

The reenactment of this great experience of deliverance is designed to rekindle our faith in God. Because of this, any reflection on the role of individuals, however heroic, is inappropriate.

Therefore, Moshe Rabbenu does not figure prominently in the *Haggadah*'s version of the story, even though in the biblical account Moshe Rabbenu is central to the events.

The *Haggadah*, by omitting Moshe's name, projects the idea that on the *seder* nights, the focus is on our relationship with God.

However, Moshe Rabbenu's name is not left out entirely. His name does appear in the report of the actual salvation, and the faith that the people then had in God and in God's servant. The name is brought in almost tangentially, but in a subtly profound way.

Misconception: After Passover, all leavened products are permissible.

Assuming that the leavened products, such as bread, have been produced in a manner consistent with dietary (*kashrut*) regulations, this does not guarantee they are permissible for eating after Passover.

The reason for this is that there is an added prohibition related to the observance of Passover. It is reasonably well known that one may not eat any leavened products on Passover or have any of these products in one's possession on Passover. They must be eaten before Passover or sold.

What is less well known is that leaven that has been in the possession of a Jew during Passover may never again be eaten by a Jew, nor may any benefit be derived therefrom. This indicates the severity of the prohibition, a prohibition so serious that the effects of neglecting its observance are far-reaching and everlasting.

Before purchasing leavened products after Passover, it is important to ascertain that these items were not owned by a Jew during Passover.

Misconception: Other than *Yom Kippur*, a fast occurring on *Shabbat* is always deferred to Sunday.

The general principle is that any commemoration of tragic events is delayed rather than advanced in time. Since it is the commemoration of an event we would rather had not taken place, it is more appropriate to push this date off to a later time, rather than to commemorate it earlier.

Thus, *Shiv'ah Asar B'Tamuz* (17th Day of Tamuz) or *Tish'ah B'Av* (9th Day of Av), when they occur on the *Shabbat*, are observed the next day. The same is true of the Fast of Gedaliah.

However, this rule does not apply to the Fast of Esther. This is the fast day that occurs prior to *Purim*. If this fast should occur on the *Shabbat*, *Purim* would fall on Sunday; we do not defer *Purim* because it is a celebrative day. It is also impossible to defer the fast until after *Purim*, since this fast was specifically established to commemorate the fasting of the Jewish community prior to *Purim*, in anticipation of the great military confrontation with those who sought to annihilate them.

It is also impossible to observe this fast on the Friday before, because the prohibition against fasting on *Shabbat* also pertains to Friday. If one fasts on Friday one enters into *Shabbat* in a fasting state, which is prohibited.

The only option left is to push the fast back to the previous Thursday, which is, indeed, the practice. The Fast of Esther is the exception to the rule. When it falls on *Shabbat*, it is not deferred to Sunday, but is observed on the previous Thursday.

Misconception: Friday is never a day for fasting.

It is prohibited to fast on *Shabbat*, because *Shabbat* is a day of fulfillment, not denial and pain; it is likewise wrong to fast on Friday. If one fasts on Friday, one enters into *Shabbat* in an afflicted state, even though that may be for only an hour. Even a minute in an afflicted state on *Shabbat* is inconsistent with the spirit of the day.

Yom Kippur (Day of Atonement) is one exception to the rule. The fast of *Yom Kippur* overrides *Shabbat* considerations and is observed on the tenth day of Tishrei, even if that should be a *Shabbat*. However, *Yom Kippur* never occurs on Friday or Sunday, so there cannot be two consecutive days when food preparation is not possible.

Most other fast days, such as the Fast of the 17th of Tamuz, *Tish'ah B'Av*, and the Fast of Gedaliah, if they occur on *Shabbat* are deferred to Sunday. In the case of the Fast of Esther, it is pushed back to the previous Thursday, as discussed on p. 82.

But there is a notable exception to this rule. That exception is the Fast of the 10th of Tevet, commemorating the surrounding of Jerusalem, presaging the destruction of the *Bet Hamikdash* and the exile of the Jewish people.

If the 10th of Tevet occurs on Friday, the fast is observed on that day, even though this means that the community enters into *Shabbat* in a weakened state. It is the only postbiblical fast that overrides *Shabbat*, but it never occurs on *Shabbat*.

However, when it does fall on Friday, it overrides *Shabbat* to the extent that the fast is held on Friday, with the unavoidable overlap into *Shabbat*.

Misconception: We mourn on *Tish'ah B'Av* because the Temple was destroyed.

The destruction of the Temple began on *Tish'ah B'Av*. Its destruction, on the heels of the ravaging of Jerusalem, was the final devastating event that presaged the exile of the Jewish people.

Mourning, however, is intended to be not just an exercise in the recollection of history. The mourning process is also designed so that we can learn from history, improve upon our present, and write a better history for the future.

Samson Raphael Hirsch points out that we mourn on *Tish'ah B'Av* not merely because the Temple was destroyed, but because it *had* to be destroyed. The community lost its cohesiveness, there was no unity of purpose, rival groups were at each other's throats, and in this atmosphere, there was no hope for any continuity. It had reached the stage where the Temple had to be destroyed; the people had to be rudely awakened so that they would realize the consequences of their bitter strife. This is not intended to excuse the enemy; it is intended to ward off excessive self-righteousness.

In mourning for the Temple, we mourn the conditions that brought on this tragic event. We hope the mourning will assure that such divisiveness and contentiousness will never again exist within the community. This is the idea and ideal behind the fasting and mourning.

3

Care of the Body

Health Maintenance
Medical Intervention
Psychological Well-being
The Scientific World

Part II

Taking Care: Physical and Spiritual

Misconception: Our fate is determined, and there is nothing we can do about it.

This argument has been used by those who overindulge in activities that may be detrimental to their health. Why should they refrain from such pleasure, they contend, when the matter of how long they will live has been firmly established by the Ultimate Power.

The logic of this position is questionable, to say the least. To whom has it been revealed that how one lives has nothing to do with how long one lives? How can we be sure that the matter of fate is an absolute rather than a contingent fate? For example, it is possible that the Divine approach to the individual is as follows: If an individual takes care of the self, this will be acknowledged by extending that person's life. However, if that person engages in questionable health practices, deliberately scoffing at the requirement to take care of one's self, then why should God care? In such instance, God may curtail the number of years given, since they are not appreciated anyway.

Using the argument of fate to justify smoking or any other unhealthy practice is a flawed argument. When the Talmud asserts that one in a hundred dies through heavenly decree, and ninety-nine in a hundred die from negligence, the Talmud is explicitly telling us that how we behave is a potent factor in the unfolding of our fate.

Misconception: Jewish law does not forbid smoking.

This conclusion may be based on having witnessed distinguished rabbis smoking, be it cigarettes, cigars, or pipes. However, with all due deference to the sagacity of rabbis, one should not derive from this that smoking is indeed permitted according to Jewish law.

Great contemporary sages have already declared publicly that according to Jewish law smoking is strictly forbidden. The fact that people may have smoked in past generations is irrelevant. They simply did not know the dangers of smoking, and so smoking was permitted. Had they known then what we know now, they would not have smoked.

Smoking has been shown, beyond any doubt, to be linked to cancer, heart disease, and other causes of premature death. It is certainly no better than poison, which according to Jewish law, is a forbidden product.

In fact, poison is prohibited to such an extent that if poison falls into a mixture, even in a ratio of one part per thousand, the entire mixture is prohibited. This is in contradistinction to a product that is prohibited because of ritual requirements, which, when falling into a mixture, becomes neutralized when the permitted mixture is only sixty times the volume of the forbidden product.

The only reason why smoking is still tolerated is because it is an old, addictive habit still catching up with the new findings. Hopefully, the next generation will have fully integrated the most up-to-date medical wisdom and will understand that because of medical truth, smoking is forbidden according to Jewish law.

Misconception: Jews were never big drinkers—so alcoholism is not a Jewish problem.

There was a time when it was believed that there was no alcoholism among Jews. This is no longer the case. Some argue that it never was the case only that we are now more aware of it as a problem. It is still true that alcoholism is not as prevalent a problem among Jews as it is among the general population, but the problem does exist.

Some contend that with the decline in religious observance, the context of drinking has changed for many Jews. Wine is not merely part of the religious context of a *Shabbat* meal, or *Simhat Torah,* or the *Purim* celebration. A drink (or many) is taken after a frustrating day at work, or becomes a necessary part of lunch to carry one through to the end of the day. It becomes habitual and part of an escape syndrome.

With no spiritual content to drinking and a pronounced increase in daily stress, the Jewish alcoholic has become a fact of modern life.

Misconception: There is nothing religious about exercising.

One of the most vital obligations that is placed upon us is to be appreciative and protective of the life that has been given to us. We are not allowed to engage in any activity that would endanger health, and we must actively pursue practices that enhance health.

Exercise increases bodily vigor, maintains good muscle tone and body equilibrium, and is, therefore, a potentially religious expression. If one exercises in order to keep one's body in good shape, to be energized for the human being's sacred calling, then, indeed, such exercise is a religious expression par excellence.

Misconception: There is nothing religious about taking a bath.

The human body is considered to be the casing for the human soul. It is a precious gift of God that one must nurture and value.

Aside from the obligation to maintain the body by well-informed health practices, the cleansing of the body is also considered to be of significant religious importance. One cleanses the body not only as a matter of health, hygiene, and good manners. It is ultimately an acknowledgment of the reality that the body is God's precious gift. The maintenance of this gift in the best possible manner is the primary way that the human being acknowledges the godliness of the body.

An ostensibly religious individual, with an unkempt, malodorous body due to self-neglect, is a contradiction of terms.

Misconception: Heeding the call of nature is not a religious experience.

The workings of the body, specifically the functioning of bowel and bladder, is one of the wonders of nature. The cleansing process is so vital that any obstruction can cause severe consequences. Kidney failure and bowel obstruction are two of the more serious malfunctions that can plague the individual.

Thus, every successful "consultation with nature" is reason enough to be grateful to God for the workings of the body, and for the fact that in this instance, everything went well.

Accordingly, upon leaving the bathroom the blessing *asher yatzar* is recited, thanking God for one's good fortune.

Misconception: There is nothing sacrilegious about not going to the bathroom when one must.

One who does not go to the bathroom when alerted by the usual bodily signals contravenes basic Jewish law. Jewish law prohibits individuals from holding themselves in, as it is an abomination. When this practice involves the urinary flow, it can compromise a man's potency. Whatever the circumstances, it is considered unhealthy and potentially dangerous to prevent waste matter from flowing out. It is therefore to be avoided.

This does not mean that every public place should become a potential privy. When the individual is alerted by the proper signals, the individual should respond with the utmost dispatch and dignity. However, in this, as in so many other instances in life, common sense should prevail. One should try to anticipate the future call, to avoid having to take leave at inappropriate times.

Misconception: Artificial insemination is never consistent with Jewish tradition.

It would be a great world if everyone who wanted children would be able to have them. Such, however, is not the case. There are instances when individuals want children, but because of the husband's impotence, natural fertilization cannot take place. Artificial insemination then becomes a practical consideration.

There are two types of *artificial insemination*: one from the collected sperm of the *husband*, called AIH; the other, called AID, from the *donor*. Although there are some contentious issues in the matter of AIH, this is generally an acceptable procedure when the natural means for effecting pregnancy are not possible.

The issue of AID, artificial insemination from a donor, is more controversial, but there are reliable authorities who permit this in the absence of any other possibility.

This discussion is not intended to render a legal decision for any particular case. Rather, it is to counterbalance the myth that such possibility is categorically rejected within Jewish tradition.

Misconception: Judaism is against abortion under all circumstances.

Under normal circumstances, the idea of aborting a fetus for convenience, or because one does not want another child, is considered abhorrent and unconscionable, and is strictly forbidden.

However, there are situations in which abortion is not only allowed, it is even mandatory. The classic example of this is when the pregnancy threatens the life of the mother. Faced with the decision to save either the baby or the mother, we consider the child to be "pursuing" the mother and as an extension of her. The *mother* is given priority, and her life is saved.

This applies not only to physiological hazard, but also to legitimate psychiatric hazard. Since this is a matter of extreme delicacy, each situation must be weighed on its own merits. However, Judaism certainly is not arbitrary in rejecting abortion as a possibility in certain situations.

Misconception: Judaism always prohibits the performance of autopsy after death.

Under normal circumstances, after death, an individual is to be accorded the appropriate honor and dignity of being buried immediately, and whole. This would normally preclude the possibility of an autopsy.

However, there are extenuating circumstances in which autopsy can be countenanced, and may even be mandatory. When there is a legitimate possibility that the autopsy will save a life, Jewish law allows it.

For example, when someone dies for no apparent reason, an autopsy may reveal the cause of death and, in turn, may save other lives. In one such situation, a child died at home for no apparent reason, and the postmortem revealed carbon monoxide poisoning. This finding led to a thorough search of the house where the child lived, and investigators found a carbon monoxide leak there. The autopsy saved the rest of the family.

When the death is the result of foul play, a postmortem may conceivably give the investigating authorities enough information so that they can then find the perpetrator of the murder. Removing a murderer from the street is also considered sufficient warrant for performing an autopsy, since by removing a murderer we actually save life. One who murders once may murder a second and a third time.

When the possibility of obvious life-saving benefit to others exists, autopsy would not only be permitted, it would be mandatory. However, autopsy just for the sake of postmortem experimentation, with no prospect of saving other lives, is not sufficient warrant for desecrating the human body.

Misconception: Judaism is opposed to organ donations.

The saving of life is of paramount importance in Judaic tradition. The desecration of the *Shabbat* is mandatory in order to save a life, and very few principles are operative in the face of life-threatening circumstances. Only idolatry, adultery, and murder are not countenanced in order to save life, even one's own.

It stands to reason that when an individual has the wherewithal to save someone else, refusal to take such action is inhumane, to say the least. "Do not stand idly as the blood of your neighbor is being spilled."

An individual who can save another person's life without placing himself or herself in danger, is obliged to do so. If donating an organ after death can save someone else's sight or someone else's life, such action is lifesaving action par excellence. Saving of sight is on the level of life-saving, since sight is a component of life itself.

Because lifesaving is of such overwhelming importance, it supersedes the general obligation to accord the donor the dignity of a full burial. There is no greater dignity that can be accorded the deceased than to know that an organ donation has saved another's life.

In all such matters, the precise circumstances need to be weighed carefully. There is the question of whether the organ donated will save a life, or just remain stored as a frozen asset for future use. There is the all-important issue of not hastening the death of the donor. Each case must be adjudicated on its own merits.

But the general principle of encouraging the saving of the lives of others is of paramount importance in Judaism. This leads to a positive stance toward the general issue of organ transplantation, as long as that is the only methodology by which the lifesaving intervention can be effected.

Misconception: Judaism has a negative attitude toward psychology.

This perception may linger in some minds, because of Freud's alleged condemnation of religion.

Freud did not condemn religion in its totality. He condemned religion that was not conducive to growth, religion that stifled rather than uplifted.

However, there is more to psychology than Freudian psychoanalysis, and there is more to Freudian psychoanalysis than meets the eye.

In the modern context, Judaism has philosophical differences with the more than 150 self-oriented schools of psychology, which to some extent posit a me-first, even a me-only approach. But effective techniques that will help individuals deal with psychological problems are eagerly welcomed within Jewish tradition.

Additionally, the process of solving a problem by sharing it with others goes back to ancient Jewish sources. In general, Judaism may not appreciate psychologies that shrink one's spiritual horizons, but would certainly welcome those that stretch human capacity.

Misconception: Self-esteem is not an operative category in Judaism.

Certain schools of thought, including the ethically oriented *musar* school, continually warn the individual of the capacity for wrongdoing and sometimes may tend to denigrate the individual. One might think that this reflects a general Judaic approach that has no patience with the notion of self-esteem.

As with most other situations, Judaism strikes a delicate balance. The idea of thinking of one's self as evil is alien to Judaism. "Do not think of yourself as wicked" is one of the ethical imperatives in classical Jewish tradition. On the other hand, the individual is constantly reminded that being human, by definition, means being finite, fallible, and always able to improve.

One must not denigrate the self; on the other hand, one must also not glorify the self. Every individual is capable of both gross evil and outstanding virtue. It is not what we are capable of doing that colors who we are; it is what we decide to do. Because of this, we are continually urged to make the right choices; but it is right choices among a host of possibilities that cover the broad scope of what it means to be human.

Think of yourself as potentially good, and then live up to that potential.

Misconception: There is no religious requirement to be happy.

The melancholy individual is unhappy with the self, unhappy with the environment, unhappy with the world. Ultimately, such an individual must have implicit, if not explicit complaints about God, and why God has placed him or her in this world. It is difficult for an individual to be grateful to God for having been given a life of misery.

Often, the miserable attitude is related to cognitive processes. Undoubtedly, there is also depression that is related to chemical imbalance. But there is also the type of depression that comes from a mental filtering that imposes dark interpretations on the world and on everything about one's life.

The happiness package, the antithesis of the sadness and depression package, includes being grateful, appreciative, and thankful for the good that one enjoys. The gratitude starts with the very simple process of saying thank you to God every morning for having restored one's soul. It continues with gratitude for every single nuance of life, from the crowing of the rooster, to the granting of sight, to the ability to walk, and so forth. Nothing is taken for granted. Everything is appreciated as a precious gift.

All this is encompassed in the exceedingly important, but unfortunately neglected, biblical imperative that we "rejoice in all the good that God has given to us and to our household." This is an obligation of surpassing importance, because it makes possible the fulfillment of so much more, with greater gusto.

Misconception: Judaism does not suffer clowns—even gladly.

The Talmud relates a fascinating story of two sages who met Elijah. They asked if there were any in the marketplace who were deserving of eternal life. None could be found until two men wandered into the marketplace. These, Elijah said, these have a claim on eternal life.

The sages, eager to discover why, approached them and asked what they did for a living. They replied that they were clowns, jesters, who sought out the sad, melancholy, and depressed in order to lift their spirits by jesting and levity.

Those who go out of their way to make others happy engage in a most vital activity. People who are sad and depressed may have embarked on a "suicide on the installment plan." By lifting a person's spirit, one actually gives him or her life. There are few endeavors more worthy.

Judaism has much room for clowns, even a need for them, as there is a need for good clinicians to help in countering depression.

Misconception: The observance of the precepts of Judaism sometimes obligates the individual to feel pain.

It is entirely possible that some individuals may feel pain while fulfilling a religious obligation. One may feel pain while fasting on *Yom Kippur* or maybe even when donating money to charity.

However, there is no commandment that the Jew is asked to fulfill where pain is necessary. That one may experience pain is incidental to the fulfillment. Pain does not enhance the observance of *Yom Kippur*. One is to abstain from eating; but the same *Torah* that requires us to fast on the tenth day of Tishrei requires us to eat on the ninth day, so that it will be easier to fast on *Yom Kippur* day. There is no desire to enervate the human being, but only to allow for total spiritual focus through the renunciation of food for that one day.

A boy is circumcised on the eighth day, when he probably feels less pain because his nerve endings are not yet well developed. However, the *brit milah* is always a joyful occasion, and very few young men have complained about it later.

Thus an individual who asserts that the observance of a specific commandment "is a pain" has obviously misconstrued the commandment and its intent.

Misconception: Judaism is against meditation.

To sit for twenty minutes and just meditate on a word is a waste of time. Judaism is against wasting time.

There are meditative "movements" that go beyond meditation and demand some form of devotion to a guru. This borders on idolatry, and is certainly inconsistent with Jewish tradition.

However, there are types of meditation that do not involve idolatry and are not a waste of time. It is possible to meditate for a useful purpose. For example, if a doctor recommends meditation as a means of relaxation to control blood pressure, then the meditation has medical value and is not a waste of time.

The choice of a meditative focus can itself be positive. For example, if one chooses to meditate on the oneness of God, on the word *ehad* (one), on the singularity of God as expressed in the *Shema* (faith affirmation), that is a positive meditation. It is meditation that infuses faith and reinforces faith. Such meditation is not only permissible; it is also desirable.

There is much to be said for the meditative moment as a basic component of prayer, that one meditates with concentration and intention when affirming faith or reciting prayers.

Jewish-oriented meditation, or meditation that provides a health benefit, unencumbered by any idolatrous trimmings, is a welcome mode of experience. If one orients the medically recommended meditation toward faith affirmation, all the better.

Misconception: Judaism and modern science are in conflict over the age of the world.

According to Jewish calculations, we are in the fifty-eighth century of the world, but science tells us that we live in a world that is billions of years old.

Ostensibly, the gap between these two views is so great as to make any rapprochement impossible. This causes no small discomfort to many Jews who feel uncomfortable with being so far outside the pale of the enlightened wisdom of modern science. Is one forced into the situation of either rejecting the Jewish view or living in the Dark Ages?

There are a few ways of approaching this issue. One is to ask scientists how old the world was at the precise moment of the Creation. In other words, did God create a world that was brand new, or did God create a world that was, by scientific standards of measurement, already billions of years old at creation? Obviously, from the fact that the first human created was immediately capable of meaningful verbal dialogue, one senses that Creation involved bringing mature human reality into a developed universe. Thus, one can accept the age of the world, according to the scientific projections, and at the same time maintain that the dialectic of human history began a little more than fifty-seven centuries ago.

Another approach is to understand the biblical chronicle of the Creation. It is spelled out as having taken place in six days, but these are six of "God's days." It is only when we start speaking about human beings and their conception of time, that the days must be translated as 24-hour days. Quite possibly, the six days of God's Creation could refer to a lengthier period. This is not to deny the possibility of God creating over a shorter span, but to indicate that the entire process may have developed through deliberate sequence, over a more extended period.

The major message in these approaches is that one need not necessarily be intimidated by scientific statements. One can retain the confidence that the Bible speaks the truth.

Misconception: Judaism cannot accept the theory of evolution.

At one time, the theory of evolution caused tremendous ripples within the religious community, because it was considered the primary challenge to the validity of religion.

In retrospect, this did not have to happen. Although the theory contains some problems of a theological nature, it does not threaten religion. However, it may threaten those who take a more fundamentalist stand and refuse to correlate science with the Bible.

A careful reading of the Bible shows that the account of the Creation follows a somewhat evolutionary pattern, starting with the creation of the simple species and culminating with the human, the most complex of all. The biblical account may be termed "creative evolution."

The scientific theory is more along the lines of "evolutionary creation." The quarrel, then, is not with the actual process, but with whether there was an architect in charge of the process. Science would have us believe that it just happened; the Bible impresses upon us that God made it happen.

A scientist who believes in God could justify the scientific theory of creation and still maintain faith. For all that science has tried to explain, it has not answered the question of first cause. Given the first drop, there are theories about how it developed into the world as we know it; but it is that all important first step—from nothing to something—that science has yet to answer, but I suspect will never be able to answer. Judaism clearly posits God as the first cause.

Thus, it is possible for an evolutionist to believe in God and for someone who firmly believes in God to accept the evolutionary process.

Misconception: Science and Judaism are on opposite tracks.

There have been historical chronicles of the antagonism between science and religion in general. Also, there are areas of science that may pose problems for Judaism, such as the theory of the age of the world, or evolution, among others.

Long ago, Maimonides articulated the position that there is nothing in science that could pose religious problems. Maimonides was confident that any position for which science could offer foolproof evidence would not contradict Judaism. He was prepared to accept the doctrine of the eternality of the universe, if it could be proven. Obviously this is a difficult proposition to prove. But on propositions that allow for proof, Judaism has never exhibited a fear of the truth; nor would it stand in opposition to scientific endeavor whose major thrust is the improvement of the human condition.

There is nothing intrinsic to the scientific endeavor that makes it impossible for one to function as a scientist while maintaining strong religious beliefs. As long as the two can coexist, there is no reason to be anything but appreciative of the contributions that science can make to our general knowledge, our appreciation of the universe, and our ability to enhance the human condition.

At the same time, science imbued by a sense of the holy, an awe-inspired respect for the majesty and intricacy of God's world, is a more sensitive, indeed, a better science.

Misconception: Miracles are an essential part of Jewish tradition.

A famous philosopher once said that miracles can be used to prove any religion; therefore, they can be used to prove none.

We do not for one moment doubt the capacity of God to perform miracles. There is no greater miracle than the creation of the world, *ex nihilo*, out of nothing. It is beyond human capacity to make something out of nothing. It is even out of the realm of human comprehension to understand how something can be made out of nothing.

But faith in God is not contingent on God performing miracles. Miracles have occurred throughout Jewish history, but the fact that a miracle does or does not occur in a specific given situation need not and should not diminish one's faith. Faith in God as Creator, Architect, and Ruler of the world transcends any miraculous manifestation or lack of it.

4

Care of the Soul

Prayer
Symbols
Blessings

Misconception: The proper name for a Jewish house of worship is synagogue or *shul*.

Synagogue is a Greek word; *shul* is a German word. The word "synagogue" has historically referred to a Jewish house of worship, a house of gathering. *Shul* is from the German for "school," reminiscent of the idea that the house of prayer was frequently also a house of learning.

Accurate and descriptive as these words may be, there are Hebrew terms that better describe a Jewish house of worship. Either *bet knesset*, literally, a "house of assembly," or *bet tefillah*, "house of prayer," is a more appropriate name.

It is ironic and perplexing that we should continue to refer to a Jewish house of worship by either a Greek or a German word, when the Hebrew term is not only as descriptive, but also much more appropriate.

Misconception: All Jews pray toward the east.

The Jews of North America do pray in the easterly direction, because Israel and Jerusalem are to their east. However, Jews of the Soviet Union pray towards the west, since Jerusalem is to their west. Countries to the north of Israel pray in a southerly direction, and countries to the south of Israel pray in a northerly direction.

All Jews face toward the same place, Jerusalem, although they do not pray in the same direction. They effectively face each other, united in the focus of their prayers.

Misconception: The *Shema* (faith affirmation) must be recited in Hebrew.

The essence of the *Shema* is affirmation of faith in God. One who is absolutely ignorant of Hebrew and has no inkling of what it means is just mouthing words rather than affirming faith.

Granted that it is possible for individuals to quickly learn the meaning of the *Shema*, yet it must be emphasized that the key to authentic recitation of the *Shema* is an appreciation of its meaning. Therefore, if that meaning can only be conveyed in a language other than Hebrew, it should be said in that language, provided that the translation is accurate.

At the same time, effort should be made to master the prayer in Hebrew and to understand its intent, because no translation of the *Shema* is a completely accurate reflection of the full impact and the delicate nuances of this all-important affirmation of faith.

Misconception: Jews did not pray until after the offering of sacrifices at the Temple ended.

This assumption is probably related to the connection between the standard prayer services of today and their link to the old sacrificial order. The *Shaharit* is in place of the daily morning sacrifice, *Minhah* is in place of the standard afternoon sacrifice, and *Maariv* is in place of certain sacrifice-related rites that took place at night.

However, it is hard to imagine that there was no prayer outside the Temple during Temple times. After all, the Temple was in Jerusalem, and sacrifices could not be brought elsewhere. This would mean that the entire community of Israel residing outside of Jerusalem did not pray at all. Such a contention is patently absurd, especially since the idea of prayer is already mentioned in the Bible.

It is true that the basic text of prayer as we know it, which has been transmitted through the generations, was first set down in broad strokes in the talmudic era. It was later firmly entrenched, primarily through the efforts of Rav Amram Gaon, in response to one Jewish community's request for guidance as to what their prayers should contain. His reply formed the basis for the *siddur* (order) of prayers.

Prayer predates the Temple, went on during Temple times, and continues to this day. The text may have differed, but the dynamics are the same.

Misconception: Nothing can be added to the prayer text found in the *siddur*.

There are certain components of the prayers that may not be adjusted, or even expanded. The adjectives for praise of God, based as they are on scriptural verse, do not allow for adding one's individual phrases.

Such prayers as the faith affirmation, called *Shema*, are likewise untouchable.

However, the main body of prayer, commonly referred to as the *Amidah* or the *Shemonah Esray* (the eighteen plus one benedictions), is a more flexible prayer. For example, in the blessing for good health, one may add a more personal request for the health of a loved one. In the prayer for wisdom, one may add a prayer for success in taking an exam.

In certain other prayers, one is permitted to insert personal requests.

Misconception: There is nothing more to Jewish prayer than what is found in the *siddur*.

The *siddur* usually contains the standard prayers for daily services, *Shabbat* services, and the festivals.

The prayers that are delineated within the *siddur* are not the maximum of prayer expression. Instead, they are the minimum prayer expression.

At the very minimum, there is an obligation to recite the *Maariv*, *Shaharit*, and *Minhah* services on a daily basis, with other prayers added on special occasions.

However, there is no reason why individuals cannot pray on their own, in their own language, or with emphasis on Psalms (*Tehilim*) or other meditative readings, for the entire day. The entire 24-hour day is an opportunity for prayer.

Put in another way, there is no time that is, by definition, inappropriate for praying.

Misconception: Reading silently is an appropriate way to pray.

The prescribed prayers in the *siddur* are to be *said,* not merely read.

Silent reading is quick and cursory, and it does not engage the individual in a spiritual experience. Emotional involvement is an important ingredient in prayer; such involvement is effected through verbal expression.

Misconception: *Maariv* may be recited only at night.

The various times for prayers are divided into zones. The one general rule is that no one time zone can, under normal circumstances, serve as the time for more than one prayer. In other words, the time zone for *Shaharit* is for morning prayers only, not for *Minhah.* When afternoon prayers are recited, *Maariv* cannot be recited.

One of the more accepted divisions is the sunset boundary, with *Minhah* taking place before sunset, and *Maariv* after sunset, or better yet, after dark.

However, in the summer, with the late onset of darkness, many congregations find it difficult to gather the necessary quorum, called a *minyan,* at 9 P.M. They thus revert to another time-zone division. The *Minhah* service is recited before *pelag haminhah* (*Minhah* divide), which is one-and-a-quarter hours before sunset, or, according to another calculation, one-and-a-quarter hours before nightfall.

These "hours" are calculated according to a different methodology. It is not a sixty-minute hour, but an "hour" which is one-twelfth of the day. Thus, a day beginning at 5:00 A.M. and concluding at 9:00 P.M. is a sixteen-hour day, and each one-twelfth is eighty minutes long. On this basis, one and a quarter "hours," amounts to 100 minutes. This places the *pelag haminhah* (dividing line) at one hour and forty minutes before 9:00 P.M. or 7:20 P.M. *Minhah* would be recited prior to 7:20 P.M., and *Maariv* would be recited after 7:20 P.M., even though it is still daylight.

The period from *pelag haminhah,* a twilight of sorts, can be appended to the next day. Thus, the time from *pelag haminhah* on is the earliest time that one can usher in the *Shabbat*; but the time before that cannot be appended to the *Shabbat* since it accrues to Friday. The time afterward can be added on to the *Shabbat,* and likewise may serve as the time zone for the evening prayer.

Misconception: Jews pray to the moon once a month.

There is an observance that is practiced once a month called *kiddush levanah* (the sanctification of the moon). It takes place during the first half of the month, on any night that the moon is visible, but after the third or fourth day of the month, depending on when the new moon was actually born.

However, in this procedure, Jews do not pray to the moon, any more than praying at the *Kotel* (Western Wall) means they are talking to a wall. Instead, the prayer is to God, in appreciation for blessing us with the luminosity of the moon. We pray to God in the ambience of the moon.

Praying to the moon itself smacks of idolatry and is theologically unacceptable.

Misconception: A *Kohen* who desecrates the *Shabbat* is unfit to recite the priestly blessing.

Many congregations have eliminated the priestly benediction from their prayer services. The benediction is recited by the cantor, but the priests do not ascend to the platform in front of the ark to pronounce the blessing.

The argument used to justify this is that today's priests are nothing special. In many instances they desecrate the *Shabbat*, and they do not have any spiritual superiority to justify their blessing the congregation.

This logic may seem foolproof at first glance, but is based on a mistaken assumption. The priests do not bless the congregation, and whether they are holy or not is irrelevant. Any blessing comes directly from the source of all blessing, namely God. The priests are merely fulfilling their responsibility to pronounce the words of the priestly blessing, and the rest is left to God. To deny the priest the opportunity to fulfill a commandment because he may be derelict in other commandments is as logical as denying individuals the right to put on *tefillin* (phylacteries) because they do not observe the dietary laws.

Misconception: One who is called to the *Torah* should pass the *tallit* over the place being read.

Passing the *tallit* over a written part of the *Torah* creates the possibility that one may erase a letter, even possibly the name of God. This is compounded if such erasure is done on the *Shabbat*.

Therefore it is recommended that one not do this, even though there are many who think that this is the proper protocol. One should make eye contact with the portion of the *Torah* that is being read for the specific *aliyah* (call to the Torah), and one may touch the *tallit* to a part of the *Torah* parchment on which there is no script. But to go over parts where there is script is potentially problematic and should therefore be avoided.

Misconception: The reading from the Prophets following the *Torah* reading is called *maftir.*

The word *maftir* does not describe a reading, but rather a person. The person who will recite the *haftorah* is the *maftir.* The word *maftir* literally means the one who recites the *Haftorah.*

The *maftir* reading is the concluding part of the *Torah* reading. The *Haftorah* is the proper term for the prophetic excerpt that is read subsequent to the *Torah* reading.

Misconception: A *Torah* may be placed in a *Torah* holder.

Many congregations, combining necessity with art, construct receptacles wherein the *Torah* is placed after it is wrapped, and before it is returned to the Ark.

However asthetically pleasing and functional these containers may be, they are far from ideal. The *Torah*, if it is outside the Ark, should never be left alone, even in a receptacle. The *Torah* must be held by a human being and accorded the dignity of being embraced, rather than being put away in aesthetic, convenient, but less-than-respectful storage.

Misconception: The *kipah* can be any size.

Our generation has witnessed the interesting phenomenon of inflation of ego and "deflation" of *kipah*. Some *kipot* (plural of *kipah*), measured from end-to-end, are probably not much bigger than bottle caps. When placed on a bushy head of hair, this size *kipah* is almost lost in the wilderness.

It is true that the *kipah* is intended to be a reminder of our responsibilities, that there is a God Whom we must serve. However, it is also the case that the head must be covered by the *kipah*. The general rule is that ideally the *kipah* should cover most of the head area that is (or was) covered by hair, but minimally should be the size of a normal hand and visible from all angles.

Misconception: Any style haircut is acceptable.

A few decades ago, the fashionable hair style for men included significant sideburns. This was fortunate, since according to Jewish law, one is not allowed to round the face. There must be some hair going down the side, a sideburn of some size, called a *pe'ah*.

According to Hirsch, this is a symbolic split between two areas of the brain, the vegetative and the animal, and symbolizes the divide-and-conquer concept wherein one gains control over one's behavior by separating out the various components of human expression. Whatever the reason, the *pe'ah* is a traditional Jewish facial feature.

In more recent times, the rounded-head style has gained many adherents. Thus, permitting the barber to style and cut your hair as he sees fit poses serious problems. The barber should not be allowed to cut corners.

Misconception: Wrapping *pe'yot* behind the ears is a sound religious practice.

Biblical law mandates that one does not destroy sideburns, that one does not round the head. Rounding of the head was considered a pagan practice, and the setting up of sideburn lines down the face is, in the words of Hirsch, an act of delineation of the various components of the brain, in line with the divide-and-conquer concept that urges individual control over the various components of human behavior.

There are those who would take this to the extreme and refrain from destroying anything that could potentially become a sideburn. This is initially achieved by wrapping the excess hair around the ears, and later, by curling the lengthening sideburns, in order to prevent them from growing to unmanageable lengths.

However, one who does not have any tangible "fuzz" or hair growth in the sideburn area, yet brings the sideburns behind the ear, is ironically contravening the biblical precept. Bringing the sideburns behind the ears effectively rounds the face, and eliminates the downward sideburn and its symbolism.

In paradoxical fashion, what is undoubtedly conceived as an act of religious meticulousness turns out to be just the opposite, a contravention of the intended regulation.

Misconception: There is a direct correlation between *tefillin* and prayer.

The *tefillin*—the leather encasements containing parchment excerpts of the *Torah*—are in some measure associated with prayer. The singular form, *tefillah*, is also the Hebrew word for prayer.

Another connection is that the *Shema*, the faith affirmation that is a basic component of the morning services, contains a statement about the obligation to wear *tefillin*. Thus, one who reads the *Shema*, ostensibly to affirm adherence to its principles, engages in self-contradiction if not wearing *tefillin* at that time. This is the primary association between *tefillin* and prayer.

But there is really no inherent limitation regarding how long one can wear the *tefillin* on the head and on the hand. Literally the entire day is appropriate for this. However, since the *tefillin* are sacred, they should not be worn in situations or circumstances that compromise their sanctity. Hence, the general practice is to not wear *tefillin* except in sacred areas, such as a sanctuary or a *bet midrash* (house of learning) or a neutral but clean place, such as a living room.

There is no reason why an individual should rush to take off the phylacteries so that immediately after the services he can dash out. It is almost as if wearing the *tefillin* for one moment longer is unnecessary, even a burden.

Thus, *tefillin* should be worn through the prayer service; and for whatever time after services that one continues to wear them, the longer the better, obviously within the constraints of having to address one's other responsibilities.

Misconception: The *tefillah* for the head may be placed on one's forehead.

The proper place for the head *tefillah* corresponds to where the fontanel is. The *tefillah* should not protrude any further than the beginning of the hairline. For a bald individual, the line is a projected boundary that would be the hairline, if he actually had hair.

Many people seem to think that the place for the *tefillah* is the forehead, but this is not the case. The *tefillah* should be placed *on the head*, rather than on the forehead.

One of the concepts suggested by *tefillin*, one of which is placed on the head and the other on the arm facing the heart, is that one should employ both the rational faculties and the emotional faculties in the covenental service of God. The hand *tefillah* is placed directly opposite the heart, and the head *tefillah* is placed on the head, the locale of the rational process. This may be the reason for placing the *tefillah* behind the hairline on top of the head, rather than on the forehead.

Misconception: The four separate portions of the head *tefillah* are easily and independently replaceable.

The head frontlet of the *tefillin* set is divided into four chambers. In each of these chambers, one of the parchment scrolls of biblical excerpts is placed. This is in contradistinction to the phylactery of the hand, wherein all of the four excerpts are printed on one parchment.

One rule among the many pertaining to these parchments is that they must have been written in sequence. This applies not only to the words of each biblical excerpt, but to the excerpts themselves. In other words, the first of the parchments should have been written before the second, the second before the third, and the third before the fourth.

Thus, if a mistake is found in the fourth of the parchments, a mistake that cannot be corrected, one cannot simply replace that parchment with perfectly written parchment. One must first ascertain that the replacement parchment was not written earlier than the other parchments. If it was written earlier, then it fails to conform to the sequential requirement and cannot be used for this *tefillin* set.

Because of the complications arising from this, when in doubt one is probably best off to replace the four parchments with an entire new set of parchments.

Misconception: If either the phylactery of the hand or the head frontlet of the *tefillin* set is missing, one should not put on *tefillin* at all.

We normally perceive the phylacteries, worn on the head and the arm, as a set, much like the four wheels of a car. Ideally, both should be worn. However, if one has only the head or the hand *tefillin*, and there is no hope of obtaining the missing part that day, one should put on the one that is available.

Misconception: The fact that you are in pain does not exempt you from having to don phylacteries.

The phylacteries or *tefillin* are sacred objects. Because they are sacred, they must be treated with extraordinary respect. One must be in a clean bodily state when donning the phylacteries, and one is obliged to concentrate on the phylacteries when they are worn. It is forbidden to don the phylacteries and then engage in trivial conversation.

If one is unable to concentrate and maintain an awareness of the phylacteries, then one is better off not putting them on. A person who is in pain and is unable to concentrate on anything else is better off waiting for the pain to subside before putting on the *tefillin*. If one is in such excruciating and steady pain with no prospect that the pain will abate, one refrains from putting on *tefillin* that day.

Misconception: *Mezuzah* is the name for the parchment that is placed on the doorpost.

Biblically, the term *mezuzah* refers to the doorpost itself. The parchment scroll, containing the faith affirmation called the *Shema* and the acceptance of the yoke of responsibility for actualizing the commandments, is to be affixed on the right entry side of the doorpost of every room.

A *mezuzah*, or doorpost, without the parchment, is a deficient doorpost. In common usage, the parchment itself has taken on the name of that to which it is affixed. Parchment and doorpost have become one, and so today we refer to the parchment by the name originally given to the doorpost.

Misconception: The most important part of a *mezuzah* is its case.

Jewish homes are obliged to have *mezuzot* on the doorpost of each doorway leading into a room, including the front and back doors of the house. The parchment enclosed within contains the affirmation of faith, the *Shema*, and the affirmation dealing with the acceptance of one's Judaic responsibilities.

The key ingredient of the *mezuzah* is this parchment, which must be written on genuine parchment by a scribe who knows how to properly write the letters of the *mezuzah* scroll.

The outer case is not nearly as crucial. Placing the *mezuzah* scroll into an attractive casing is important because it adorns the *mitzvah* (commandment). Just doing it does not suffice; we insist on doing it beautifully.

But if one has only limited funds available for the purchase of *mezuzot*, the priority should be to purchase parchment scrolls that are of superior quality, and the balance to be used for the cases.

Misconception: The *mezuzah* is placed on the doorpost in a slanted position merely as a decorative nuance.

There is a difference of opinion among religious authorities as to whether the *mezuzah* is to be affixed on the doorpost in a horizontal or vertical position.

The *mezuzah* is placed on a slant, somewhere between the horizontal and the vertical position, with the top part of the *mezuzah* facing inward toward the house or the room. This compromise incorporates a little bit of each of the views.

Incidentally, the Sephardic community places the *mezuzah* in a vertical position, pointing upwards to the heavens.

Misconception: Mistakes in a *mezuzah* or *tefillin* scroll are easily corrected by a scribe.

According to Jewish law, the portions of the *Torah* that are on the *mezuzah* and *tefillin* parchments must be written in order. They cannot be written backwards, out of sequence, or any other way that is different from the way they appear in the Torah.

Were a mistake to occur in a word at the beginning or middle, the correction of that word effectively means that this word is being written "now." That word, in the middle, has been written "after" whatever comes subsequent to it. Thus, even though the mistake is technically corrected, it does not result in a parchment scroll that is usable.

The last words of the last excerpts of both the *mezuzah* and the *tefillin* parchments could be corrected, with the proviso that what follows subsequently does not include God's name (God's name may not be erased).

Misconception: A house of prayer needs a *mezuzah* on its doorpost.

The *mezuzah*, the parchment scroll containing the reminder of our responsibilities, is visible as we enter and leave the home. It must be affixed on a dwelling place.

A place that is used for storage is exempt from having a *mezuzah* on it. Likewise, and surprisingly, a place that is used for prayer does not need a *mezuzah*. It is not a dwelling place, and one is not permitted to eat in the room designated for prayer.

A congregational complex of many rooms, some of which are used for eating or for meeting, among other activities, would need a *mezuzah* on the right entry side of the eating or meeting rooms. Likewise, the main entrance to a complex that contains prayer rooms and rooms for other purposes would also need a *mezuzah*. But the entry to the prayer room proper need not have a *mezuzah* on its door.

Misconception: Good news does not require any special reaction.

Good news requires that one react with the recitation of a *brakhah* (blessing). If it is good news only for the recipient of the news, then the blessing is *sheheheyanu* (Who has kept us alive and maintained us, enabling us to reach this moment).

If the news is good not only for oneself but also for others, then the blessing is *hatov v'hamaytiv* (Who is good, and Who does good for others).

If one's investment went up, *sheheheyanu* is in order. If this was a joint investment, which is good news for others, the *hatov v'hamaytiv* blessing is in order.

Misconception: There is no special greeting that one extends to a person one has not seen for a long period of time.

If one has not seen a close friend or relative for more than a year, then one greets this individual with more than a warm Hello.

There is a special blessing for such an occasion: "Blessed be the One Who resurrects the dead."

After an absence of a year, it is as if the individual had been totally removed from one's consciousness. Seeing the person after the year, with its attendant joy, should evoke a feeling akin to meeting someone who has come back from another world. Hence this blessing.

Misconception: There is no special greeting that one should recite upon seeing someone who has recovered from illness.

Aside from the obvious joy that one has at seeing someone who has recovered from illness, there is also a blessing to be recited in gratitude to God for having granted this individual the restoration of health.

That blessing thanks God for having given the recovered person to us and not to the dust. On any appropriate occasion, we express our gratitude to the Ultimate Bestower of blessing for every good fortune.

Misconception: There is no blessing recited at the birth of a child.

There is a specific blessing for the birth of a child. For the birth of a female child, the blessing is *sheheheyanu*. For the birth of a male child, it is *hatov v'hamaytiv*.

Misconception: Admiring nature shows sensitivity to our world, but it has no religious significance.

There are many outstanding components to the world, including rainbows, great rivers or mountains, the appearance of the first fruits on the tree, thunder, and lightning.

All these have specific blessings attached to them. The individual who experiences these great manifestations of nature recites a *brakhah* (blessing), expressing awe of God as the architect of the experienced beauty.

The precise blessings depend on the aspect of nature involved and are contingent on the seasons and/or time elapsed between the last experience of that manifestation and the present experience of it. But the obligation to express one's appreciation to God for these is well entrenched in Jewish tradition.

Misconception: Buying a car is a purely business matter, with no religious implications.

Whenever one purchases something significant, new clothing, or other items the individual is excited about, one recites the blessing of *sheheheyanu* (Who has kept us alive and maintained us, enabling us to reach this moment).

Therefore, when one purchases a car, and one may assume that the purchase of a car is a significant event that makes the individual happy, one should recite the *sheheheyanu* blessing. We link the joy of acquisition with gratitude to God.

If the car will be used by many drivers, including the children, then a different blessing is recited, that is, *hatov v'hamaytiv* (Who is good and does good for others).

Part III

Eros
and
Thanatos

5

Marriage and Divorce

Before
During
After

Misconception: Matchmaking is an archaic way to bring couples together.

In this age of computer dating, one of the more sophisticated ways of introducing men and women, the old-style *shadkhan* (matchmaker) seems to be in trouble. After all, how can one compete with modern technology and psychological expertise? However, it should be realized that the *shadkhan* does not impose; the *shadkhan* proposes. The *shadkhan's* methods may be scientifically less precise, but this does not mean that they are any less accurate.

In this process of matchmaking, primary emphasis is placed on the families involved, their traditions, their genealogy, their affirmations. Obviously, the personalities of the prospective bride and groom are of overwhelming importance, including their values and their characters. Ideally, the *shadkhan* is concerned not only with present compatibility, but with long-range sharing of destiny. This is so vital in marriage, but it is an intangible that escapes many a computer matchmaker.

This is not to suggest that there are no abuses in the *shadkhan* "industry." Probably the greatest problem within the *shadkhan* system is that too often the information provided, whether first- or secondhand, is not on the level. In the rush to marry, there are some who would distort the truth. In the end, this is a favor to no one, least of all the couple, who are unsuspecting victims of the false information.

With all the problems, the basic thrust and approach within the *shadkhan* system is arguably superior to technological matchmaking.

Misconception: The more religious may agree to marry without seeing the spouse-to-be.

In previous generations, because of the continual peril in which Jewish families lived, marriages were sometimes arranged between parents, on behalf of their still very young children. To a large extent, this was a survival mechanism. If two families agreed that their children should marry at an appropriate time in the future, they thereby immediately guaranteed two sets of parents for these vulnerable children. A child whose parents might be killed in a pogrom had a greater chance of survival because the child would be cared for by the future parents-in-law until reaching the age of marriage. People may poke fun at this arrangement today, but in its historical context it was a serious matter, not a joke.

However, barring necessities born of emergency, under normal circumstances it is forbidden for a bride and a groom to marry without seeing each other. Quite possibly, if they meet for the first time at the wedding, they may not like what they see, and will be united in a climate of enmity, thereby contravening the basic obligation of "love your neighbor as yourself."

How much "seeing" must precede "believing" is a matter best left to individual discretion. Some people see each other for ten years before getting married, but this does not guarantee that the marriage will last. Others may see each other for only ten days, but may learn enough so that it is possible to proceed to the destiny–sharing of marriage.

But marrying a mate who is "out of sight" is not consistent with Jewish tradition.

Misconception: No weddings may take place between *Pesah* and *Shavuot*.

The *Omer* period, between *Pesah* and *Shavuot*, is one of semi-mourning, linked primarily to the staggering loss of the many thousands of students of Rabbi Akiva, which occurred in this time period. The semi-mourning mood was further entrenched because of the blood libels against the Jews, and the post-Passover tragic implications of these absurd accusations.

However, the period of semi-mourning does not extend though the entire period. It is a semi-mourning period only for thirty-three of the forty-nine days. There are varying customs as to whether one takes the first thirty-three days or the last thirty-three days, or other combinations, for the semi-mourning expression.

Those who observe the first thirty-three days as semi-mourning may have weddings from *Lag B'Omer* (the thirty-third day of the *Omer*) in the morning until the end. Those who observe the last days may have weddings up until *Rosh Hodesh* Iyar, which is the fifteenth day.

Interestingly, many authorities allow those who are invited to a wedding during the period of their own observance of the *Omer*, but which is not in the mourning custom of the hosts, to attend that wedding.

It would be wrong to unnecessarily extend the thirty-three-day mourning period into a forty-nine-day mourning period. Where possible, communities are best advised to establish one custom for the entire community, so that the approximately sixteen remaining days are not unnecessarily relegated to semi-mourning.

Misconception: It is permitted to have a wedding at any hour on *Lag B'Omer*.

There are two approaches to the observance of the thirty-three-day semi-mourning period between *Pesah* and *Shavuot*. One custom is to observe the first thirty-three days, starting from the second night of *Pesah*. The other custom is to observe the last thirty-three days.

Those who follow the second custom incorporate the thirty-three days, aside from *Lag B'Omer* itself, into the calculation. For those who observe this custom, *Lag B'Omer*, from nightfall until the end of the next day, is a time when weddings are permitted.

However, for those who maintain the custom of the first thirty-three days, were they to conduct marriages on the night of *Lag B'Omer*, they would then effectively be left with only thirty-two days of semi-mourning. The adherents to the first custom must incorporate *Lag B'Omer* evening and a short time of *Lag B'Omer* morning to complete the required thirty-three days. Only subsequent to that can weddings be held.

A small part (even a few minutes) of the day is considered to be like the complete day. A little bit of the day of *Lag B'Omer* is considered as the totality of that day, so that the semi-mourning period is considered completed, and marriages can take place from then on.

Misconception: Bride and groom are not allowed to see each other for the seven days before the wedding.

There are many brides and grooms who avoid seeing each other for the seven-day period prior to the wedding. However, this is not a law that is codified in Jewish legal sources. Instead, it is a custom undoubtedly related to the proposition that absence makes the heart grow fonder. By not seeing each other for the seven-day period prior to the wedding, the bride and groom intensify their anticipation of the great moment, and thus approach it with heightened expectation. The custom is designed to make the joy of the wedding an even more celebrative event, by virtue of its impact on the emotions of the bride and the groom.

Since this is a custom that itself is not explicitly codified as an entrenched practice, it is difficult to say that bride and groom are prohibited from seeing each other. Instead, it is better to say that they are best advised, consistent with the tradition, not to see each other for the seven-day period prior to the wedding, so that their coming together on the wedding day is an even more blissful experience.

In Sephardic tradition, bride and groom refrain from seeing each other only prior to the ceremony on the day of the wedding. The idea of absence has currency even here, albeit a little less of it.

Misconception: A house of prayer is the ideal setting for a wedding.

Since a wedding is a sacred event, and a house of prayer is a sacred place, it would seem as if the house of prayer is an ideal place for a wedding. It is where sacred meets sacred.

There are many authorities who, to this day, look with disfavor on the idea of having a wedding in a house of prayer. Their feeling is that a house of prayer is dedicated specifically for the purpose of prayer, and any activity other than prayer compromises its sanctity.

This by no means diminishes the importance of weddings. It is only to indicate that because the house of prayer has a specific purpose, no other activity should take place there.

The ideal place for a wedding is a dignified setting, preferably under the sky, under the aura of heavenly majesty.

In contemporary times, most houses of prayer do in fact encourage weddings to take place on the premises. It is likely that houses of prayer are built with weddings in mind. In other words, they are built not only for prayer, but for other sacred activities such as weddings. This being the case, there is little problem with weddings taking place in houses of prayer.

Even though the standard practice is to recommend the house of prayer for weddings, it is important to be aware that this well-entrenched custom is not free of difficulty.

Misconception: For a Jewish marriage to be legally binding, a rabbi must be present.

The truth is that one does not need a rabbi in order to be
married. The only requirements for a marriage are a man, a
woman, an item of value, two cups of wine, two reliable witnesses, who are unrelated to each other or to the couple, and a
marriage document, called a *ketubah*.

The man and the woman are needed to effect the union.
The item of value is necessary for the husband to transmit to his
soon-to-be wife. The cups of wine are necessary for the recitation of the appropriate blessings, giving religious imprimatur
to the wedding. The *ketubah* is necessary as the legally binding
contract establishing the guidelines for the marital union.

The two witnesses are needed to testify and assure that all
procedures for establishing a legally binding marriage have
been properly carried out.

It is assumed that a rabbi would be singularly qualified in
this regard, and is therefore usually present and can serve as one
of the witnesses to the marriage. Even if not serving as a witness
to the marriage, the rabbi is instrumental in assuring that all the
legal requirements are met.

But this does not mean that it cannot be done without a
rabbi. It is highly advisable to have a rabbi officiate and supervise the marriage ceremony. However, it is also important to
recognize that the rabbi's role is not to pronounce the marriage
as official, but rather to assure that what has been contracted
and how it has been effected is in keeping with Jewish tradition.

Misconception: The rabbi who presides at a wedding ceremony recites the blessings on his own behalf.

The first two blessings pronounced under the *hupah* are referred to as *Birkhot Erusin* (blessings of betrothal).

These blessings should, by right, be pronounced by the groom. However, problems may arise if the groom is not capable of reciting these blessings. The practice has therefore evolved that the rabbi recites these blessings on behalf of the groom.

It is important to realize this, both from the point of view of the rabbi and the groom, who should know for whom the blessings are being recited.

Misconception: When the groom gives the ring to the bride, the couple are married.

The ceremony that takes place under the *hupah* is actually a combination of two components that unite husband and wife. The first component is the betrothal; the second is the marriage.

In previous generations there was a space of about a year between betrothal and marriage. In betrothal, the husband and wife reserved themselves for each other. They did not yet marry, but were committed to marrying. If there was a change of heart, then it was necessary to obtain a *get* (Jewish divorce), because the betrothal was a legally binding commitment. Marriage was the sanctification of the union—the coming together, uniting as one.

The betrothal is called *kidushin* (sanctification), in which each makes the self sacred and reserved for the other. The marriage is called *nisuin* (uplifting), or the mutual transcendence of the couple into the sphere of matrimony.

Under the *hupah,* when the groom gives the ring to the bride, they are merely betrothed, or in modern parlance, engaged but not yet married. The second stage, being together under one roof, symbolized by the *hupah,* is *nisuin.* It culminates in an action that takes place after the wedding ceremony, when the bride and groom retire to a private room for a specific length of time. It is then that they establish themselves legally as husband and wife.

Misconception: Only a ring can be used to effect betrothal.

The betrothal component of the marriage ceremony invariably involves the giving of a ring from groom to bride. According to the Talmud, such betrothal could be effected not only by a ring, but by any material item of solid value.

"Solid value" means any item whose value is clear and not subject to misinterpretation. Thus, a diamond is not of solid value because of its volatility, and because it may sometimes be assumed to be worth more than it really is. Therefore, a solid metal substance is always preferred. It could be a gold, silver, or platinum ring, or a less expensive metal, but it must be an item whose value is clear.

Additionally, betrothal may be effected through a contract. A ring was chosen as the traditional means for this because it is worn on a hand and is thus a continual visible reminder of one's marital status. The ring binds and reminds.

Misconception: Prenuptial agreements have no place in Judaism.

Most people assume that prenuptial agreements are a recent invention. In fact, prenuptial agreements already existed in the time of the Talmud.

Under normal circumstances, when a man and woman married, there was a division of responsibilities between them. The husband was responsible to provide for the home, and the wife was responsible for its upkeep. The husband earned the bread, the wife baked it.

However, this type of trade-off was not hard and fast, nor was it beyond negotiation. The wife, both prior to and during marriage, could assert her preference for a different arrangement. She could tell her husband that she did not expect to be supported by him, and that he should therefore not expect her to be responsible for the housekeeping.

As a general rule, it was the wife's desires that were the more decisive. If she wanted to venture out on her own and not be sustained by her husband, this is the way it was. Special arrangements for the status of property during and after marriage were also negotiable.

Prenuptial agreements are not new. There may not be an exact replication in some of the more intricate prenuptial agreements that are prepared in contemporary times, but the idea of negotiating some of the parameters of the marital compact already existed in talmudic times.

Misconception: The *ketubah,* given by the husband to his wife during the marriage ceremony, is only a symbolic document.

This assumption may be related to the feeling that the *ketubah* has no legal status in a secular court.

However, the couple, married within the framework of Jewish tradition, are bound by Jewish law to certain obligations that are spelled out in the *ketubah.* In Israel the *ketubah* has significant legal status, especially since the precise financial terms for the marital compact are spelled out in fine detail in the *ketubah.*

Aside from this, the *ketubah* is the document of responsibility, which makes it more difficult for the husband, in particular, to gain easy exit from the marriage.

So important is the *ketubah* to the integrity of the marital union that the sages forbade husband and wife to be together even one hour without a *ketubah.*

Misconception: A glass is broken under the *hupah* at the wedding ceremony to commemorate the destruction of the Temple.

This is the conventional wisdom, and, in fact, such a reason is cited in some of the sources explaining Judaic custom. However, the original root of this custom has little connection with the destruction of the Temple.

The custom traces back to an incident reported in the Talmud, of a wedding in which the participants went slightly berserk. The rabbis, to inject a note of sobriety into the festivities, took an expensive crystal object and smashed it on the floor. This brought the people to their senses. They realized that they were overdoing it. In their happiness, they had forgotten the seriousness of the event and were uncontrolled and giddy.

The breaking of the glass to culminate the marriage ceremony is to remind the couple, and all who are about to celebrate the joy of the wedding, that they should not get drunk and lose control. Instead, they should be seriously and soberly happy. The happiness should be of the type that on the next day, the joy of yesterday can be recalled and fully appreciated.

Misconception: Following the wedding, bride and groom are obligated to have *sheva berakhot* celebrations and meals for the wedding day and the next six days.

It is customary that in the period following the wedding, the seven blessings, called the *sheva berakhot* are recited in the presence of a *minyan* (quorum). This is done on the day of the wedding and for the next six days.

However, it is *not* obligatory to put together the quorum for the meal. The general rule is that if a quorum does gather, it is obligatory to recite these seven blessings, provided that one of the members of the quorum is a new face, a fresh face, to reinvigorate the sense of joy and thus to justify the recitation of the *sheva berakhot*.

Many go out of their way to schedule a series of *sheva berakhot* meals for the days following the wedding. This is definitely joyful but not obligatory.

Misconception: Judaism has a prudish attitude about sex.

Judaism views the sexual relationship between husband and wife not as something of which to be ashamed, but as something that is sacred.

The reluctance to discuss sexual matters in a public forum does not stem from the feeling that sex is dirty or a topic to be avoided. It stems from the feeling that sex is a matter that is so sacred, that one dare not trivialize it through public discourse.

There is much practical and good advice in the Talmud, and rabbinic sources discuss the dignified and effective manner by which the sexual relationship should be experienced.

In the words of the author of "The Holy Letter," sexual relations, when engaged in properly are holy and pure, a blissful experience surpassing any other experience in life.

Misconception: There is no blessing recited for the sexual experience.

For almost every enjoyment of this world, there is a blessing. If there would be no blessing for the sexual experience, it would be one of the rare exceptions, even more pointedly because the sexual experience is so basic a component of human life.

The *Shema* prayer (affirmation of faith recited before retiring at night) starts with the word *hamapil*. In this lengthier than usual blessing, one requests of God: "May my bed be complete before you." This, says Rabbi Yaakov Emden, a sage who lived a few generations ago is the blessing for a meaningful sexual experience, and appropriately so, since the sexual relationship, properly experienced, is indeed a blessing.

Misconception: Sex in marriage is a demand of the husband that the wife must fulfill.

The sexual relationship, like other components of marriage, demands mutuality, but even more acutely. It should be free of demands and must be characterized by love and mutual desire. The husband has absolutely no right to coerce his wife, by taunts, threats, or other unacceptable behavior, into the sexual relationship. Such behavior is considered abusive and demeaning.

Neither of the partners is allowed to deliberately withhold sex from the other, but neither can demands be made. Genuine love, which results in a meaningful union, is the primary ingredient in marriage, and thus, in the sexual relationship.

Misconception: A woman after childbirth, or during menstruation, is unclean.

"Unclean" is a terrible word to describe a woman at this or any other time, but it is the usual English translation of the biblical word *tamay*. The Hebrew word *tamay* relates to ritual distancing, to a check against becoming involved in certain ritual expressions.

An individual who has come in contact with a corpse is *tamay* and may not enter into the Temple area. This ritual distancing is a way of conveying to the individual that he or she should be affected and sobered by the experience of coming in contact with a corpse, and should therefore contemplate life in its full significance and with greater intensity.

There is a sense of loss of life involved in the childbirth process, since the life that was within the womb is now born. In the case of menstruation, it is the loss of potential life that is involved.

In both these instances, the woman experiencing these physiological changes is asked to go through a period of distancing from active involvement in matters that require religious intensity, in order to fully appreciate the implications of what is happening.

In the instance of menstruation or childbirth, there is also a suspension of marital relations. But the woman is not unclean; she is rather in a state of ritual distance, which is a more accurate, but perhaps awkward translation of *tamay*.

Misconception: The husband and wife separate during menstruation just for separation's sake.

The Talmud discusses the matter of why husband and wife must separate during the wife's menstrual cycle. It asks the question: Why does the Torah prohibit marital relations during this period of time? It is uncharacteristic for the Talmud to inquire about the purpose of biblical legislation, but in this instance, the Talmud suggests that the reason is so that the husband and wife will later reunite in a spirit of renewal that is reminiscent of their wedding day.

In other words, the Talmud states clearly that the husband and wife separate not for the sake of separation, but for the sake of togetherness.

Misconception: It is important to look one's best in public.

The building blocks of the Jewish community are the individual families. Families can only be building blocks if individuals within the community acknowledge that the family is their number one priority.

That being the case, it would be more vital that one looks one's best in the confines of the home. Historically, ornaments were given for individuals to be attractive to their partners, not to others.

Although this idea may sound foreign, it really is not. After all, does it make sense that individuals should dress in their best clothes because they are going to the theater or because they are going to work, yet look disheveled in the presence of the individual who means the most, namely the spouse?

This is not to suggest that one should be unkempt in public. It is to suggest that one should put one's best foot forward in the place that matters the most, namely at home with one's mate. Would not marriage be enhanced if the husband took a shower and shaved in the evening, after work, rather than before it, thereby looking his freshest for his wife? Should not the wife do the same for her husband? It would be a powerful and profound statement, an expression much more eloquent than words.

Misconception: A wig is a superior means for a married woman to cover her hair.

The religious obligation for a married woman to cover her hair is consistent with the importance placed on modest bearing rather than exhibitionism.

One finds it hard to reconcile the general posture of modesty with a *sheitel* (wig) that looks as natural as one's own hair and is often anything but modest.

It is true that the wig has become the major fashion for head covering within the religious community, but it is not entirely clear this is the preferable way to cover the hair. Arguably, a hat, beret, or kerchief are superior means for covering the hair.

Misconception: Incest has never been permitted.

There is no instance of the Torah explicitly allowing incest. It would thus seem as if incest is never permitted, since it is explicitly prohibited.

However, it is instructive to go all the way back to the creation, to Adam and Eve, and their children. We know that Adam and Eve parented Cain and Abel, but whom did Cain and Abel marry? If Adam and Eve only had sons, then the world could not have gone on. But they also had daughters, and the world proliferated through the marriage of these siblings.

If this union between brothers and sisters was prohibited at that time, then all children born of these marriages would have been illegitimate. That illegitimacy would have carried down, through the generations, to the present.

One must, therefore, reach the unavoidable conclusion that incest is a prohibited relationship when viable alternatives to that incest are available. For the children of Adam and Eve, there was no alternative, and therefore no incest.

But not long afterward, many alternatives became available, and therefore an incestuous relationship became prohibited.

If, God forbid, a nuclear holocaust should engulf the world, and the only two survivors were a brother and a sister, they could renew the human race as husband and wife, without fear that this would be incest. Far from being a forbidden union, it would be highly recommended, in order to prevent the total extinction of humanity.

Misconception: Judaism is against bigamy.

In western countries, one is unlikely to find a man who is married to more than one woman at a time. This is a social convention that has become part of our legal code, a code that prohibits having more than one spouse at a time.

In biblical law, however, a man was allowed to have more than one wife at one time. Abraham, the first patriarch, and Jacob, the third of the patriarchs, both had more than one wife. King David had many, and King Solomon, even more.

Later on, monogamy became the norm, and eventually Rabbenu Gershom issued an edict forbidding any Jew within the province of his rabbinical authority to have more than one wife at a time.

Even today there are some communities, such as Morocco, that have never accepted this edict. There, a Jewish home may be comprised of a husband and a number of wives, and, of course, many children.

The fact that in the western world Jewish families today have only a one man–one wife configuration is the result of the continuing application and renewed validity of the edict of Rabbenu Gershom, in conjunction and compliance with the prevailing laws of western society.

Misconception: The Jewish community does not suffer from a significant divorce problem.

Unfortunately, this myth was exploded some time ago. In the past, the rate of divorce in the Jewish community was quite low, and even today it is lower than the national average. However, it is increasing, and the increase is disturbing because cohesive Jewish families are all-important for Jewish continuity.

This is not to suggest that following divorce, Jewish expression must perforce disappear; rather, it becomes more difficult, since community expression is couple-oriented.

The rate of divorce may differ depending on which segment of the community is involved, but there is literally no segment of the community that is immune from the problem, including the very religious. Although the rate of divorce is lower in the very religious community, even here there has been a notable increase in the number of broken homes.

Of greater importance is the impression of many that even in situations when the family stays together, the happiness and intrinsic contentment that may have been the hallmark of the Jewish home of earlier generations does not prevail today. And, after all, the bottom line is not merely the statistical measure, but the all-important issue of whether the married couple is content.

Children who grow up in unhappy homes, where father and mother do not get along, carry that baggage with them. Sometimes the repercussion of such a marriage is that the children are disinclined to getting married themselves. At other times, the behavior patterns with which they grew up are in turn transmitted to their spouses and children, entrenching an unfortunate syndrome and a downward spiral of unhappiness and misery.

Lamentably, there is not only a divorce problem in the Jewish community, but a marriage problem as well.

Misconception: Judaism is prejudiced against divorcees.

This may be subconsciously related to the fact that according to biblical law, a *kohen* is forbidden to marry a divorcee. This suggests that a *kohen*, who occupies a more sacred trust within the community, is compromising that trust by marrying someone who is "tainted" with the stigma of a failed marriage.

The prohibition against marrying a divorcee may be traced back to an interesting process. In Temple times, a woman would go to the Temple to bring an offering following childbirth. Private offerings such as this were usually preceded by conversation with a priest.

Immediately after childbirth, a woman was emotionally vulnerable, having experienced an exhilirating, yet potentially traumatic experience. In pouring her heart out to the priest, she may have found him to be much more understanding than her own husband. This realization may have understandably caused her to regret her choice of mate, and may even have led her to want to divorce her husband and marry the priest.

This potential scenario would have likely caused the husband to think twice about letting his wife go to the Temple in the first place, thus sabotaging a major conduit for legitimate religious expression. Possibly to avoid such scenarios, the Bible prohibited a *kohen* from marrying a divorcee. There would be less worry about anything improper transpiring between the woman and the priest, since any romantic trysts would be automatically ruled out. This, among other reasons, may be the rationale for this prohibition. It makes no statement about a divorced woman being inferior.

In the contemporary arena, some divorcees are made to feel uncomfortable because of public discussion, and even rabbinic harangue, about the importance of keeping families together and lamenting the increasing rate of divorce among Jews.

This is an unfortunate, but understandable interpretation. The Judaic attitude is to be for marriage, happiness, and contentment and against the unhappiness that leads to divorce. Being against unhappiness and divorce is a far cry from being against those who divorce.

Mistakes can happen, and if divorce is the only way out of a bad situation, it is authorized in the Bible. The exit option is clearly designed to give individuals the opportunity to find the contentment in life that they deserve.

Misconception: Divorce is a sin.

It may sound suprising, but actually divorce is a *mitzvah*. But before anyone jumps to conclusions, this should be explained. Obviously, the ideal is that a married couple are happy, content, and harmonious throughout the duration of their marriage.

However, there are times when marriage simply does not work, when circumstances or conditions result in the dissolution of the union. In such instances, it is obligatory for the husband and wife to separate from each other through the process of granting a *get* (religious divorce). This is a religious obligation.

In other words, if the marriage must be terminated, then it should be terminated via a *get*. This is the *mitzvah*.

There are commandments that are obligatory, others that are conditional. They depend on a certain set of circumstances. If such circumstances unfold, the *mitzvah* becomes operational. The mitzvah to grant a *get* may be seen as an imperative to behave like a *mensch* (decent person), even under the most trying of circumstances.

Although it is a *mitzvah* to divorce via a *get*, it is obviously a greater *mitzvah* fulfillment for the couple to make each other so happy that they can think of nothing better than being together.

Misconception: Judaism countenances only limited grounds
for divorce.

The reasons why one may demand a divorce are quite wide-
ranging. Either partner in the marriage may demand and have a
legitimate right to divorce, if the other refuses conjugal union.
The husband or wife who refuses to live sexually with the mate
can be sued for divorce.

The same is true if the husband does not support his wife in
the way that he is obliged to. Similarly, the wife who does not
abide by her obligation to maintain the home can also be sued
for divorce.

If either of the spouses has an extramarital affair, the other
has the full prerogative to leave the union.

Only some grounds for divorce have been delineated here. It
is also understood that if both husband and wife agree that they
are not simply compatible, that it is imperative to part so that
each might find a more suitable partner, there should be no
problem in their obtaining a *get*.

The Jewish family has maintained its stability for generations, in spite of the fact that divorce could be relatively easy to
arrange. Perhaps the knowledge that divorce was possible
placed a greater obligation on both partners to make sure that
the need for divorce would not materialize.

Misconception: A woman cannot sue for divorce.

This is untrue, even though it is a popular assumption. It is true that in the divorce procedure, it is the husband who instructs the scribe to write the *get*, and it is the husband who delivers the bill of divorce to the wife, much as, in marriage, it is the man who gives something of value to the woman in order to effect betrothal.

However, insofar as initiating divorce proceedings is concerned, both are equal. Actually, the wife probably is more favored in this regard.

Both can sue for divorce if the other denies conjugal relations, if the other fails to live up to basic support and maintenance requirements, or if the other imposes unlivable conditions.

For example, if the husband works in a tannery and comes home with an unbearable stench, the wife can sue for divorce, even if she knew before marriage that the husband would be working in a tannery. The wife can sue for divorce if the husband insists on bringing his mother into the home, and the wife finds her mother-in-law unbearable and impossible to live with.

The court, upon hearing the wife's complaint, and finding no way out, orders the husband to divorce the wife. In a case when the husband and the wife argue against each other's claims, the court usually takes the word of the woman.

The husband would have no choice but to heed the court's directive. Failure to do so would place him in contempt and make him a likely candidate for *herem* (excommunication). Excommunication itself is not a light matter. It means that no one is allowed to have any commercial relations with the individual, the individual is not allowed to be part of the prayer service, and is even denied basic burial rights in the communal cemetery.

The procedure of giving the divorce is from husband to wife, but the right to initiate the procedure and to insist upon it is equally the province of the woman.

Misconception: A woman who is divorced may remarry immediately.

There is a mandatory wait of ninety complete days, excluding the day of divorce and subsequent remarriage, before a woman may remarry.

The reason for this is that a marriage that is contracted almost immediately after the termination of a previous marriage may pose a serious problem. Should the woman give birth seven months after the second marriage was finalized, there will be doubt about who is the father of the child. Is the baby a seven-month baby from the second father, or a nine-month baby from the first father? This is a vital matter, not just a curiosity. It is the all-important matter of who is obligated to support the child, to raise the child, to take responsibility for the child's complete welfare. This issue is too vital to leave to chance or to mediation.

Therefore, the intervening 90-day period is mandated in order to ascertain who is the child's father.

No distinction is made between women who are of childbearing age and women who are beyond that stage. The law is not concerned with whether a woman has reached menopause. It is no one's business, and the best way to guard against intrusive speculation is to make this 90-day-plus waiting period mandatory for 95-year-old women as well as for 25-year-old women.

One exception to the waiting rule is when the woman remarries the man she had divorced. Since paternity is not at issue, they can remarry immediately.

Misconception: A man whose wife dies may not remarry immediately.

In actual point of law, there is no prohibition against remarrying soon after the death of one's wife.

However, such remarriage should certainly not take place during the mourning period for the wife. Even subsequent to that, it is advisable that the bereaved husband pass one cycle of the three major festivals of the year before remarrying. This is not because he is obliged to mourn for a year. The actual mourning period for anyone other than a parent is thirty days.

However, it is important to go through the throes of mourning, in order to better handle the responsibilities of the new marriage, not the least of which is the obligation to make one's wife happy. This is hardly possible if one is in a state of melancholy.

Even though this is the advised practice, in a situation of extreme urgency, one may marry earlier, but this is the exception rather than the rule.

Misconception: A man is always permitted to remarry the woman he has divorced.

If in the intervening period following divorce a former wife has remarried, then by biblical law, one can not remarry that former mate. However, if in the intervening period there has been no legal union with another, then one may return to one's former spouse.

However, a *kohen*, who may not marry a divorcee, may not remarry his ex-wife, even if she had not remarried in the intervening period. For a *kohen*, divorce is forever.

Misconception: A couple, once divorced, ceases to have any relationship with each other.

Obviously, a couple who divorce after having children are united in the common concern for their offspring. In their endeavors to raise the children, their primary concern should be what is best for the children, and any personal agenda should be removed from the consideration of the children's welfare.

Even when there are no children, the fact that the couple have divorced does not mean that they are permanently and totally disconnected. The Talmud applies the verse, "From your own flesh be not oblivious," to an individual who has divorced his wife. When married, they were as one. Divorce unhinges the relationship but does not destroy the reality of their original oneness. There are tangible aspects of this obligation; for example, one should not allow one's former wife to fall into extreme poverty.

Marriage, it turns out, is indeed forever, even after divorce.

6

Illness, Death, and Beyond

Illness
Funeral
Mourning
Aftermath

Misconception: Any time is appropriate for visiting the sick.

One does not visit the sick just to do a good deed. Visiting the sick is a *mitzvah*, an act of lovingkindness, that must be permeated with the concerns of a person who is loving and kind. Thus, one must be sensitive to the wishes of the one who is ill. When visiting, one must be especially careful not to speak in a discouraging manner or to overextend one's stay.

Many people think that more is better. This does not apply to sermons, nor does it apply to visiting the sick. Often those who are not well are too polite to ask the visitors to leave, because they do not want the visitors to feel bad. It is the visitor who must show extra sensitivity to the needs of the sick person by not staying for an extended period of time.

A sick person who prefers no visitors has that right. No one should impose on the sick person, justifying the visit as a *mitzvah* that the sick person must, therefore, permit. There is no *mitzvah* when the visit causes pain, anguish, or discomfort to the sick person.

Misconception: The *mitzvah* to visit the sick is fulfilled in the visit itself.

There is no question that there is much benefit to be derived from a useful and positive visit to a sick individual. Ideally, through the visit, the sick individual should feel encouraged or, at least, more comfortable.

However, this is only one component of the *mitzvah*. The true fulfillment of the *mitzvah* contains one other ingredient. The visitor should pray for the recovery of the sick individual. One who visits the sick should be so concerned and so moved by the sick person's plight as to entreat God on behalf of the sick person. This shows ultimate concern, free from ulterior motive, and profound in its expression.

Misconception: Death is a tragic component of life.

The loss of a relative or friend is a difficult experience. The reaction to death, including its prescribed period of mourning, reinforces the view that the death of an individual is a tragedy, not so much for the one who has died, but for those who have survived.

All this does not relate to the more general question of whether the fact of death is, in itself, a tragedy. To better understand what this suggests, one should contemplate how our lives would be affected if we lived forever. Would humanity be better off if people never died? Some people may think so, but anyone who lives with a guaranteed life contract is more likely to slough off, once assured of such an arrangement.

The thought that one will live forever gives one the prerogative of forestalling any action, of delaying any confrontation with one's responsibility. If you have forever, then you can delay forever.

The fact that the human being is finite means that each person has only a limited time in which to address the responsibilities of life in a most meaningful way. Delay, procrastination, any stalling tactic is unfathomable when one will be blessed only with a finite life span.

It is for this reason that King David, when he contemplated the fact of death, actually burst forth in song. He realized that because of death, life itself has enhanced meaning.

This is an interesting dialectic, to some extent paradoxical, but ultimately profoundly intelligible.

Misconception: The person who commits suicide is denied burial rights.

The problem with this assertion is that the legal definition of suicide and the Judaic understanding of the term are poles apart.

In ordinary terminology, suicide refers to anyone who deliberately kills himself or herself. However, the Judaic term for suicide is *me'abed atzmo la'daat* ("one who destroys the self with one's full wits").

The proviso, "with one's full wits," is the key element in this issue. Who commits suicide with full wits? Usually, the one who commits suicide is at wits' end. Considering the option of suicide like an accountant, putting all the advantages of life on one side of the ledger and all the disadvantages on the other side, checking if the debits outweigh the credits, and then rationally deciding to jump to a conclusion, is more a theoretical construct than a real one. The suicide rushes to judgment and certainly not on the basis of rational choice. It is usually done in the throes of depression, of despondency, or desperation. It is certainly not with one's full wits. Thus, what society would call a suicide would not be considered a suicide in Jewish tradition.

Additionally, even if an individual may have been in possession of all his wits at the beginning of the act of suicide, we have no assurance that he did not have a change of heart in the midst of the act of suicide. Thus, an individual who drowns can be assumed to have experienced remorse in the agony of the actual drowning. Even the fact that a suicide has left a note is insufficient reason to associate the action with the note. Suicide is a serious offense, and we have no right to make such an accusation unless the facts are clear.

Without such proof, the individual is not branded as a suicide, and there is no reason to withhold any final respects.

In effect, Jewish tradition condemns suicide, but refuses to rush to brand such action as *me'abed atzmo la'daat*. For all intents and purposes, it can be assumed that one who commits suicide did so without full wits, and there is no justifiable reason to refrain from a respectful farewell and burial.

Misconception: The tasks that the *Chevra Kadisha* (Jewish Burial Society) fulfill are duties not expected of anyone else.

A *Chevra Kadisha* is found in almost every city of significant Jewish population. They are a group of men and women who have undertaken, often voluntarily, to be available should anyone die. They are on call to make the appropriate arrangements, to assure the proper dignity of the deceased, to cleanse and prepare the body for burial, and then to assist in the funeral, up to and including interment.

But whose work is the *Chevra Kadisha* actually doing? It is wrong to assume that the *Chevra Kadisha* is doing its own work. It is wrong because this denies a fundamental obligation that rests upon each member of the community.

Whenever anyone passes away, there is an immediate obligation placed on every member of the community, to cease all activity in order to assist in the preparation of the departed for interment.

Any community would find it difficult to function if after any death, all its members would drop everything and concern themselves only with the departed. The organization known as the *Chevra Kadisha*, in undertaking to accord the final dignities to the deceased, is actually doing the work of the community. It is the community that must be involved in the final arrangements, with no individual member of the community being able to say it is someone else's responsibility and not mine.

Thus, any community that has a *Chevra Kadisha* is fortunate, for this holy society (literal translation of *Chevra Kadisha*) has openly declared: "We will assume responsibility for the communal obligation."

Misconception: The blessing of *Dayan haEmet* (Blessed be the True Judge) is made only following the death of one of the seven close relatives.

The blessing of *Dayan haEmet* is appropriate for all situations when an individual would normally feel intense pain. This includes the death of one of the seven close relatives — father, mother, sister, brother, son, daughter, and spouse.

This blessing would be appropriate for the pain and agony of suffering a business collapse, although not necessarily bankruptcy. Declaration of bankruptcy is more a means for attaining solvency and is probably not the great tragedy it used to be.

But for obvious and painful losses, whether the destruction of one's property, the death of a pet, or the turning of one's wine into vinegar, the recitation of the blessing *Dayan haEmet* is appropriate.

Misconception: It is proper to tear a ribbon instead of an article of clothing upon the death of one of the seven close relatives.

There is an obligation to tear one's clothing upon learning of the death of one of the seven close relatives. This obligation reflects the feeling that something precious has been torn away, that one feels a tear in one's very being.

The proper way to do this is to tear one of the basic garments. For a man the proper garment for this purpose is a shirt; for a woman, a blouse. These are the appropriate choices because they are garments that are part of one's regular dress, not artificial additions.

A ribbon placed on the clothing is an artificial addition and is really a way of avoiding the tearing procedure. If the tearing is to express the grief at what has been torn away, the garment of choice must be something that is basic and necessary, rather than superimposed and superficial.

Misconception: The only time to rend a garment is at the death of one of the seven close relatives.

The seven close relatives are father, mother, sister, brother, spouse, son, and daughter. Although it is true that a garment is rent for the death of such relatives, there are other instances in which a garment is rent.

One must rend a garment upon hearing of the death of one's *rebbe*, from whom one has learned the majority of one's knowledge and wisdom.

Additionally, there is a requirement to rend one's garment upon coming into visual proximity of the original site of the Temple, provided that at least thirty days have elapsed since having last been in the proximity of the Temple mount.

Misconception: The garment that is torn prior to the funeral must be worn for the thirty-day period called *shloshim*.

The garment that is torn prior to the funeral symbolizes that something significant has been torn away from the mourner. This garment is worn during the *shivah* as a continual reminder of the terrible rupture in the mourner's life.

However, there is no requirement to wear this garment beyond the seven-day period, excluding of course the *Shabbat*, when the torn garment is never worn.

The reason why some people think that this garment must be worn for thirty days is related to the talmudic discussion about when, how, and under what circumstances the torn garment may be resewn. After a thirty-day period, the garment may either be tied together or resewn perfectly, depending on whether the mourning was for a parent or for one of the other close relatives. Some may have thus drawn the conclusion that one must wear the garment for thirty days. But this is a wrong reading of the text, and hence an incorrect application of the norms.

Misconception: Mourners should wear black clothing.

In mourning, one's dress should not be a matter of concern. Obviously, it is inconsistent with the melancholy feeling of mourning to dress in loud, bright colors. Subdued colors—brown, blue, or black—are more consistent with how one feels, with the mood one *should* feel. But there is no specific obligation to wear only black clothing.

Misconception: Pregnant women are not allowed to attend funerals.

Generally speaking, pregnant women have avoided attending funerals, and it is erroneously assumed that this is because they are not permitted.

In actuality, pregnant women were discouraged from attending funerals simply because of the fear that the trauma attached to such an experience might upset them and possibly even cause a miscarriage.

If the danger period for miscarriage has passed, then there should be no real argument against attending.

Misconception: Once buried, the interred cannot be moved.

Under normal circumstances, once an individual is buried, the body should not be moved from the burial site. However, there are some significant exceptions.

If the body is being moved to a permanent burial site in Israel, then it is permissible.

Additionally, if the purpose is to bring the individual to a family plot, from an area far removed from that of other members of the family, this too is permissible.

When there is an expectation that there may be a desire to move the individual, the family should explicitly state, just prior to interment, that this is only a temporary interment, and that there is an intention to move the deceased to a permanent resting place afterward.

Obviously, it is preferable that the deceased be immediately interred in the final resting place, but this is sometimes impossible. In such situations, a future move to a more appropriate site may be contemplated.

Misconception: Mirrors are covered in the house of mourning for superstitious reasons.

There are varying reasons given for the practice of covering the mirrors in a house of mourning. One reason is that mirrors are usually used to fine-tune one's looks. However, in the midst of mourning, how one looks should be unimportant.

Another reason is related to the fear that one may inadvertently look in the mirror and see how badly traumatized one actually looks. Shocked by one's appearance, the mourner may feel even worse.

Thus, the reasons for covering the mirror are hardly superstitious. They address the mourning situation in either a prescriptive or a descriptive manner; but either way, the reasons are rooted in a sober understanding of human experience.

Misconception: The chairs on which one sits during *shivah* must be uncomfortable.

There is absolutely no reason why the chair that one sits on during *shivah* must be uncomfortable. The basic rule is that the *shivah* chair must be low to the ground—in fact, no higher than approximately one foot above the floor. As long as the chair is at that height (and one may remove the cushion from a couch to accomplish this), it can be a comfortable chair. There is no obligation to break one's back during the *shivah* period.

In previous generations, and in certain places even today, the practice was to sit on the floor.

Sitting in a raised chair is a sign of majesty. The mourner sits on a lower stool to reflect the melancholy, the sadness of the seven-day period—feeling low and, therefore, sitting low.

The "getting up" from *shivah* involves being raised from the depths of despair, to once again confront life with all of its responsibilities.

Misconception: The *shivah* period lasts for seven days.

The word *shivah* means seven, but the actual sitting of *shivah* never really extends for seven complete days, each twenty-four hours in duration.

The reason for this is that a part of the first and last days of mourning count as complete days. For example, if a funeral takes place on Tuesday afternoon, and the *shivah* commences before sundown on Tuesday, then the entire day of Tuesday is considered the first day. This is the case even if one sits *shivah* for only five or ten minutes of that day.

Then, Wednesday, Thursday, Friday, Saturday, and Sunday are complete days of *shivah*, and the *shivah* concludes on Monday. However, the *shivah* does not conclude at the end of the day. Instead, it concludes Monday morning, after a short duration of actual sitting, following the morning services.

So while the *shivah* extends over a seven-day period, the actual sitting is not for seven complete days.

Misconception: There is no *shivah* observance on *Shabbat*.

Shabbat is a day when one refrains from any public display of mourning. Though one must wear the torn garment and leather-free shoes as part of the *shivah* observance, one reverts to regular dress and shoes on *Shabbat*.

However, *Shabbat* is included as one of the seven days of mourning. Even though there are no public manifestations of mourning, one still mourns on *Shabbat*.

For example, during the *shivah* period, marital relations are prohibited. This prohibition applies even for *Shabbat*. Since this expression of mourning is in the category of a private matter, it does not compromise the general spirit of *Shabbat*.

Misconception: If a funeral is held on Sunday, and the *shivah* begins on Sunday, then the *shivah* ends on Friday.

This is a popular misconception, probably related, in some small measure, to the fact that the actual seventh day in such an instance would be *Shabbat*. Because there is no public mourning permitted on *Shabbat*, one might assume the mourning ends on Friday. However, this is faulty reasoning.

In the first place, *Shabbat* is one of the seven days of mourning, and if the mourning should end on *Shabbat*, then it ends on *Shabbat*.

The normal time allowance for *Shabbat* preparation on Friday afternoon would also be the appropriate practice in this instance. Since the *shivah* ends on *Shabbat* morning, it more or less dissolves, without the formal procedure of getting up and walking around the block, as is the case when the *shivah* ends during the week.

Getting up and walking around the block is merely a symbolic gesture on the part of the mourners. During the mourning period, they are restricted in their movements and should remain indoors except for attending services if there is none at the house of *shivah*, and if necessary returning home at night to sleep. At the conclusion of *shivah*, they leave the house in one direction, and return from another direction, symbolizing the hope that they will embark on a path that will bring them better news. The mere fact of going outdoors for a walk signals their reentry into the social matrix.

On *Shabbat*, one leaves the house in the morning, but proceeds directly to prayer services. For mourning that commences on a Sunday, the *shivah* ends *Shabbat* morning.

Misconception: For a *shivah* that continues into *Shabbat*, one can interrupt at noon on Friday.

Friday seems to get short-changed in the *shivah* observance. There is no public manifestation of *shivah* on *Shabbat*, and one is allowed to make necessary preparations for the *Shabbat* on Friday afternoon, but this should take no more than about an hour. In the winter months, when *Shabbat* is ushered in earlier, preparations may begin at about 3 P.M. One rises from sitting *shivah* at this time.

But it is a mistake to transpose this timeframe to the summer, when *Shabbat* does not arrive until late. In such instance one should wait until the twilight period, called *Pelag Haminhah*, before making *Shabbat* preparations. Prior to that, one should not interrupt the sitting of *shivah*.

Misconception: The *shivah* can never end on Friday morning.

For *shivah* to legitimately end on Friday morning, the onset of the mourning period must have taken place on *Shabbat*. Under normal circumstances, *shivah* does not begin on *Shabbat*, and the *shivah* could not end on Friday.

For *shivah* to start on *Shabbat*, the funeral would have had to take place on *Shabbat*, which cannot occur.

However, there are unique circumstances when the *shivah* does actually begin on *Shabbat*, even though the funeral did not take place on that day.

For example, if a person passes away during *Pesah*, and the funeral takes place on one of the intermediate days, called *Hol HaMoed*, the observance of the *shivah* is deferred until after Passover.

However, if the first day of Passover is a *Shabbat*, the last day is also *Shabbat*; that last day is actually counted as the first day of *shivah*, because it is the eighth day of Passover, and observed only outside Israel and is not a biblically mandated festival day. (This is also the case if the eighth day is an ordinary weekday.) For this *Shabbat* day, private manifestations of mourning are in force, but not public manifestations. Since the *shivah* has begun on the *Shabbat*, it concludes on the following Friday morning.

There is another circumstance when *shivah* may end on Friday morning. That is if an individual receives news on *Shabbat* about a relative who died within the last thirty days and was already interred. Having received such news on *Shabbat*, the private manifestation of *shivah* begins immediately, and the *shivah* would therefore conclude on the following Friday morning.

Misconception: In the case of *shivah* that ends on *Shabbat* morning, one must sit for a short while on Saturday evening.

When the *shivah* period comes to an end, it is closed. There is no reason to add on to it an eighth day, and there is absolutely no purpose nor any requirement to sit for that extra time.

Misconception: Anytime is appropriate for visiting mourners.

Visiting mourners is obviously a vital fulfillment. Those who are in mourning are in genuine need of comfort and need to know that even though they are in intense grief, there are significant friends within the community who care. It is hard to overestimate the importance of commiserating with mourners, giving them a chance to express their sense of loss and enabling them to feel a connectedness at the very time when they feel a sense of disconnection.

However, if the object of visiting mourners is to comfort, it is important to gauge when the possibilities of comfort are actually realistic. In the heightened moment of grief, it is absurd to try and comfort the mourner. The readiness for comfort comes only after the passage of some time after the actual interment.

Thus, those who wish to visit individuals who are sitting *shivah* should not visit until the morning of the third day. It is assumed that the day of the funeral and the day after are days of such intense grief that the mourner is not ready for conversation, and visits at that point are ill advised.

In the visit itself, the accent should be on extending comfort, rather than on discharging an obligation. Paradoxically, it is precisely by being sensitive to how one can comfort the other that one discharges one's obligation.

Misconception: When visiting mourners during *shivah*, one is obliged to initiate conversation.

One cannot know the state of mind of individuals who are going through the mourning process. They may be in the mood to talk, or they may not. Even if they are ready for conversation, one can never be sure whether they are in a frame of mind to talk about the departed.

When visiting the mourner, the primary concern should not be the discharge of an obligation. The focus should be on the situation of the mourner, to thus assure that the visit will, indeed, be a comfort to the mourner. Sometimes the mourner is comforted just by the presence of others; at other times, it may be not merely the presence, but also the shared conversation.

Jewish law states that when visiting a mourner, one should wait for the mourner to initiate conversation. Only in this way can we be reasonably certain that the conversation will reflect the mourner's state of mind, and may thus be of some comfort to him or her.

Misconception: Parents can excuse their children from the obligation to observe the *shivah* period.

The *shivah* period is the mandated time that close relatives, namely father, mother, sister, brother, son, daughter, or spouse, are obliged to sit in mourning to contemplate their loss and to come to grips with the new reality.

To say that anyone can excuse another from an obligation implies that it is in their hands. However, the obligation to observe the period of *shivah* is a legal requirement directed to those who have survived. It is they who feel the agony, the pain, and the torment of the situation, and it is they who must go through the period of grief to absorb the full implications of the loss.

No relative can excuse another member of the family from such an obligation, any more than they can excuse a member of the family from keeping other basic practices.

Misconception: Parents can never waive their child's mourning obligations.

There are certain obligations in the mourning process that are absolute, and it is beyond the capacity of any individual to release others from such observance.

However, there are other mourning obligations of a different nature.

The *shivah* obligation to mourn intensely for seven days overlaps into the thirty-day mourning period, which is incumbent upon all primary relatives—father, mother, sister, brother, son, daughter, and spouse.

However, the mourning period for a deceased parent extends beyond thirty days, to an entire year. This is in recognition of the special role that parents have in the child's existence and development. It is based on the requirement to honor one's parents, an obligation that pertains in life and extends even after the death of the parents.

However, since the year's mourning, approximately eleven months following the conclusion of the thirty days, is predicated on the obligation to honor one's parents, the parents have the right to waive that honor requirement in advance of their death. They may release the child from the post-thirty day obligation, to allow him or her for example, to attend weddings.

The parents cannot, before death, waive the *shivah* or the *shloshim* (thirty days) mourning observance, but they may release their children from the post-*shloshim* mourning that is uniquely for parents.

Misconception: A parent who is in the midst of *shivah* may not attend a child's wedding.

A parent who suffered the loss of one of the seven close relatives, whose mourning period actually occurs at the time of a child's scheduled date for marriage, is faced with a most agonizing dilemma. One does not relish the prospect of compromising the period of mourning, nor does one have any desire to miss a child's wedding.

Jewish law gives the joy of bride and groom the highest priority. It is assumed that the presence of parents is vitally important to bride and groom, and the absence of the parents may be deemed potentially devastating. In order not to diminish the joy of the marriage, with the impact that a parent's absence may have on the mood of the bride and the groom as they embark on their life together, the parent, even in the midst of the *shivah* period, is allowed and encouraged to attend a child's wedding.

There is also no need to eliminate music from the wedding, since by so doing the joy of the occasion might be diminished. The option to do so remains, but there is no such legal requirement.

Obviously, Jewish law cannot dictate emotions. The parent attending the marriage is distraught, and no amount of legislation can take away the mourning emotions. Jewish law, however, can suggest norms and guides to steer the concerned individual on the proper course.

Misconception: There is no *shivah* mandated for one's parents-in-law.

Presently, it is unheard of that one should sit *shivah* for one's parents-in-law.

However, in generations long past, a son-in-law or a daughter-in-law actually joined his or her spouse in mourning for a parent. This respect was expressed for both the spouse and the spouse's parents, whom one must look upon also as parents and respect accordingly.

Misconception: When someone dies all the deceased's shoes must be discarded.

Following death, the utmost respect is accorded to the deceased. The deceased individual is prepared for burial in a dignified way, and the entire body is usually returned to the earth.

Respect is even accorded to anything that may have absorbed from the deceased, including the shoes. The tradition of not wearing the shoes that the deceased was wearing at the time of death is based on the notion that respect for the deceased extends even to the deceased's perspiration, which is in the shoes, or it may be related to deathly poisons that remain in the shoes at the time of death.

However, it is erroneous to assume that all shoes belonging to the deceased must be thrown away. This is wrong and a terrible waste of useful clothing.

More respect is accorded to the deceased when whatever the deceased left behind, shoes included, can be put to good use by people in need. The charity lives on.

Misconception: The *Kaddish* is a prayer for the dead.

The *Kaddish* makes absolutely no mention of the deceased, or even of death, for that matter. *Kaddish* is not only an affirmation recited by mourners; it is also part of the ordinary prayer service. It is a sanctification and glorification of God. Simply put, it is an affirmation of faith. The special meaning of *Kaddish* for mourners relates to the anticipation that the mourner, battered by the agonizing and traumatic experience of loss, may understandably experience a weakening of faith and a compromise of the sense of purpose.

The *Kaddish*, recited over the course of a prolonged period (eleven months), is intended to rekindle that faith and to revive that sense of purpose, so that the individual can continue in life, energized by the memory and example of the departed.

Misconception: It is forbidden to visit a cemetery in the year following the death of one of the seven close relatives.

There is no truth to this custom. Those who are in mourning are not encouraged to make excessive visitations to the gravesite, but occasional visits and the recitation of prayers at the gravesite are appropriate.

There is a custom among some to actually visit the gravesite immediately upon arising from *shivah*. In many places, including Israel, the memorial at the establishment of the monument takes place at the conclusion of the thirty-day mourning period called *shloshim*.

It is thus apparent that the first year carries with it no prohibition against visiting the cemetery.

Misconception: *Yahrzeit* corresponds to the day of death on the secular calendar.

Yahrzeit, literally meaning a year's time, refers to the commemorative day of remembrance of the passing of a loved one. It is a day spent in contemplation, marked by the recitation of the sanctification prayer called *Kaddish,* and for some, as a day of fasting.

This day is observed yearly, on the day corresponding to the original Hebrew date of death. It is not calculated according to the secular calendar, but according to the Hebrew calendar. In other words, the precise Hebrew date of death is the *yahrzeit* that is observed from year to year. Because of this, there will be a variety of secular dates on which the *yahrzeit* occurs. Often, the *yahrzeit* is observed weeks apart from the secular date of death.

An important factor in calculating the *yahrzeit* date is the precise moment of death. If death occurred before sunset, then the *yahrzeit* would be on one day, whereas if the death occurred after nightfall, the *yahrzeit* would be on the next Hebrew date, even though the secular date for both is the same.

Misconception: A *yahrzeit* is observed only once a year.

In most circumstances, a *yahrzeit* observance would only be once a year. But this is not always the case. In some years, a *yahrzeit* may actually be observed twice.

If death occurred in the Hebrew month of Adar in an ordinary year, then in a Hebrew leap year, when two Adars, Adar 1 and Adar 2, are on the calendar the *yahrzeit* is observed twice. It is observed in Adar 1 and Adar 2 on the date corresponding to the date of death.

Misconception: Sending out those who are not required to recite the *Yizkor* during the services is pure superstition.

It is hard to relegate to the realm of superstition a practice that has been in vogue for centuries.

The *Yizkor* prayer, the prayer of remembrance of loved ones, is recited on *Yom Kippur,* as well as on the last day of *Pesah,* of *Shavuot,* and on *Shmini Azeret,* following the Tabernacle festival of *Sukkot.*

Yizkor, a memorial prayer, is recited by those who have lost a loved one, whereas those who have not suffered such a loss do not recite the *Yizkor;* in fact they leave the sanctuary for the duration of the *Yizkor* service.

In this generation, as in previous generations, there are some who have suggested that there is absolutely no logical reason why those who do not recite the memorial prayer should leave during the time when this memorial prayer is recited.

The superstitious reasoning for this would be that being in the midst of those who are reciting memorial prayers may invite the undertaker. A logical mind would have difficulty with this reasoning, even as it would have difficulty with the proposition that people who have never suffered the loss of a loved one should leave the sanctuary when others are reciting the *Kaddish* (sanctification), the prayer recited during the period immediately following the loss of a close relative. No one has suggested this; therefore, it would seem that there is no reason why others should leave during the recitation of the *Yizkor.*

However, the Jewish people have never really placed much stock in superstition, the "evil eye" notwithstanding, and a custom such as this must be based on more than just superstition.

It is based on a profound understanding of the dynamics of the *Yizkor* prayer. Those who recite the prayer evoke the memory of loved ones. In all likelihood, this is an emotional experience when many may weep. It is logical and psychologically realistic to suggest that individuals experiencing such an emotional upheaval will feel much more comfortable if they are not being observed by others who have not experienced such trauma. They are much better off within a group that has shared this experience.

In fairness to those reciting the *Yizkor*, those who are not required to recite the *Yizkor* should not impose their presence. They gracefully leave the sanctuary to allow the unimpeded emotional flow of those evoking the memories of their loved ones.

Misconception: There is no logical reason not to recite the *Yizkor* during the year following the death of a parent, even if one has never recited the *Yizkor* before.

The reason for this is logical, and may be related to why those who need not recite *Yizkor* temporarily leave the sanctuary during that service. Those whose loss is still fresh will probably be even more emotional than those who have lived through at least a year of coming to grips with the tragic event. They may make it uncomfortable for those who, although crying, are still emotionally in control. These mourners wait for a period of a year, to come to terms with their grief, before becoming part of the *Yizkor* service.

Others suggest that remembering is only appropriate when forgetting is more likely to occur, namely after a one-year period. Whatever the reason, we are dealing here more with psychological wisdom than with superstition.

Misconception: The memorial ceremony at the gravestone is appropriately called an unveiling.

The word "unveiling" implies the removal of a veil. This obviously refers to the practice of placing a cloth over the grave stone, covering it until members of the family respectfully remove it at the ceremony. However, there is nothing in the tradition to indicate that this is a necessity.

It has become some sort of a hocus-pocus. First the stone is put up, then it is covered, then it is uncovered. The real purpose of gathering is to recite prayers at the site, to remember the departed, and to honor the memory of the departed. This is more appropriately called, in Hebrew, *hakamat matzayvah*, which means "the setting up of the memorial stone."

This is a more accurate terminology than "unveiling," which is associated with plaques and other paraphernalia that are unveiled for display in various ceremonies. Veiling and unveiling may be desirable when one wants to impress the public with the beauty of a painting or other such items that remain covered to arouse the public's curiosity. It really does not have a legitimate place at the *hakamat matzayvah* ceremony.

Misconception: The *hakamat Matzayvah* should take place a year after death.

There is a difference between setting up a stone and the cere-mony attached to this. The obligation to set a gravestone at the site of burial dates back to the Bible itself. With regard to when this is done, there is no question that the earlier the better. This is a signal mark of respect for the departed, and it is fitting that the gravesite be appropriately delineated as soon as possible. In Israel, for example, many culminate the thirty-day mourning period with a visit to the gravesite, with the memorial stone already in place.

Certainly, if family members cannot come together for quite a long time, because they live too far apart, or for other reasons, this should not deter those immediately involved from having the stone put in place almost immediately, weather permitting. The ceremony erroneously called "unveiling" may be deferred, but the placing of the stone should not be delayed.

Misconception: Belief in the future world has no currency in this age of rationalism.

There is an assumption that a thinking individual cannot comprehend the idea of a world beyond this world.

The Talmud adduces some measure of proof for the existence of a future beyond this world by arguing as follows: One who has never existed is born into life. How much more so is it likely that one who has once lived should again be born into life!

The purist will argue that this is no proof, and the purist is technically correct. It is not a proof, but it is an argument that serves to at least counter the claim that belief in a future world is preposterous. There is evidence for such future world eventualities in day-to-day encounters.

Put another way, the idea that after life there is nothing, that death signifies the absolute end to life, is fraught with difficulties of its own. If it is true that death is the absolute finale for an individual, then this is true for society as a whole. What then is the meaning of life, if it all ends in nothingness?

Belief in an afterlife simply means that death is not the end of life; just as there must have been something before birth, so must there be something beyond death. We do not know the precise details of that future life, but the idea that there is a future is not as irrational as it may seem. One may even argue that the rejection of such belief leads to more irrational, even irresponsible behavior.

Part IV

PEOPLE

7

Parents and Teachers

To Honor
To Discipline
To Teach and Respect

Misconception: The honoring of one's parents is a person-to-person obligation.

Jewish law may be divided into the primary categories of person-to-God legislation, and person-to-person legislation. Although there is significant overlap in many of the regulations, the division is itself instructive.

Insofar as honoring of one's parents is concerned, this is found in the Ten Commandments. The Ten Commandments are themselves divided into two sections, five on the first tablet, and five on the second. The first tablet contains regulations governing one's relationship to God, including the prohibitions against idolatry and creation of images.

The second tablet contains regulations relating to one's societal responsibilities, including the prohibitions of adultery, murder, false testimony, and coveting that which belongs to one's neighbor.

One would expect that the legislation regarding one's obligation to parents would be found in the second tablet. However, this is not the case. The obligation to honor one's parents, the proverbial fifth commandment, is the last commandment on the first tablet. Since the first tablet deals with one's obligation to God, the obligation to honor one's parents is projected as a person-to-God obligation.

We honor our parents because they were instrumental in bringing us into the world and we are grateful for this. There is a natural progression backwards, if one follows through, in that one should likewise be grateful to our grandparents for bringing our parents into the world and we are grateful for this. Carried to the limit, we go back to the original husband and wife, Adam and Eve, and then to the ultimate Creator of all parents. Intervening generations should not blind us to the reality that it is God who generated the creative process. We acknowledge our immediate parents, and at the same time our ultimate Parent, through the honor that is bestowed upon father and mother.

Misconception: We are obliged to love our parents.

The biblical injunctions concerning parents are twofold. One is the obligation to honor one's parents. The other is the obligation to be in awe of one's parents.

Honor of parents involves feeding the parent, clothing the parent, taking the parent out, bringing the parent in. Being in awe of the parent involves specific expressions of respect, such as not sitting in the parent's chair, not contradicting the parent, or doing anything that would diminish the esteem in which a parent should be held.

Nowhere does the Bible legislate an obligation for children to love their parents. Love is an emotion, a feeling that is impossible to legislate. One can legislate behavioral norms such as respect and honor, but one can hardly legislate feelings. It is hoped that through interaction, the child will come to appreciate all that the parent has done and will reciprocate the parent's love, but this must be left to unfold naturally and is not a matter for legislation.

Misconception: There are no religious implications connected with kissing one's parents.

The primary obligation of children toward their parents is to honor them. Honoring parents means an active show of appreciation to them, especially when the parents are growing older and they need the reinforcement of others' concern. The primary obligation to care for parents in this situation rests upon the children. There are many ways one may show concern and provide help at this point in their lives. Providing food and clothing, or just being with them are some of the more typical ways.

Additionally, showering the parents with love, showing that they are important and treasured, is of inestimable importance. A meaningful kiss, therefore, is totally consistent with the obligation to honor one's parents.

Since the obligation to honor one's parents extends also to grandparents and great-grandparents, it is reasonable to assume that kissing them is likewise a matter of great importance. One may even suggest that it is a *mitzvah* to go out of one's way to kiss one's parents and grandparents.

Misconception: Cursing a parent may not be nice, but it is not a crime.

The Bible specifically prohibits the cursing of a parent. Not only is cursing a parent prohibited, but it is also considered a capital crime.

In Jewish law, capital punishment can only be administered if the crime was committed in the presence of two independent witnesses, after the criminal was adequately forewarned. Thus, it is difficult to conceive of a circumstance in which conviction for cursing a parent could actually materialize.

Cursing would probably occur in the privacy of the home, and more suddenly rather than with prior notice. Because of this, prosecution for such crime could not ordinarily take place. However, the action itself is still prohibited and roundly condemned.

The specific type of curse that is a capital offense is one in which the child invokes God's name to pronounce a curse on the parent. However, any cursing of the parent is also prohibited.

Misconception: Hitting a parent is worse than cursing a parent.

Hitting a parent, thereby drawing blood, and cursing a parent are both considered capital offenses. This indicates how important respect for parents is considered. This is primarily a theoretical yet vital concept, since satisfying the legal requirements necessary to carry out the death penalty is quite difficult. The action usually occurs in the home, where the witnesses are likely to be relatives, who may not testify against kin.

The specific death penalty was more severe for cursing. For hitting, the penalty was death by choking; for cursing, it was death by stoning. Since death by stoning was a more severe penalty, it is clear that the *Torah* considers cursing worse than hitting. Hitting may hurt more, but cursing is a more serious breach.

Cursing, which involves invoking God's name, is a compound felony. It combines abuse of parent and abuse of God. Hitting, however inexcusable, does not involve a direct abuse of God, although the physical attack is by definition a denial of a Godly obligation.

Today, we do not administer the punishment, but we can absorb the lesson.

Misconception: A doctor may perform surgery on his or her own parent.

According to biblical law, it is forbidden for a child to wound a parent. Wounding a parent and drawing blood in the process is a capital offense.

Obviously, a doctor operating on a parent, and thereby drawing blood in the process, is doing so not to wound but to heal. Nevertheless, because there is a prohibition against drawing blood from a parent, a surgeon is better advised against performing surgery on a parent. There is no issue of such surgery being considered a capital offense; but in order to avoid drawing of blood, this practice is discouraged.

However, if the surgeon is the outstanding expert in the field, and if the interests of the parent would be best served, there is no question but that the surgery should be performed by the child.

The idea that a physician should not perform surgery on a parent has an emotional side to it, which is quite understandable. Based on the assumption that there is an intense feeling between parent and child, the surgeon may be overcome with emotion and will thus be hampered, and his professional skills could be compromised. As a general rule, it may be better to have someone not so close to the patient performing the surgery.

Misconception: A Jewish old-age home is the ideal place for the elderly.

The biblical obligation to honor one's parents is given an interesting tangible expression in the Talmud. There it is stated that one honors one's parents by feeding them, by clothing them, by taking them out, and by bringing them in.

The obvious question arises: Is this not what parents do for the children? Is it not the parents who feed and clothe the children, rather than the reverse?

The Talmud addresses the general pattern of role reversal that takes place in the parent–child relationship. The child starts off being dependent primarily on the parents. As the years go by and the parents age, it is they who become more dependent; and it is the children who, by biblical fiat, must honor their parents by doing for them in their later years as the parents did for their children.

The ideal is that when individuals grow older, their children should care for them. Buying such care from an institution or agency is too often an evasion of primary responsibility. There are instances when children are totally incapable of taking care of their parents' needs, because the parents must have special professional care, but that is more the exception than the rule. Under normal circumstances, the appropriate Jewish response to the question "What should we do for our aging parents?" is "Bring them into your homes." That is where they belong.

Misconception: It is wrong for parents to hit their young children.

During the early stages of a child's development, there may be occasions when a less-than-gentle smack on the child's seat, harmless but transmitting a particular message, is necessary.

In such instances, parents certainly have the discretionary right to transmit a message in this manner. Parents should not abuse this right, but one cannot brand this reaction as wrong. The smack should not be administered in anger or retribution; it should be administered out of love and concern for the child. It should not be the result of a temperamental explosion; it must be administered under full control and in proper measure.

Once the child reaches the age when disciplinary lessons can be transmitted by verbal communication, hitting the child is prohibited. Hitting when we should be talking incites the child to anger, to bad feelings about the parents, and even to the contemplation of evil for the parents. In placing such a "stumbling block before the blind," (the blind in this case being the unsuspecting child), the parent behaves in a forbidden manner.

Hitting a child is permitted in the early childhood years; in the later years, it is forbidden.

Misconception: Parents are obligated to feed their children.

Parents do have obligations to their children; they are obliged to bring children into the world, to care for them during their youth, and to give them a headstart by educating them and preparing them for a profession.

However, from a strictly legal point of view a parent is not obliged even to feed the child beyond the age of six. Before rushing to hasty conclusions, it should be noted that this is not to provide justification for parents to throw their children out of the home, telling them to fend for themselves. It merely establishes that beyond the early years, the parent who feeds the child is actually doing so as an act of charity. There is no legal obligation; there is a moral obligation, but feeding the child is a charitable act.

This is useful information, especially for those parents who are sometimes confronted by their rebellious teenagers, who arrogantly ask, "What have you ever done for me?" The parent usually counters this declaration of independence and arrogance with a sheepish reference to the agony of childbirth, the years of training, feeding and clothing, and great sacrifice. The child counters with "But you had an obligation to do that." The parent can now confidently tell the child that there is no such obligation, that it is an act of charity.

One act of charity deserves another. So, it would be most fitting if the children were charitable, kind, and appreciative of their parents.

Misconception: Parents are no longer responsible for children who have reached the age of religious responsibility.

This assumption may be gleaned from the fact that when a child reaches the age of responsibility, the parent thanks God for being relieved of any culpability for the child's misbehavior.

However, to translate this into a total release from responsibility for the child is inaccurate. Before reaching the age of responsibility, 13 years plus for a boy and 12 years plus for a girl, the child behaves like a child. There may be different levels of maturity during this early stage of life, but in general one cannot assume that the child will behave in a disciplined and adult manner. Because of this, any action of the child that is dramatically wrong can be attributed to the fact that the parents did not properly monitor the child's behavior.

Once the child reaches the age of responsibility, the parents can relax their control, allowing the child to develop, albeit with continued parental guidance. The parent is no longer responsible for the child's misbehavior, since the child should be adult enough to know right from wrong. But there are other issues in the natural maturation process for which a child needs a parent, and for this there is no exemption.

Misconception: There are no Jewish juvenile delinquents.

Even in the days when the Jewish community was a well-integrated and self-contained entity, there were probably behavioral problems among children as they went through the various stages of childhood and adolescence. However, the opportunities for delinquent expression were not that readily available.

Today, there are unfortunately many enticements beyond the home, including addictive substances and alternate families—cults—to which children may run. Alas, the proportion of Jews in cults is alarmingly high. In addition, it is not true that Jews are not involved with drugs. The problem may not be of epidemic proportions, but it is certainly a matter of concern.

It may be that juvenile delinquency, like assimilation, is the price that one pays for being in a free and open society. Explanations, however, do not solve problems, nor do they make the families of runaway or addicted children any happier.

Misconception: The parent–child obligations are one-sided in Judaism; children are obliged to respect their parents, but the reverse is not true.

The Bible does not specifically spell out any obligations that the parents may have insofar as respecting their children is concerned. However, this matter is discussed in rabbinic literature, with distinct implications for the parents' obligation to respect the children.

Parents are generally under an umbrella regulation (do not put a stumbling block before the blind) which forbids them from doing anything that would cause the child to be disrespectful to them. Children who are aware of this regulation may distort its intent and challenge the parents' authority whenever it interferes with the fulfillment of their own desires. But this is an abuse of the basic principle.

The principle provides that in situations of necessary discipline, for example, when the child is old enough to understand discussion of a matter, hitting the child is ruled out. If the child understands, then talk, do not hit. This is a primary example of the parental obligation not to incite the child to behave disrespectfully. Other examples include being demanding of the child, or standing on ceremony in forcing the child to honor and respect the parent. By inciting the child, the parent puts a stumbling block in front of the blind, "the blind" meaning the child. Because of parental abuse, the child spontaneously reacts by insulting or even hitting the parent. The child is not exonerated because of such actions, but neither is the parent permitted to abuse parental authority.

Misconception: One's parents are more important than one's teacher.

Parents are important, not only for biological reasons, but also for spiritual reasons. It is the obligation of parents not only to bring children into the world; it is also their obligation to shape the new entity into a respectful, caring, and committed individual. In other words, parents are obliged to be the child's primary teacher.

Unfortunately, in the present educational system, it often seems that everyone but the parents becomes the child's teachers. The child does not have one mentor or guide from infancy to adulthood. That job is shared by many over a long period of time.

But a child who has a mentor, someone who provides guidance in the path of Judaism from infancy to adulthood, would be obliged to give greater deference to that teacher than to a parent who does not teach. In the words of the Talmud, the parent in such instance has merely brought the child into this world, but the teacher has through the educational process brought the child into the future world.

This value judgment, although it may run contrary to conventional logic, indicates how important education is in the Jewish sphere of things. Without knowledge and without commitment based on knowledge we are lost.

Misconception: It is best to have specialized teachers.

This is an age of specialization, and the specialization syndrome extends even to the classroom. Departmentalization, with teachers for specific subjects, is the order of the day. In medicine, in science, in almost every sphere, areas of knowledge are being more sharply delineated, and new areas of specialization continue to appear. The tendency is to try to gain as much as possible from each specialist.

Throughout the generations, the Jewish community developed the concept of a *rebbe,* a teacher or master who gave his entire being over to his students, who in turn spent days, months, and even years learning from the master.

Ideally, it is the father who should occupy this role of teacher; but failing that, a *rebbe* to whom one can relate on a personal level, over an extended period of time, is the ideal guide to help the child develop in a wholesome way.

In the present generation, students have many teachers, but not one *rebbe.* This is unfortunate and certainly not ideal. The whole is more than the sum of all the parts. In departmentalization, one may be exposed to all the parts but is denied a sense of the whole.

Misconception: Jewish teachers have the right to go out on strike.

The right to strike is a fundamental component of democratic society. Aside from preventive legislation that states, provinces, or countries may invoke for essential services, individuals are generally permitted to strike as a protest against working conditions, salary, or other items that are pertinent to the contractual arrangement with their employers.

Jewish teachers, who are in the employ of school boards, where the contractual agreement allows for the right to strike, are certainly part of that framework. But this does not apply to Jewish teachers who teach Jewish students in Jewish schools.

Teaching is considered a sacred calling that transcends matters of salary or working conditions and precludes the right to strike, except in extenuating circumstances, where a living wage is not being paid and hence the teacher cannot teach. Ideally, individuals should be inspired to teach regardless of monetary considerations, but this is not always possible.

As a means of differentiating between the payment for teaching and other work, tradition suggests that teachers are paid, not for teaching per se, but for the time they have given to this calling, which they could have used for other employment. This may seem to be a fine-line distinction, even dialectic hair-splitting, but it is intended to convey an important message. Theoretically, at least, the obligation to teach and to share wisdom with others is not a matter that is related to salary. It is an obligation that every knowledgeable individual carries with him or her every day, an obligation that must be exercised even without remuneration.

The awareness that teachers are so obliged should not be translated by the administration of Jewish schools as *carte blanche* to do as they please in an insensitive fashion. Too often, advantage is taken of teachers who are reluctant to protest unfair treatment by striking. This fact places as much responsibility on the employers as it does on the employees.

Misconception: Judaism does not look with favor upon sex education.

The matter of proper sexual relations is too important to be approached haphazardly. Since it is one of the most vital building blocks of the family, both partners in the marriage need to know the intricacies of the sexual relationship and the parameters of responsibility in full detail.

The question is not whether sex education is necessary. The question is: What is the best medium for effectively transmitting sex education? Is it in a classroom among children who are years away from marriage? Is it in a manner that trivializes, even "biologizes," the sexual relationship? Should it be taught by individuals who do not have a deep appreciation of the holiness of the sexual relationship?

These are the questions that need to be addressed in formulating an approach to sex education. Obviously, in contemporary times, when there is so much that passes for enlightened information, so much that is bombarding our unsuspecting children, it is important to investigate how this can be neutralized through the proper transmission of a value-imbued appreciation of the sexual relationship.

A good insight into the importance of sex education is revealed in the famous talmudic episode of a student who sneaked into his *rebbe*'s bedroom and stayed under the bed while the *rebbe* and his wife engaged in conjugal union. The student started talking to himself in startled reaction to his *rebbe*'s passionate lovemaking, which understandably elicited a reaction from the *rebbe*. The *rebbe* asked the student what he was doing there. The student responded, "It is *Torah*, and I need to learn."

There is no evidence from the Talmud that the *rebbe* became angry at the student, although one can assume that the student was politely asked to leave.

But the message of this illuminating episode is clear. Sex education is *Torah*, and this generation, just like all other generations, needs to know.

Misconception: Giving one's seat to an older individual is nice but not obligatory.

There is a biblical obligation to rise for individuals who are 70 years old or older.

Obviously, people do not go around with placards announcing their age, so if it seems that the individual is approximately 70 years old, it is advisable to err on the side of showing respect.

Standing for one who is "sage with age" means more than just giving up one's seat on a bus or a train. It also means standing in the presence of that person. This is a sign of deference and respect that we owe to individuals who attain the age of 70.

8

Women and Men

Disparity
Fairness
Setting the Record Straight

Misconception: God is a man.

Many references to God, in Scriptures, in prayer, as well as in other Judaic literature, employ male terms.

However, God is gender-free. As Maimonides points out, it is impossible to posit attributes of God such as tall or short, thin or heavy, male or female. References to God's hand or other such usages are anthropomorphic. They employ human terms for the purpose of conveying a message that can be apprehended by the finite human mind. But this does not imply that God actually has a hand. It only means that we experience some event or phenomenon as if it were a hand, the hand of God.

The not-infrequent reference to God in masculine terminology reflects a linguistic convention; and such usage is not intended to impute masculinity to God, any more than feminine terminology, such as *Shekhinah*, employed to describe God, means that God is a woman.

Misconception: The Bible paints a negative picture of women.

If anything, the reverse is the truth. In biblical situations of a man and a woman confronting each other, whether it is Abraham and Sarah concerning Yishmael, or Isaac and Rebecca concerning their children, or Yehudah and Tamar concerning each other, the woman is acknowledged either for her superior insight, her greater understanding, or her integrity.

There is a negative picture painted of some individuals in the Bible, but invariably they are males rather than females. Think of Esau, Korah, Datan, and Abiram, among others.

Episodes in the Bible dealing with rebellion all involved men.

Misconception: Women occupy an inferior position in Jewish thinking.

Different yes, inferior no. In the present generation, we have experienced a dramatic shift from a home-based Judaism to an institution-based Judaism. In this change, the woman's importance has not been as obvious as it was in previous generations, when the home was the focal point of Jewish expression.

It should be noted that even though emphasis was placed on the home, women were not, by definition, excluded from the social matrix. If women had been perceived as intrinsically inferior and second rate, it would have been impossible for Deborah, a prophet in the time of the Judges, to rise to the rank of leader of the Jewish community. Such a rise through the ranks would have been beyond contemplation, had Deborah been relegated to an inferior class by virtue of being female. This was not the case then, nor has it ever been the case.

There is no question that women and men have never been the same in classical Jewish thinking, but the differences between them are just that—differences. They are of equal importance, but in uniquely different dimensions.

Misconception: Men regularly thank God for not having been created as women, proving that men are superior to women.

There is a blessing that is recited every day to this effect. One may wonder why the blessing is not more assertive—thanking God for "having made me a man."

The context of the blessing indicates that the issue here is the obligation to fulfill commandments. Women, who for specific positive reasons are exempt from certain commandments, have less responsibilities of an obligatory nature. The men have more, and in the opening exercise of their daily prayers, express acceptance of this responsibility for more obligation with gratitude and thanks.

However, they do not say, "Thank you for making me a man," because being a man, living up to the responsibilities of a man, is something that they have yet to achieve. They are not made as complete individuals; instead they have to work toward that completeness. Hence, the "not having made me a woman" text is employed.

The blessing certainly was never intended to denigrate women, or to affirm, with chauvinistic pride, the superiority of men. Any interpretation to that effect distorts the meaning and intent of the blessing.

Misconception: In Jewish law, a father has the full right to sell his daughter.

The father did indeed have the right to sell his daughter. However, before jumping to any conclusions concerning this right, it is important to recognize what it means.

The reason for this was to give the father an option in a situation of extreme poverty, in which there was literally not enough on the table to sustain the daughter. In such instance, the father could transfer the responsibility for sustaining the daughter to another family, where there was legitimate prospect that the daughter could marry a member of that family. In so doing, the father had another option for rescuing his daughter from the agony of extreme poverty and starvation.

The daughter always had the right to reject the potential marital options, if she so desired. The permission to sell is nothing more than an escape hatch from the terrible circumstances of poverty. Rather than locking the father and daughter into a situation without hope, this option was made available for use only in extreme emergencies.

Permission is granted, but permissiveness did not enter into this issue.

Misconception: Daughters have no claim on the estate of their father.

The biblical rules concerning inheritance give priority to the sons. Although this is interpreted by some as disadvantageous to women, this is not the intent, nor is it the case. Since men have the primary obligation for sustaining their families, it is they who are given the benefits of the estate so that when they marry, they can share that estate with their partners in life. A daughter may not be the beneficiary of her father's estate, but upon marriage, she will benefit from the estate that will be shared with her husband. Thus, on a communal basis, it levels out.

In specific instances when the father died and left no sons, the daughters gained title to the estate. Additionally, and quite importantly, all this is applicable only once the question of immediate sustenance of the daughters is addressed. If there is still money left in the estate, beyond the monies needed to sustain the daughters, that goes to the sons. However, if all that is contained in the estate is just enough to sustain either the sons or the daughters, this is transmitted directly to the daughters, and the sons must fend for themselves.

Misconception: Allowing a man to have many wives is unfair to women.

In biblical law, a man may have many wives, but a wife may have only one husband at a time. This seems unfair, at least at face value. Why should a woman not have the same choice as a man?

The answer relates to elementary biology. When a man has many wives, one always knows who is the father of the child. However, if a woman has many husbands, paternity is uncertain.

Clear knowledge of who is the child's father and mother is considered absolutely essential. Otherwise, each possible father can claim it is the other husband's child, and thus no one will take paternal responsibility.

To prevent this, the Bible forbade a situation that would almost unavoidably lead to the chaos of uncertain paternity.

Therefore, a woman can have only one husband at a time. With regard to the disparity itself, it should also be pointed out that if, upon marriage, it was clearly understood between husband and wife that no other women would be welcome to the domain, then the husband had no right to marry another. This could only be done with the wife's permission.

Additionally, the woman, in choosing a mate, was given a much wider range of choice because of the biblical permission. She could choose to marry either an already married man, who had the means to sustain more than one wife, or she could choose to marry someone who was unmarried but perhaps poor and not even capable of supporting one woman. The woman had the choice of opting either for a romantic but economically shaky marriage, or an economically stable but perhaps less romantic relationship.

The choice was hers; she was not forced to marry anyone contrary to her own desire. What, at first glance, seems to be unfair turns out to be the creation of more marital options for the woman.

Misconception: Women are obligated to have children.

The first biblical commandment is to "be fruitful and multiply," the minimal standard for species replacement. This means that a married couple should have at least one boy and one girl.

The *mitzvah* to procreate is directed at the male partner. The Torah does not oblige the woman to have children.

It seems incongruous that the woman who carries the child in her womb for nine months, is under no obligation to do so. She is obviously part of the obligation to assure that the earth is "not desolate but inhabited," yet from a legal perspective, it is the husband who must have children. Why is this so?

For the husband, the childbearing process starts with pleasure, and it is free from the direct experience of pain. All the pain associated with the carrying of the child and the subsequent birth is experienced and endured by the woman. Since the woman must often suffer excruciating pain to bear children, God refuses to place such an inordinate burden on the woman. It is unfair to obligate her to endure pain in order to fulfill a commandment.

It is effectively up to her to decide whether she desires children. For the man, whose role in the childbearing process is a distinct pleasure, there are no barriers to imposing an obligation.

The dynamics of the marital union are thus more clearly delineated in this biblical directive. The man who is obliged to have children must endear himself to a woman who, although not obligated to have children, will be so enamored with her spouse that she will want to share everything with him, to build a future with him, even if at times it may be painful for her to do so.

Misconception: Only a woman can commit adultery.

A man who has an affair with a married woman is guilty of having engaged in an adulterous union. This is regardless of whether the man is married or single.

A woman can be guilty of adultery only if she is married. A man, on the other hand, can be guilty of the crime of adultery even if he is single.

In the minds of many, adultery implies a lack of faith, infidelity to a partner. It is thus more difficult to understand the concept that one can be guilty of adultery when single. In the case of a man who has an affair with a married woman, his breach of faith inheres in his invading the sacred domain of an already existing marriage.

Misconception: A woman may be divorced against her will.

In biblical times, a man was allowed to have more than one wife. This was essentially intended to provide greater choices for the woman. If she so desired, she could marry a man of obvious wealth who offered the prospect of financial security. Because there were relatively few such men, she would have to share this individual with other women. She was never forced into such a marriage; this possibility was only made available to her. Some women preferred financial security, even if this meant sharing a husband. The choice was proposed, not imposed.

However, this option could only be viable if the wealthy husbands were allowed an escape hatch, should they experience a sudden change of fortune. If they knew they would be locked into their many marriages forever, they would not take the risk. Then, the possibility of marriage offering financial security, coupled, of course, with love, would not have existed. For this reason, the available option included with it the right of the husband to divorce his wife, even against her will, and to provide the divorced wife with the prearranged settlement as spelled out in the *ketubah*.

In the course of time, the situation changed dramatically. Approximately one thousand years ago, Rabbenu Gershom established that a Jew was not allowed to have more than one wife at a time. At the same time, the right of the husband to divorce his wife against her will was taken away.

This makes eminent sense. A marriage for financial convenience required the availability of relatively easy exit. Once marriage was established on a one-to-one basis only, there was no longer any reason why the husband should be allowed to force divorce upon his wife. Mutual consent then became the primary basis for divorce. If marriage is a one-to-one relationship, then the relationship is one of mutual responsibility and equality during and after marriage.

Misconception: Men are obligated to observe more commandments because they are more holy.

The *mitzvot* were given to us in order to shape us through disciplined adherence to responsibility. The *mitzvot* are designed to bring out the best in us.

Obviously, the better we are, the less discipline we need. An outstanding child is less restricted by a parent, whereas a child with irresponsible tendencies will be given a more exacting set of behavioral guidelines.

The fact that men have been given more commandments indicates that they are in greater need of discipline. Women, on the other hand, have throughout history exhibited a greater faith and adherence to responsibility. They need not be reminded of this as often and as concretely as do men.

It is precisely because of deficiencies that men have more commandments, rather than the reverse. If anything, one would gain from this the notion of female superiority within Judaism, although it is distasteful to make judgments between the sexes. Certainly, the argument that women are inferior because they do not put on *tefillin* has been shown, through this logic, to be absolutely wrong.

Part V

FOOD FOR THOUGHT— THOUGHT FOR FOOD

9

Food for Thought

Judaism as a Legal System
The Commandments
Comparative Religion
Superstitions and Other Matters

Misconception: Judaism is a religion.

The truth is that Judaism is not a religion. It is more a way of life that is predicated upon a religious belief. Judaism has been lumped together with other religions such as Christianity and Islam, and is therefore painted with the same brush.

If religion is defined as a relationship of faith, then certainly that ingredient is very significant within Judaism. However, the matter of faith is merely the foundation, the ground upon which Judaism is built.

It is difficult to legislate a relationship. An individual cannot be told to marry someone else. However, once two individuals agree to marry, then certain rules and regulations apply for their marital compact.

In a similar sense, an individual cannot be ordered to believe in God. Leading Jewish thinkers of the past refused to include belief in God as one of the commandments. The relationship itself cannot be commanded. That must stem from within the individual.

However, once that relationship is firmly established, it is possible to propose the parameters for that relationship. In other words, once an individual professes faith in God, Judaism projects the rules and regulations that should govern that faith relationship. Faith is a given—it is presumed.

We refuse to relegate the notion of faith in God to being a mere abstraction. Instead, through various affirmations, testimonies, and fulfillments of obligation, we affirm, entrench, and solidify that faith. The commandments are the tangible expression of our faith, which at once reinforce the relationship and enhance our lives.

Misconception: Judaism is nothing more than a conglomerate of laws and rules.

There is no denying the fact that Judaism contains an abundance of laws and rules. The question that is open to discussion is: Why all the rules, why all the laws?

The absolutely wrong explanation for this is that God desired to create mechanical people who only stick to the letter of law and go by the rules. The absolutely right understanding is that the laws are the guideposts, the common denominators, the framework and parameters within which one's behavior should be expressed.

The law teaches what is considered important and asks individuals to understand not only the regulation, but also the meaning and thrust behind it. From the vast legislation concerning honoring one's parents, one should learn how to keep to the letter of the law and also how to appreciate one's parents to whatever extent possible.

Kashrut (food edibility) regulations have an impact not only on diet, but also on sensitivity to creatures and on one's sense of disciplined control.

There is the letter of the law, and there is the spirit of the law. There is the boundary of the law, and there is the area within the boundary. It is within the boundary and through living the spirit of the message that the law conveys, that one apprehends the full scope and profundity of the Jewish way.

Misconception: Judaism is based on democratic ideals.

This impression may be based on the fact that the modern State of Israel is seemingly modeled along the lines of Western democracies, with an elected Knesset and with each individual given the right to vote.

However, it is questionable whether Judaism itself espouses the democratic ideals basic to Western civilization. The two ideals that will be focused upon are the right of every individual to hold office and the right of free speech.

Insofar as holding of office is concerned, there are obvious limitations. An individual who would have liked to be a judge within the community could not say "I want to be a judge," and run for that office. In ancestral times, the individual who desired to serve in such capacity would have had to show competence in Jewish law before being eligible for the position. Appointments to this position were based on merit rather than on popularity.

Once individuals became members of the *Sanhedrin* (Rabbinic Court), they took part on an equal footing in the deliberations of the court. For capital cases the court, comprised of twenty-three judges, worked on the basis of a majority vote—specifically, a majority plus one, or thirteen. Thirteen votes were required for conviction in a capital case. The defendant would be declared guilty, and the appropriate penalty was meted out.

A king was not elected; he was either appointed or assumed the throne as the next in line in the dynasty. Prophets were not elected; they attained their position within the community based on personal merit, as judged by God.

Insofar as freedom of speech is concerned, individuals within the Judaic theocracy were prohibited from uttering statements that were either blasphemous or insurrectionist. Aside from this, any speech that was insulting, degrading, deceitful, or irresponsible was prohibited. This is as true today as it was then, except that it is impossible to enforce.

Individuals are free, but they are only free within the context of adherence to a set of principles and guidelines. To a certain extent, this is true even of Western-style democracies, which do not countenance statements of rebellion, bigotry, or slander. There are some checks on free speech, but they are not as far-reaching as in the Judaic system.

If democracy means the freedom and dignity of the individual, there is significant affinity between such ideals and Judaism. But the major concern of democracy is to allow individual freedom in an open society without threatening that society. In Judaism, the major concern is to forge personal and communal growth through adherence to transcending values. There may be some overlap, but there is also a world of difference.

Misconception: In Jewish law, the majority rules.

Normally, there are few items that are decided by vote. The fact that 90 percent of a community does not adhere to the dietary regulations does not therefore mean that the entire community is exempt from such religious practice.

However, in certain matters, a vote may be necessary in order to adjudicate a complicated situation.

Specifically, this procedure was standard for any legal matter that came to a Jewish court. A financial matter that came before a court of three judges would be decided by a vote among the three, and here the majority would prevail.

However, in cases involving capital punishment, the situation was not quite the same. Such cases could not be decided by a court of three; they could only be decided by a court of twenty-three individuals who were properly ordained for judging these very serious matters.

If the vote in the matter of capital implications was 12 to 11 in favor of conviction, the court could not render a guilty verdict. A majority of one was not sufficient in such instances. Instead, at the very minimum, a majority of two was required, but since the court was comprised of twenty-three judges, for all intents and purposes this meant that a majority of three would be needed to obtain a conviction.

Outside the legal sphere, however, Judaism is guided mainly by *vox Dei*, not *vox populi*.

Misconception: Jewish law is punishment oriented.

A reading of the Bible would seem to indicate that punishments play a very significant role in Jewish law. There are delineated consequences for the many potential breaches of the law, a vast array of punitive measures ranging all the way from the administering of stripes (flogging) to a court-imposed death penalty.

It should be noted that in Jewish law, the death penalty was rarely employed.

Additionally, the various requirements necessary to impose the death penalty were impossible to satisfy in many cases. In these instances, the death penalty remained a theoretical matter rather than a practical reality.

The question then arises: If the punishments were not, and in some instances could not be administered, then why speak about them at all? The answer to this strikes at the very root of the role of punishment in biblical law. We only know from the punishments what the Bible considers to be essential to society. From the fact that cursing one's parent is considered a capital crime, we learn how much importance is placed on honoring one's parents. The same is true concerning the capital punishment associated with the desecration of the *Shabbat*. The punishment hierarchy sets up a value priority, a clear statement of what is considered of capital importance, and what is considered of somewhat lesser importance. This is vital in terms of making judgments when there is a clash of values. For example, one who is faced with an unavoidable choice of either desecrating the *Shabbat*, or eating something which is not kosher, should choose to eat the non-kosher food, since the penalty (flogging) for eating non-kosher items is less severe than the capital penalty for desecration of the *Shabbat*. The punishment hierarchy, in effect, sets into motion a legislation of its own.

The main message, however, is that the punishments are more a means toward an understanding of the full scope of

Jewish law including the value priorities. It is difficult to state that one law is more important than another. By indicating the theoretical penalty, the Bible effectively tells us what is of most immediate importance.

Misconception: The Judaic legal system is primitive and outdated.

One of the major features of the Judaic legal system is the absence of a jury system. Instead, cases are tried in the presence of experts in law, with a court of twenty-three being mandatory for cases of capital import. Another feature is that circumstantial evidence in cases of criminal culpability is inadmissable as evidence. A third feature provides that conviction for a capital crime can only result from direct witnessing of the act by at least two individuals, preceded by a forewarning of the consequences of the act to the would-be perpetrator. This serves as a precaution against the individual being insane. Finally, there is no prison system in the biblical legal framework. Instead, the accent is on restitutive rehabilitation.

These are some of the basic guidelines that are operative in the Jewish administration of justice. One may argue that far from being primitive and outdated, this system is quite instructive for the contemporary situation. In democratic societies with their overcrowded prisons, there is much pressure to reassess the system. Aside from the overcrowding, there is great debate as to whether a prison sentence teaches a lesson or hardens the individual to become an even worse criminal. The Jewish approach of rehabilitation through restitution, such as working for the victim, is a much more instructive and helpful model for the correcting of societal ills, and for the reeducation of those who have deviated from the path of justice.

One may argue about the wisdom of refusing to admit circumstantial evidence. The refusal is in order to obviate the possibility that the death penalty might be administered for a crime the convicted person did not commit. For example, Judaism goes to extremes to avoid such unwarranted capital punishment. It only sanctions capital punishment when the individual, having been forewarned of the consequences of an action, brazenly asserts a willingness to die just to have the satisfaction of perpetrating the act of murder.

It should be emphasized that the administrators of justice in Judaic society, the rabbinic scholars, always had the power to enact regulations that were deemed necessary to protect society. Thus, they had the power to put into social isolation one who was obviously guilty of murder, but who could not be convicted along biblical lines because of some technicality.

It turns out that the Judaic system of justice is an enlightened model that has stood the test of time and would undoubtedly withstand the test of modern times as well.

Misconception: Judaism supports capital punishment.

This assumption is based on the many instances in which the Bible imposes the death penalty for committing certain crimes, ranging from adultery to murder to idolatry.

However, to jump from this to the conclusion that capital punishment was countenanced and encouraged would be erroneous. In theory, capital punishment was a possibility. In fact, it was almost an impossibility.

For capital punishment to be possible, the potential perpetrator must have been forewarned by two witnesses who admonished him not to commit the crime and indicated the consequences of the crime.

Having been forewarned, the perpetrator must accept the warning and say, "Even with the consequences, I am still going ahead with the crime." This is an indication that the perpetrator was aware of the gravity of the situation, was of sound mind, and was willing to accept the consequences.

The crime must have been committed in full view of two witnesses, who then testified that they saw the crime committed. Circumstantial evidence would not suffice, however conclusive it might have been.

Relatives could not be witnesses, nor could intimate friends. (Relatives or friends are either very supportive or very antagonistic, and therefore cannot serve as witnesses.)

When the witnesses testified, they were scrupulously cross-examined by the judges, and if there was the slightest discrepancy the witnesses were dismissed. If one said the victim's eyes were blue, and another said that the victim's eyes were green, the testimony was thrown out.

The entire court procedure weighed heavily in favor of the defendant. Assuring a conviction for a capital crime was almost an impossibility; in one talmudic view, any court that administered the death penalty even once in seventy years was considered a murderous court.

The Bible contains much talk about capital punishment, but it is mainly theoretical. Capital punishment was rare, almost an impossibility, considering, for example, that most violent crimes take place within the home and certainly not within the view of witnesses.

Why, then, does the Bible speak about capital punishment so frequently? The answer is simply, that there was no question that a murderer deserved to be put to death. However, that is just theoretically stating that anyone who takes another's life does not deserve to live.

But in practice, everything was done to prevent the court from taking a life. If the individual was truly guilty of a crime worthy of capital punishment but eluded the sentence because of a technicality, the court had the right to incarcerate him as a protective measure for society. As for the ultimate justice that the individual would confront, that was left to God, the Ultimate Authority.

Misconception: Judaism espouses "an eye for an eye."

This misconception is based on a biblical verse that states that in the case of inflicted damage, one is obliged to pay "an eye for an eye." The more literal translation is "an eye under an eye."

The Talmud, which is the authentic explication of the Bible, speaks of the many difficulties in applying this exhortation literally. For example, if the aggressor is already blind in one eye and is now to be punished by having the second eye gouged out for having gouged out an eye of the victim, we would then make the aggressor totally blind, while the victim could still see with one eye. Or, in the reverse, if the victim is already blind in one eye, and through the aggressor's actions is now totally blind, by the court's blinding only one of his eyes, the aggressor would still be able to see. Surely this is not equitable.

Moreover, how can any court in administering such a punishment, be sure that the inflicted damage will only be the blinding of an eye. How can the court be sure that, in the process, more serious damage will not be incurred, perhaps even killing the individual.

The Talmud thus concludes with absolute certainty that the statement "an eye for an eye" means that the aggressor must pay the victim the *worth* of an eye.

If such is the case, why does the Bible speak in such categorical terms, terms that may even seem misleading? It is because the Bible desired to state in unequivocal terms how seriously it views the act of blinding someone, or inflicting other forms of irreparable damage. By right, the victimizer in such situations deserves to have an eye gouged out, but the actual punishment is much more merciful. The Bible tells us the deserved punishment; the Talmud gives us the actual punishment.

Misconception: The Bible endorses slavery.

There is discussion in the *Torah* of the regulations concerning slaves that would lead one to believe that Judaism endorses slavery.

This is based on the erroneous assumption that the body of legislation concerning the *eved* (wrongly translated as "slave," but really meaning "worker"), is a replication of what is normally implied by the term "slavery."

The two instances in which an individual may become enslaved to a fellow Jew are either for having stolen and not being able to repay, or by selling oneself into slavery because one is destitute.

In the case of not being able to repay, the servitude is penalty for the act of theft. The penalty itself is quite instructive. Instead of placing the convicted felon in jail, where nothing is gained by felon or by victim, the law places the criminal in the home of the victim and literally forces victim and victimizer to live together. The felon hopefully learns that the victim is not an insensitive "fat cat," and the victim learns that the felon has more than just a few saving graces. By working for the victim, the felon at once makes material recompense and social reconnection. This is a rehabilitative penalty with obvious implications for those who would like to improve the present prison system.

In the case of a person selling himself because of extreme poverty, it is more like entering into the employ of another, akin to a personal services contract.

In both of these instances, the rules concerning the relationship between slave and master are quite clear, with the primary onus on the master never to subjugate the worker, never to refer to him as a slave, or to in any other way afflict him.

In fact, if it ever reached the point where there was only one pillow available, the rule was that the servant gets the pillow.

This is what the Bible means when it deals with the "slave" institution. It is not slavery at all; it is nothing more than enlightened employment.

Misconception: Judaism affirms that learning is the highest value.

Learning is a high value, a very important value, but not the highest value. We learn in order to know, but we know in order to do. The full extent of one's manifold responsibilities can only be fully appreciated through learning about them. It is only when one knows how to go about the observance of honoring parents, respecting others, fulfilling the *Shabbat*-related imperatives, among others, that one can observe these commandments properly and with reinforced meaning.

Ignorance is an impediment to proper appreciation of the thrust and intent of Jewish life. Additionally, there is hardly any purpose in being intellectually aware of everything one must do, but then refusing to do it. One must know in order to do. The doing is the essence of Jewish life.

Misconception: Intelligence is a defining characteristic of Jews.

There are those who would have us believe that Jews are more intelligent than the average non-Jew. Novelist C. P. Snow ventured that since rabbis are the most learned among the Jews, and since they usually proliferate in great numbers, Jews therefore have a superior gene pool of intelligence.

However, it is wrong to insist that there is a correlation between I.Q. and Jewishness. One need not pass an intelligence test in order to become Jewish, nor does one forfeit Jewishness because of a low score on an intelligence test.

Judaism does place a great emphasis on learning, because one cannot behave properly without knowledge. But this should not be transformed into prejudice against those who are not blessed with "above-average brains."

There are defining characteristics, traits by which Jews can and should be recognized. These are (1) the capacity for compassion and mercy, (2) a sense of remorse after wrong-doing, and (3) a propensity to act with kindness toward others. These are the hallmarks of the Jew, because they are the most vital characteristics of Judaism.

Misconception: There are 613 commandments.

The 613 commandments are sometimes referred to as the *taryag mitzvot*, with TaRYaG being the numerical equivalent of 613. The T (*tav*) equals 400, the R (*resh*) equals 200, the Y (*yud*) equals 10, and the G (*gimmel*) equals 3.

The word *Torah* has the numerical equivalent of 611. T (*tav*) equals 400, V (*vav*) equals 6, R (*resh*) equals 200, and H (*heh*) equals 5, adding up to 611.

The differential between 613 and 611 is 2. Since the first two commandments were given directly by God, then what remains are the 611 that were transmitted by Moshe; hence, the *Torah* of Moshe.

However, to think that there are only 611 obligations derived from the *Torah* is a mistake. There are abundant obligations that stem from the *Torah*. The construct of TaRYaG is merely numerically reminiscent of *Torah* itself and pertains to the main basic commands which number 613.

In reality there are many more than 613 commands in the *Torah*. *Sefer Haredim*, a treatise written by the 16th century kabbalist Eliezer Azikri, on the commandments deriving from the *Torah*, lists many more commandments than the primary 613.

Misconception: Ritual commandments are more important than ethical commandments.

It is exceedingly difficult to categorically state which commandments are more important and which less important. Certainly, the categorical substitution of one set of commands for another set is unwarranted. Judaism is a package, and any diminution of a part has a negative impact on the total package.

In actuality, the ritual and ethical regulations are interrelated. One reinforces the other. The ritual commandments cement the individual's dialectic with God, and the ethical commandments address human interactional obligation.

Though these may seem to be separate compartments, there is a significant overlap in that every ethical imperative is founded on a sense of the holy, one's sacred obligations, and one's appreciation of the absolute holiness of all other individuals, indeed the holiness of life in its totality.

One example will illustrate the interface of ritual with ethical. The dietary regulations, which forge a disciplined approach to what one may and may not eat, contain a specific set of rules for how one prepares an animal from the eligible species for slaughter. There is meticulous ritual surrounding the actual preparation of the animal, including the use of a knife that is 100 percent nick-free, the uninterrupted cutting action free of excessive force, and other considerations. In other words, one may only eat from the animal species if one has prepared the animal with sensitivity, free of even a split second of unnecessary pain.

This kosher legislation has obvious impact on one's ethical stance, whether it is sensitivity to animals, or to humans who certainly should not be approached with less respect than animals. If unnecessary pain may not be inflicted upon animals, verbal pain should never be inflicted upon human beings.

The legislation regarding the *Shabbat*, which obviously has person–God implications, establishes a day that is free from all work. This entrenches the idea that human beings, although employed, should not be overworked or the work required should not be beyond humane limits. They have an intrinsic dignity that may not be compromised, a dignity that is reaffirmed once a week because they are free from any work obligations. Thus, what appears to be a purely ritualistic observance has definite ethical overtones and implications.

In essence, the ritual and the ethical reinforce each other. The ritual infuses the ethical with the sense of the holy, the ethical infuses the ritual with the sense of immediate relevance for the human context. You cannot have one without the other.

Misconception: The observance of *Shabbat* and the dietary laws are the most complicated Judaic fulfillments.

There is no question that the observance of *Shabbat* and *kashrut* may pose difficulties. These difficulties are most acutely felt in societies where there is much activity on the *Shabbat* and where there is much non-kosher food available. However, the experience of freedom has brought with it a work week in which the *Shabbat* can remain sacrosanct. So, too, there is the ready availability of kosher alternatives to almost any food item.

What, then, qualifies as the most difficult commandment to observe? Arguably, it may be a *mitzvah* that to many may be a total revelation. The *Torah* legislates the various festivals and then exhorts that we are to rejoice in those festivals. Accordingly, this translates as an imperative to be happy during the period of the festival.

To be happy on these days means to avoid any anger, to avoid any upset, to avoid any feeling of melancholy or sadness. Such consummate control of one's emotions and feelings is the most complicated of fulfillments. It requires discipline, it requires dedication, it requires concentration. In the end, it is worth it.

Misconception: It is hypocrisy to observe that which one does not understand.

By that logic, one would never learn to swim. Some philosophers have claimed that they did not observe one or more of the biblical commands because they were "not yet ready for it." One can only learn to swim while in the water. One becomes ready for the commandment by actually doing it.

Is it hypocrisy to abide by the dietary laws when one does not understand their meaning? There are two major problems with such an approach. The first is that we will probably never understand the full meaning of the commandment. The second is that if it were left to everyone to decide what they should observe and when they were ready to observe it, it would create a community of chaos rather than a community of common affirmation.

Is it the human being who must develop the readiness for the command, or is it the command that inspires the individual to attain loftier heights? In truth, it is probably the second alternative that should be operative, for the commandments were given in order to shape humankind. It is precisely when we are out of spiritual shape that we should jump into the spiritual waters of religious fulfillment. One is most ready when one is not ready.

Misconception: Stricter is better.

There are obviously circumstances in which being more careful and scrupulous is better. The stricter one is with regard to being honest, with regard to being careful of the dignity of others, with regard to not trespassing on ethical boundaries, obviously the better.

However, with regard to observance of other fulfillments, this does not always follow. For example, one who adopts a strict interpretation of the biblical passages regarding the *Shabbat* and consequently will not get off his chair or leave the home becomes a shut-in; this may be stricter, but it is not better —it is much worse. Such strictness has destroyed the spirit of the *Shabbat*.

One who is so careful with regard to the possible abuse of one's sensual desires to the point of not marrying has taken matters to a strict, but sinful extreme. The classic example of strictness leading to outlandish, dangerous conclusions is the foolish pietist who refuses to save a drowning woman, with the "rationale" that it is unseemly to look at women.

As long as strictness has not distorted the perspective and the intent of the commandment, but has enhanced it, that strictness is an improvement. Otherwise it is an unwarranted intrusion. At all times, one must be singularly aware of the boundary where legal requirement ends and personal stringency begins. When the stringency becomes the main element, one has lost focus. This is the beginning of value distortion.

Misconception: Experiencing pleasure is sinful.

It would seem unlikely that anyone would dare suggest that experiencing pleasure is sinful. However, there are too many who identify religion with denial, who see pleasure as almost antireligious.

It therefore comes as a surprise that not only is pleasure not sinful; in fact it is a *mitzvah*. We are asked to rejoice in all the good that God has given to us; we are asked to be happy and enjoy the world. We are obliged to make our spouse happy in marriage, primarily through our caring, our sensitivity, and also through the sensual experiences.

After all, it is difficult for individuals to be grateful to God for having been placed on this earth, if they are under obligation to renounce all possible joyful and pleasurable experiences. An individual who, in the context of a meaningful and disciplined approach, enjoys and appreciates the good that God has placed in the world, is more likely to be grateful to God, happy about being here, and eager to make a positive contribution to the world.

The experience of pleasure is, therefore, essential for meaningful Judaic expression.

Misconception: Fasting is a sign of superiority.

There may be some ideological correlation between an individual's fasting and more intense religiosity. It is an indication of sacrifice for God's sake, or at least that is what some assume.

Certainly, insofar as the prescribed fast days in the Jewish calendar are concerned, the observance of these fasts in the proper manner is an expression of a religious commitment.

The addition of more fast days to one's personal calendar, with the intention that these fasts are also spiritual offerings, is another matter. If it is based on the premise that by denying oneself, one gains God's favor, then it is faulty reasoning. Mere fasting for fasting's sake, subjecting oneself to privation for no reason, is a questionable religious practice. Judaism does not espouse denial; it rejects denial for denial's sake as a religious expression. The Nazarite who vows to abstain only from wine is considered a sinner. How much more so, says the Talmud, is one who abstains from more than wine considered a sinner.

If the fasting is intended to create the proper conditions to focus on self-improvement, this is another matter. In such instance, the fasting is not an end in itself; it is a means toward a very important spiritual end. Such fasting, which focuses on the positive rather than on denial, is an affirmative act.

However, any individual contemplating such activity must be able to convincingly argue that the process of spiritual improvement could occur only by fasting. One would venture to guess that in the overwhelming majority of cases this is hardly true.

Misconception: It is all right to make vows as long as you fulfill them.

Obviously, making a vow and not fulfilling it is a serious breach. However, it is not at all clear that making a vow is the best way to express oneself even if one has every intention of fulfilling the vow, and even if one does, indeed, fulfill that vow.

The best way, according to talmudic wisdom, is not to make vows at all. One should just go about the business of doing good deeds without talking about them in advance or placing oneself in a position of possibly breaking the vow.

Misconception: A sinner is stigmatized forever.

Many people in society are unforgiving of those who have done wrong. However, no one is perfect or free from taint.

Repentance, the regretting of a previous wrong coupled with resolve for future improvement, is an essential feature of Judaism. It is what *Yom Kippur*, the Day of Atonement, is all about. Nor is this process restricted to *Yom Kippur*. The process of self-improvement, of making up for past breaches and offenses, is a perpetual exercise.

We are told that with our proper repentance, God forgives. If it is good enough for God, it should be good enough for us.

There is also a certain amount of arrogance in the refusal to forgive. The unforgiving individual names someone else a sinner, asserting that the other is permanently stuck with such a stigma. Who relegates such omnipotence to any individual? Forgiving individuals are much more likely to be forgiven individuals. This makes for better relationships.

Misconception: A *hasid* is more religious than other people.

The original definition of a *hasid* is one who is pious. This term was used to describe an individual who seriously and diligently undertakes to fulfill responsibilities.

However, in more modern parlance, the term *hasid* describes a disciple of a specific sect that is led by a *rebbe* (sage). Belonging to such a sect, or being a disciple (*hasid*) of a certain *rebbe,* does not necessarily imply a greater sense of commitment or religiosity.

A *mitnagid,* one who takes serious issue with the basic ethos of one or another hasidic group, may be even more religious (if that can be measured). Whether one belongs or does not belong to a certain sect is not an accurate barometer of religiosity.

Misconception: An alternate name for the books of the Scriptures is the Old Testament.

Many people do refer to the Bible, the Prophets, and the Scriptures, the *TeNaKh*, as the Old Testament. However, even though this may be in vogue, it is certainly not a Judaic usage.

According to Christian belief, the *TeNaKh* has been superseded by the New Testament. Thus, "Old Testament" has a pejorative ring, suggesting that it is now past history, archaic, no longer relevant.

Jewish belief is that the Bible, the *TeNaKh*, is ever relevant. It is not old; it is timeless.

Misconception: The Jews are the chosen people.

There are many references in Scriptures and in later literature, as well as in the prayers, that testify to a special relationship between God and the Jewish people.

However, the idea of "chosen" as descriptive of this relationship is slightly misleading. The famous adage states:

> How odd of God
> To choose the Jews.
> It's not so odd.
> The Jews chose God.

Jews are essentially the choosing people. They chose to embrace God's word and to live by that word. God's choosing the Jews was an act of appreciating the people who chose to live by God's word, thus making that people into God's nation.

There is nothing to suggest exclusivity in this relationship. One need not be of a specific color, race, or previous persuasion to be eligible to embrace God's word. In other words, anyone who makes the decision to live by God's word, by the *Torah*, would immediately be "chosen" too.

The idea of choosing is the more crucial element in the relationship. Being chosen is almost an automatic outgrowth of the choosing. The act of choosing and the experience of being chosen are not to be interpreted as indications of superiority or translated into religiously imbued arrogance. Choosing is the embrace of a profound responsibility. It is not a burden, but neither is it a boast.

Misconception: It is not important to spend extra money on the fulfillment of precepts.

An individual who can only afford styrofoam or plastic cups for the *Kiddush* (sanctification over wine on the *Shabbat*) is not required to go into debt to purchase an expensive wine cup.

However, an individual who chooses to recite the *Kiddush* with a styrofoam cup, or who affixes the *mezuzah* scroll in cellophane surrounded by aluminum foil, or who places *tefillin* in a paper bag, and at the same time adorns the home with expensive chandeliers, wallpaper, carpeting, and the like, projects a value distortion — that expensive decorations or luxuries are a necessity, but for the expression of the holy, cheaper is better.

Adorning the precepts, beautifying that which is associated with religious fulfillment, indicates that one attributes a sense of importance to these precepts. For those who cannot afford anything more than inexpensive decoration, that too is most beautiful.

Misconception: Islam has less in common with Judaism than does Christianity.

It would seem as if Christianity is more directly linked to Judaism, since Christianity evolved from Judaism, and at one time was only a small, insignificant sect within the Jewish community.

Islam, not having such a primary historical association with Judaism, would seem to be less connected, to have much less in common with Judaism.

Yet, in spite of the historical connection, Christianity has moved far away from Judaism. It has renounced the primary affirmations of Judaism, ranging from the Oneness of God, to *Shabbat*, to *kashrut*, to ritual immersion in the *mikvah* water. In establishing itself as a distinct alternative to Judaism, it went in another direction.

On the other hand, Muhammad was greatly interested in attracting the Jewish masses to his new religion, and he went out of his way to accommodate the Jews by offering a reasonably compatible theological platform.

Muhammad posited the idea of the Unity of God, originally accepted the notion of a Day of Atonement, which later became a voluntary fast, and maintained some semblance of regulatory practice concerning the dietary laws, such as the prohibition of pork.

This is not to suggest that the relationship between the Koran, the basic document of Islam, and the Bible, is one of total agreement. As much as Muhammad may have related positively to Judaic tradition, he later deviated from this approach because he realized that Jews were not flocking to his ranks.

Nevertheless, there are interesting and arguably more positive connections, at least in theory, between Islam and Judaism than between Christianity and Judaism.

Misconception: *Goy* is a term that only describes a non-Jew.

The nations of the world are often referred to as *goyim* (nations) in scriptures. Many use the term *goy* to describe a member of the nations of the world, a non-Jew.

It will come as a surprise to some that the Jewish people are themselves referred to by this term. Every *Shabbat* afternoon, in the *Minhah* service, we refer to the people of Israel as a unique *goy* (nation).

Usage notwithstanding, Israel is one of the *goyim* of the world.

Misconception: The Hebrew calendar is lunar based.

This would seem to be true, based on the realization that the Hebrew month is usually twenty-nine or thirty days, in order to balance out the lunar month, which is approximately twenty-nine-and-a-half days.

A lunar year is 354 days, or eleven days fewer than a solar year. If eleven days were to be lost to the calendar every year then the seasonal correlation of the festivals would go awry. Passover eventually would occur in the winter (not in the springtime); the Tabernacle festival of *Sukkot* would be not in the fall, but in the most intense winter season. Since these festivals must occur in their appropriate seasons, some method had to be introduced to correct the eleven-day discrepancy between the lunar and solar calendars. This is achieved by the addition of one extra month (a second month of Adar) seven times every nineteen years. Eleven multiplied by nineteen is approximately 210, divided by seven is thirty. Adding those thirty-day blocks seven times every nineteen years more or less corrects the eleven-day discrepancy and allows for the festivals to be correlated with the seasons.

The Hebrew calendar, although firmly rooted in the lunar system, is more accurately a correlation of solar and lunar cycles.

Misconception: The Hebrew calendar has always been fixed, and no adjustments or changes have ever been made.

This has been true ever since the permanent calendar was established in the second century by Hillel II.

However, this should not lead to the conclusion that the calendar is an unyielding instrument. In the days of the Temple, one did not know from one month to the next whether the previous month was 29 or 30 days, nor was the adding of another month to the year a matter that could be known years in advance.

In a year that was particularly rainy, making the pilgrimage to Jerusalem for Passover quite difficult, the high court (*Sanhedrin*), in their wisdom, would add another month, thus affording time for the weather to improve and the roads to dry, so that the paths to Jerusalem would be more accessible.

Other considerations, such as famine, could come into play in affecting the decision of the *Sanhedrin* as to whether a leap year should be declared.

In the Jewish scheme of things, at least originally, the calendar was there to serve the people.

Misconception: Judaism does not place any value on astrology.

Stargazing, or the attempt to understand one's self better by knowing one's time of birth and the attendant astrological implications, seems at first glance to be alien to Judaism.

However, there are statements within Judaic tradition that seemingly take on an astrological bent. For example, the Talmud relates that one who is born in the constellation of Mars will be a shedder of blood.

The problem with astrology is not that it may establish some framework, boundary, or context for a specific person. It is that the person may give this too much credence, thereby feeling helpless to counter whatever is determined by that astrological connection.

Thus, the Talmud, in stating that someone born in the constellation of Mars may be a shedder of blood, immediately states that this is not a compromise of individual free will. This does not condemn the Mars person to being a murderer. Perhaps the person will be a murderer; but, on the other hand, the person could be a doctor or, perhaps, a ritual slaughterer, or another profession that involves the shedding of blood.

Every human being has by his or her nature some restrictive parameters. One who is short is probably less likely to be a center on a basketball team; one who is tall is less likely to be a jockey; one who is born into a rich family has a different set of possibilities than one born into poverty. In all instances, the fact that the individual may have certain restrictions is not a compromise of free will.

If free will is taken to mean freedom from any limitations, or unlimited opportunity to choose from all possibilities, then no individual is free. On the other hand, if free will is nothing more or less than the freedom to either accept or reject the values that hallow life, a "freedom toward" instead of "freedom from," then no individual, no matter what the restriction, is necessarily constrained in such choice.

Thus, if astrological parameters are seen as guideposts for individual expression, they do not restrict individual free will. The individual always retains the capacity to affirm life's values under any circumstances.

To deify astrology would go against Jewish tradition. To explore one's self through astrology, but with full awareness that choice is always operative and must always be exercised, is not necessarily inconsistent with Jewish tradition.

Misconception: Judaism opposes the use of magic.

Magic *per se* is inherently neutral. Taking rabbits out of hats, swallowing fire, or making coins appear magically, are enjoyable tricks. They do not become problematic as long as there are no religious overtones attached to these tricks.

However, if the magic is used as a means to convince individuals of the truth of a certain idolatry, then this type of magic becomes prohibited.

The biblical prohibition against sorcery is directed more at the intent of the sorcery, which is to mislead individuals into idolatrous expression.

Misconception: The belief in evil spirits or demons is an irrational superstition.

The idea that an individual may be possessed by an evil spirit, or that one may have been invaded by a demon that needs to be exorcised, certainly smacks of irrationality. A modern, scientifically oriented individual has great difficulty understanding such weird notions.

However, in going beyond the superficial implication, evil spirits and demons are not as irrational as they may first appear. For example, people often say, "We don't know what possessed him (or her) to do that." We say that there was probably an evil spirit, or something drove the individual out of control, or the individual's behavior seems psychotic.

Consider the situation of an individual who is overcome by melancholy, by depression. Such an individual seems more often than not to have been taken over by a demon, not to be himself (or herself), but almost someone else. This is also the case with a manic–depressive person who suffers from alternating fits of depression and equally irrational fits of exultation.

What in modern terminology has been branded as psychosis or depression bears a similarity to what was referred to as an evil spirit or demon in other eras. The terminologies are different, but the ideas are the same.

The idea of a demon needing to be exorcised is, in modern parlance, a depression that must be cured by therapy. A good therapist will be able to hopefully "exorcise" a depression, a depression being a foreign, demon-like force that enters the system, terrorizes it, and eventually overwhelms it.

Earlier rabbinic literature may have given arms and legs, head and body to the demon, dressing it up as a life-size force. By so doing, the rabbis projected the immense power that such demons have, giving a tangible projection of a subtle but potent force that all too often overcomes the individual. Perhaps the language today is more sophisticated and science more advanced, but the general idea is time proof.

Misconception: The idea of the *ayin hara* is pure superstition.

The idea of *ayin hara* is, surprisingly, a very rational concept. In its original sense, it refers to the effect that ostentation may have on people's emotions. For example, an individual who openly flaunts wealth may evoke the jealousy of others. In a larger sense, this type of jealousy may incite the envying ones to either rob or vandalize the wealthy person. They may see the wealthy person as the one who exploited them or prevented them from raising their own living standards.

Of course, vandalizing or stealing is not legitimate for any reason. However, it is vital to recognize that open flaunting does have a harmful effect and can cause even violent reaction. Thus, it is advisable to behave modestly and not be exhibitionistic with material things.

The evil eye or the envying eye that is incited by ostentation, is thus a psychologically understandable concept. The Talmud warns individuals to be wary of the evil eye. It warns individuals not to evoke the evil eye, and, at the same time it cautions against employing the evil eye, for its effects drive a person out of the world. An evil eye is unhealthy, both for the one who elicits it and for the one who uses it.

Admittedly, there is more to *ayin hara* than the dynamics explained here. Some of it goes beyond this rationale, but at least the fundamental basis for the evil eye can be understood in intelligible, rational terms.

Misconception: Knocking on wood is an innocuous habit.

Knocking on wood is a cultural habit, or at least it seems so. People do this in the course of conversation, when they refer to something that has gone well. "Knock on wood, my business is growing"; or "knock on wood, my children are doing nicely in school"; or "knock on wood, my car drives without any problem"; and so forth. The phrase expresses the hope that things will continue to go well.

However, "knocking on wood" is untenable as a Jewish expression. The notion of touching wood is related to the wooden cross, and the idea that the cross brings good luck. It is Christian in origin, not Jewish, and is an act to be avoided.

There are some, especially among Yiddish-speaking people, who will use the expression "poo poo" as their way of hoping that everything will continue to be okay, although this is not a direct equivalent.

Jews are best off using the phrase *bli ayin hara* (without an evil eye), expressing the hope that no one will cast an evil eye on that which has gone well.

Misconception: Thirteen is an unlucky number.

The number 13 is quite significant in many ways. The attributes of God, the manifestations of God expressed in the human context, number 13. The basic principles through which the *Torah* is extrapolated also number 13.

A boy, having reached 13 years of age becomes an adult obligated in the commandments. A girl becomes so obligated upon entry into the thirteenth year.

There is nothing unlucky about the number 13. Not listing it on an elevator or avoiding it in other ways is an absurdity.

Judaism does not subscribe the notion of unlucky numbers. There are significant numbers, but luck and numbers do not mix.

Misconception: Judaism is essentially anti-art.

There are those who point to one of the Ten Commandments' prohibition of the making of images of human beings or animals, as evidence of Judaism's anti-art posture.

However, the embellishment of religious artifacts is one area open to Jewish artists. No effort was spared to make the Temple in Jerusalem (or subsequently other houses of worship) as inspiring and beautiful as possible. God is glorified in the beauty with which religious artifacts are invested.

Cecil Roth points out that the major reason for the lack of Jewish involvement in art throughout early history was that most art was directly involved with the glorification of the church. Understandably, Jews would not have been involved in this type of activity.

In later generations a unique form of Jewish art developed, which focused not on human or animal figures but on shapes, forms, and other abstractions.

Continuing a longstanding tradition going back many generations, artwork for the Passover *Haggadah* or the marriage *ketubah,* among other Jewish objects, has produced exciting and innovative work.

Judaism is only against art that is anti-Jewish, inconsistent with Jewish values and affirmations. However, art that fits within the context of Jewish law and enhances our appreciation of life is eagerly welcomed.

Misconception: It is appropriate to fully decorate the Jewish home.

The Jewish home is the most vital of all institutions in Jewish life. It is the place where children are educated, where traditional values are transmitted. The home is the place where Judaism is not only taught, it is the place where Judaism is lived. Therefore, it makes sense that the place where Judaism is lived to the fullest should be appropriately decorated to reflect the importance of the home and its centrality.

However, when speaking about the beauty of the home, one refers to a value-inspired beauty, not to ostentation. Often, what is value-inspired is consistent with what is asthetically beautiful. But this is not always the case.

For example, ever since the destruction of the Temple, the Jewish people have continually reminded themselves of this missing link to their historical past. There are many manifestations of this, including the observance of the Fast of *Tish'ah B'Av*, as well as other fast days that are reminders of destruction and exile. Within the home, there should also be a continual reminder, an area one cubit by one cubit (one- and a-half square feet) left undecorated, as a sign of our incompleteness because of the destruction of the Temple.

The beauty of the home reflects its importance. Likewise, the stark contrast of the bare part of the home signifies the missing link, the beauty that was.

Misconception: The *magen David* is a religious symbol.

The *magen David*, literally the shield of David, is a hexagram, a six-pointed star comprised of two triangles placed upon each other in opposite directions.

Its origins are not really Jewish, and this Star of David did not become a popular symbol until the nineteenth century. Some earlier kabbalists had given the shield a messianic symbolism.

The star was adopted as a sign to symbolize Judaism, in contradistinction to the cross that identified Christianity.

The Zionists adopted this sign, and its meaning was intensified when the Nazis made the star a badge of Jewish shame. Today, we have turned it into a symbol of pride as the flag of the State of Israel.

But the star is not a religious symbol. It evokes memories, but is itself not holy, only very significant.

Misconception: A doormat with the word *shalom* (peace) on it is a suitable furnishing for a Jewish home.

The word *shalom* means many things. It means hello, it means goodbye, it means peace, completeness, harmony. It is a word with many implications.

Since the home should be a place of peace, and it is a place where people are welcomed and greeted, a *shalom* doormat would seem to be most appropriate.

However, there is a problem, and not a small problem at that. *Shalom* is such a powerful word, with so many connotations, and with so many pleasant implications, that it is associated with God. Peace is not merely the absence of belligerence; it is more a harmony that is rooted in an appreciation of the God-like qualities of all individuals.

Furthermore, *shalom* is one of the names of God. In other words, *shalom* is one of the many appellations by which God is identified. This means that *shalom* on the doormat is really the name of God on the doormat. People who enter the home are stepping on God's name. It therefore becomes quite obvious that *shalom* so used is inappropriate. The idea behind it might be sound, but in practical terms it does not belong on a doormat.

A much more appropriate phrase on a doormat would be *brukhim haba'im* (blessed are those who have come), or simply "welcome." These project the idea of *shalom* without spelling out the word.

Misconception: Exciting, thrilling experiences are welcome additions to one's life.

The experience of nature is an important conduit to more fully appreciating God's majesty. However, there are different ways of experiencing nature, some of them involving hazard and others being quite safe.

Thus, watching a sunset or the flow of the Niagara Falls, or beholding the Grand Canyon or the Swiss Alps are truly inspirational experiences. They are so important that one should go out of the way to experience them.

However, there are other experiences of nature that though overwhelming in their impact are hazardous. Mountain climbing or rafting down a particularly dangerous river, though it may imbue the individual with a sense of the holy, may also cause injury or death. Nature is wondrous, but life is sacred. One should thus do as much as possible to experience the glory of nature, at the same time assuring, within the limits of human capacity, that the experience of nature is not dangerous and life-threatening.

Misconception: Shaving with a razor blade is permissible.

In past generations, one of the distinguishing features of the Jew was his beard. A priest was referred to as a *galah*, literally meaning "shaven one." The fact that one was clean-shaven was considered a distinguishing characteristic by which he could be recognized as a non-Jew.

In the days prior to the electric shaver, when the major option available was a razor, Jews could not shave in a permitted way, since putting a knife to the face was biblically proscribed. Today, with the invention of electric shavers, there is an option available for shaving in a permissible manner. The shaver uses a scissor-type action to cut the facial hair and usually does not cut below the surface.

10

Thought for Food

Misconception: One is permitted to eat anything that is kosher.

There is an adage that says, "If you cannot pronounce it, do not eat it."

In contemporary times, shelf-life has become an important issue for mass producers of food. To extend shelf-life, certain ingredients that may be harmful are added to the food. The exact extent of the potential damage is often unclear, but it is clear that people would be better off without these preservatives. The food is preserved by the chemicals, but the person is not.

One does not know what the cumulative effect of the chemicals may be, but it is wrong to assume that simply because an item is free from any ritually forbidden ingredients, it therefore may be eaten.

Someone with high blood pressure, who has been told by the doctor to avoid foods high in sodium, is, in fact, forbidden to eat such foods. That is a dereliction of the responsibility to preserve oneself.

If the weight of evidence concerning a specific food suggests that it is unfit or ill-advised for human consumption, then it is highly questionable whether one is allowed to eat such food.

Misconception: There is nothing wrong with being obese.

We are taught to be very careful of others' feelings, taking care not to say anything insulting to them. One of the more sensitive issues with regard to others is their appearance. Telling someone who is already self-conscious that she looks overweight, or even pleasantly plump, can be very hurtful.

Therefore, any judgment one would make about the condition of obesity must not be construed as a condemnation of the obese person; it is merely a judgment about the condition itself.

There are individuals who are obese because of metabolism problems. Often these individuals do not eat more than the normal, but the body translates their intake in a distorted fashion. This is as much an illness as any other, and it should be appreciated as such. One always has sympathy for others who are afflicted with any malady, and this should be no different.

However, there are situations of obesity that come from lack of self-control. There are people who are obviously overweight because they overeat, and they do not overeat just a little. Again, one does know the circumstances that give rise to overeating—anxiety, problems in the home, problems with employment, or perhaps a food addiction. It is not anyone's role to be judgmental and condemnatory about this.

What is clear is that the general condition of obesity, because of its harmful effects on the individual's health, is to be avoided. The individual who embarks on a life-style consistent with the basic principles of Judaism should incorporate the obligation for health maintenance as one of the primary obligations for "The dead cannot praise God."

In other words, all that we do should enhance life. This affects the attitude toward smoking, drinking, and of course, toward undereating or overeating. A balanced diet, with proper nutrition, should be the desired norm. We should all do our level best to conform to that norm.

The issue of concern for health goes beyond eating. Overworking, excessive stress, and other avoidable hazards are likewise to be shunned.

Misconception: Judaism has nothing to say about one's eating habits.

Eating habits have potentially significant implications for individual health. Since maintenance of one's health is of paramount importance in the Jewish way of thinking, it makes sense that Judaism should have much to say about eating habits.

Eating in a relaxed atmosphere, eating the proper balance of foods that are conducive to good health, and eating in moderation are considerations arising from the Judaic ethic of eating.

Misconception: A food item is either kosher for everyone or not kosher for everyone.

This presumes that the rules of *kashrut* are absolute, black and white. Either an item is kosher, or it is not kosher.

Before rushing to judgment, it is worth contemplating whether this is the case. What makes a food kosher, fit to be eaten? A food, especially meat, is permissible if, coming from the permitted species, it is properly prepared through the cutting action of the *shohet* (ritual slaughterer), the loose blood is allowed to run off, the forbidden fats are excised, and the meat is properly salted or roasted.

Another important category in determining if the meat is permissible centers around whether it came from an animal that is blemish-free. What type of blemish renders an animal suspect? Essentially, any wound or deficiency that would make it impossible for the animal to live under normal conditions for more than a period of 12 months. Thus, an animal with a hole in the heart, or a broken leg, or other such infirmities, is not kosher, because under such circumstances it could not live for 12 months.

One does not know with surety that an animal is blemish-free. Checking every animal thoroughly from top to bottom introduces a variable to the meat-preparation process that would greatly complicate matters. Instead, if there is no reason to be suspicious, we rely on the assumption that everything is okay.

The only exception is the area of greatest vulnerability, namely, the lungs. The lungs are inspected to make sure there are no adhesions; adhesions being quite usual, many are of the type that render the animal unfit to be eaten. Thus, the animal's being kosher is an assumed state, rather than an assured one.

There are also questions (relating to the permissibility of the meat) that are subject to debate among the religious authorities. In such instances, a rabbi may be called upon to make a definitive judgment on the matter.

When there is a doubt, the rabbi may give different verdicts to different people. A rich person coming with a question may be told to refrain from eating the questionable item, since a rich person could readily afford to purchase different meat. On the other hand, a poor person, if deprived of that meat, would thereby be deprived of any sustenance, not having the means to purchase anything more. Thus, a poor person may be told that it is permitted. This is all because there are issues in *kashrut* that are not always black and white; they are grey, and may become white for the poor and black for the rich.

Courageous rabbis explicitly stated that they would rather answer to God for having stated that something not kosher is kosher, than to answer for having deprived the poor person of desperately needed sustenance.

This, by the way, is eminently kosher reasoning.

Misconception: Dill pickles, smoked meat, chicken soup, knishes, and bagels and lox are "Jewish food."

There is hardly anything Jewish about smoked meat, dill pickles, knishes, and bagels and lox. Even *gefilte* fish is not Jewish food.

What is Jewish food? Jewish food is food that is mandated as fundamental to Jewish commitment. Thus, the obligation to eat *matzah* on Passover, could categorize *matzah* as a Jewish food.

Another candidate for qualifying as Jewish food is *cholent*. This is a mixture of meat, potatoes, beans, and what not, that is placed on a slow burning fire prior to the *Shabbat*. It is cooked enough before *Shabbat* so that it is edible when *Shabbat* begins, but remains on the stove for the *Shabbat* lunch meal.

What is Jewish about this? It is a Jewish way of addressing the prohibition of cooking on *Shabbat*, and at the same time, having a hot *Shabbat* lunch.

The word *cholent*, referring to the *Shabbat*-day food, has some interesting linguistic implications. Some suggest that it comes from the word *shelan*, meaning that it has rested overnight, referring to the fact that this food was cooked over the Friday-night period.

Others suggest that it may be associated with the idea that this is the meal that is eaten at the conclusion of prayer services on *Shabbat* morning, when "*shul* ends" (*cholent*).

Spicy food, whether dill pickles, or smoked meat, may have some ingredients that link it culturally with Judaism. For a people who had been denied the delights of life, who lived in an exile that was devoid of any spice, it was natural that they should try to spice up their life in the only manner that was available to them, namely by spicing the food.

Misconception: Vegetarianism is consistent with Jewish tradition.

Over the course of the centuries, there have been prominent Jewish religious leaders who refrained from eating meat. If one refrains from eating meat because it does not agree with the individual, or because one genuinely dislikes meat, or because one is not sure about its *kashrut*, such "vegetarianism" is understandable and not antithetical to Jewish tradition.

When the objection to eating meat is based on the argument that the process of preparing the meat is cruel to animals, this is a different matter. Making such value judgments is a form of being "holier than thou." In this instance, "thou" is none other than God. Since permission has been granted to eat meat, and since eating of meat is linked to the joy of the festivals, the vegetarian then becomes one who actually questions God. The individual says that he or she knows better about the animal species and can make better value judgments about them than God, Who has specifically permitted and even ordained occasions when meat must be eaten.

Vegetarianism rooted in this approach is inconsistent with Jewish tradition.

Misconception: Fruit and vegetables are always kosher.

In ancient Israel, there were certain obligations that had to be carried out before one was able to eat fruit. There were portions that had to be separated out for the Priest, the Levite, and the poor, a practice that prevailed when the Temple was the spiritual focal point.

Today, this is done in token fashion, since the Priest–Levite institution that existed in Temple times no longer exists. But if it is not done, the fruit is not yet kosher, not yet fit to be eaten.

Additionally, no fruit of a tree may be eaten in the first three years after planting. In the fourth year, fruit may be eaten after the redemption procedure.

Recently a concern has arisen regarding certain vegetables, particularly lettuce, which may have almost invisible worms on its surface. These worms are ritually forbidden and since they are on the lettuce, they render the lettuce problematic. Thorough cleansing is an absolute requirement before such lettuce is consumed.

In any event, it should not be assumed that fruits and vegetables are automatically kosher. There may be nothing intrinsically wrong with fruit or vegetables, as is the case with meat, but other issues may create problems.

The tithing may not have been separated out, or other items such as worms may have attached themselves. If these concerns have not been appropriately addressed, the fruit or vegetables are not fit to be eaten.

Misconception: Meat may be eaten without any restrictions.

The context of this statement deals with meat that is kosher (fit, acceptable), in which there are no impediments to the meat's edibility.

This is the opposite of the vegetarian argument, the other extreme. Jewish law concerning meat projects an interesting balance. Meat is permitted, but it certainly should not be part of the daily diet. One of the ways in which the joy of the festivals— *Pesah, Shavuot,* and *Sukkot*—is manifested is in the eating of meat. If meat were part of the daily diet, and one would eat meat every day, it is difficult to understand why there would be any special joy attached to its being eaten on the festivals. Obviously, the joyfulness of meat on the festivals inheres in meat being something special, which is eaten only on rare occasions.

The Bible states quite clearly that meat may be eaten only when one has an appetite for it. While permission for preparing an animal to be eaten is part of the legal structure, abuse of animals is also prohibited. We may eat meat, but we should not eat too much of it. It should retain its sense of being special, for only when there is a specific appetite for it, or a purpose, is there enough justification for the use of animals as food.

Use is permitted, abuse is not.

Misconception: The process of salting draws all the blood out of the meat.

By biblical law, blood is a forbidden substance. However, it may be argued that blood is such an intrinsic part of meat that one can hardly avoid actually digesting some of it when one eats meat.

If the *Torah* forbids blood but permits meat, then our understanding of the salting process needs some modification. Obviously, a small amount of salt sprinkled over the surface of a large piece of meat can hardly be expected to take out all the blood.

Salting removes blood that is in the meat and muscles, and could loosen during cooking, what may be called capillary blood. It is the blood that may separate from its source that is the problem, a problem that is solved by salting.

Loose blood is prohibited; blood that is firmly imbedded in the meat fibers is part of the meat, and therefore is permitted.

Misconception: Pork is prohibited because it is not kosher.

The term kosher literally means fit or proper. Applied to food, it means that the food is fit to be eaten, that it is proper according to Jewish law to eat that food.

Kosher or not kosher applies to those animals that are permitted to be eaten if properly prepared. For example, a cow or sheep must be approached by an expert (*shohet*) in the ritual preparation of the animal. The *shohet* applies a sharp-edged, nick-free knife to the animal's neck with a quick to-and-fro motion, severing the carotid arteries and jugular veins in the process of separating but not detaching the head from the rest of the body.

This quick action, if done properly, without any unnecessary delays or physical abuse of the animal, is the first step in making the animal kosher. The blood is then allowed to flow from the animal, after which the animal is soaked and salted, or roasted, depending on the situation and desire. The animal meat has then been prepared properly, and it is kosher (fit), to be eaten.

If the expert in this preparation would apply the same procedure to a horse, a tiger, a lion, or a swine, it would be meaningless, because no matter how such an animal is prepared, it still cannot be eaten. These animals cannot become kosher, because they are in the category of *tamay*, or ritually unfit.

Thus, pork is not unkosher, simply because it can never reach the stage to which the categories of kosher or not kosher apply. Pork is *tamay*.

Misconception: Pork is forbidden because it is unhealthy to eat it.

It is wrong to suggest that there is absolutely no health component in the biblically legislated regulations concerning which foods are permitted and which are prohibited. Whether the food has a physiological or spiritual impact on the individual is a matter of debate, but there is an impact.

However, it is a mistake in logic to jump from acknowledging that there is a physical or spiritual health component to the kosher code, to asserting that it is *only* a health legislation. The next step would be to say that since it is merely a health legislation, we are now able to counter the health problem associated with a specific food, so that such food should be permitted.

The original assumption is wrong, and the subsequent conclusion is equally erroneous. It is convenient to be able to grasp onto a rational hook for a commandment, but it is dangerous to assume that the hook is the only link. One may grasp a relevant component, but this does not necessarily mean that one has grasped the whole. The whole is probably beyond grasp.

Pork may be unhealthy, but it was prohibited and remains prohibited even if it can be shown to be beneficial to health.

Misconception: It is correct to believe that Jews have a natural aversion to pork.

The idea of a Jewish stomach that rejects alien items such as pork is questionable.

If one would reduce Judaism to a mere cultural expression, then one could see dietary preferences as part of this culture. It is one of the rules of the club that people must keep.

However, the pork prohibition is not reducible to cultural expression. It is a transcending legislation with more than mere culinary implications.

In the words of the sages, one should not say that one abhors pork, or that it is impossible for one to digest it. Rather, one should say that one could easily eat it, but that God has dictated that it not be eaten. The higher level of commitment is one that is based on an understanding of the ideological base, the theological underpinnings of the legislation, rather than reducing the theology to a personal aversion.

Misconception: Of all the forbidden foods one can eat, pork is the worst.

The biblical legislation concerning foods that are permissible and foods that are prohibited does not make value judgments as to which is better and which is worse. They are all equally prohibited. Tiger meat is as bad as horse meat, which in turn is as bad as porkchops. What then, explains the special aversion that seems to have developed concerning pork?

The species that are eligible for eating are those that have two signs: (1) the animal rechews its food, and (2) the animal has cloven hooves. Usually an animal is of the either-or type. Either it has both of these signs, or it has neither of the signs.

There are a number of exceptions. Some animals chew their food, but do not have cloven hooves. The pig is unique among the species in that it has cloven hooves, but it does not rechew its food. It is this singular feature of the pig that is probably related to its being so abhorred.

From the outside the swine looks kosher. However, from the inside, it is not. The pig has thus come to symbolize hypocrisy or projecting a false image of purity.

Misconception: Kosher milk is an appropriate term to describe *"cholov Yisroel"* (milk prepared in the presence of a Jew).

In previous generations, there was a fear that milk would be mixed with forbidden fatty substances, and therefore prohibited to drink. Because of this, a Jew would watch the milking process, and thus assure that the milk was pure, with no questionable ingredients. This was known as *"cholov Yisroel,"* milk that was prepared in the presence of a Jew.

Today, the preparation of milk is under government regulation in most countries, and one can assume that all milk is pure and kosher and fit for drinking.

However, there are those who, in spite of this, still insist on maintaining the practice of having a Jew present during the milking process. Some people have fallen into the habit of referring to *cholov Yisroel* milk as "kosher milk." This is a faulty terminology, most importantly because it gives the impression that any other milk is not kosher. This type of implication is itself not kosher.

Misconception: Mother's milk is dairy.

Milk from cows is considered dairy, but mother's milk is actually neutral, or *pareve* (neither meat nor dairy). A mother who has fed a young child some meat need not wait before nursing that child. There is absolutely no consideration that this is a mixture of meat and milk, and there would be no reason to make such separation even as a matter of education for the child. Meat must be separated from cow's milk; meat and mother's milk go together.

Likewise, an adult who for whatever reason drinks mother's milk need not wait the usual time interval before eating meat.

Misconception: Chicken is meat.

The general practice is to refrain from having chicken with any dairy products. It is considered as meat and is not mixed together with cheese or milk.

However, chicken is a species of its own. It is not dairy, but it is also not comparable to the animal species. It is in the category of fowl. It is unclear whether fowl should attain the status of meat. This is a contentious issue in the Talmud; one opinion suggests that chicken is neutral (*pareve*) and may be eaten together with milk.

The final decision of the Talmud is that chicken should be considered as meat, primarily because it looks like meat. Were people to have chicken together with milk, the unsuspecting onlookers would deduce that meat and milk together is permissible.

The knowledge that chicken is technically not meat, but is only considered like meat, is useful in serious situations when one such as a nursing mother must have sufficient protein, plus milk. For such individuals, one may contemplate, through adjudication by a proper rabbinic authority, having a chicken meal, and then not waiting the usual period of six hours (or thereabouts) before drinking milk.

Misconception: Milk–meat separation is part of the kosher code.

The word kosher means fit, and with regard to eating, that which is kosher is fit to be eaten, and that which is forbidden or not kosher, is unfit to be eaten. It would seem as if the forbidden meat–milk mixture would belong to the kosher code.

To a certain extent this is correct. However, in explicating the kosher code in the *Torah*, the meat–milk separation is not included. Instead, we have a listing of the various species that are permitted and from which one may partake after having appropriately prepared them. This legislation is related primarily to the diet.

On the other hand, the rules that govern the mixture of meat and milk belong in the context of other biblical legislation concerning species differentiation. For example, there is a law that one may not wear a mixture of wool and linen, wool being the growth of sheep, linen being vegetative material. Meat and milk likewise represent the animal side (the meat) and the vegetative side (the milk), since the cow's grazings are the primary food that produces the milk.

The maintenance of a separation between the vegetable and the animal sides, both in eating and in clothing, transmits a message that we must appreciate the uniqueness of creation and must also maintain behavioral control through the separation of the animal and vegetable domains. There is no reason to jump to the conclusion that anything of animal origin must be separated from anything of vegetable origin; one manifestation suffices.

Of course, there are other examples of species differentiation, such as the legislation prohibiting the planting of wheat and grapes together.

Meat and milk, once together, may not be eaten, but each on its own is permitted. It is a case of two permitted things coming together—and their very coming together causes the entire mixture to become prohibited. Although one may technically consider this to be part of the dietary restrictions, it is legislation of a different genre.

Misconception: Jewish people wait six hours between meat and dairy meals.

It should first be noted that the six-hour interval begins after every meat meal, but not necessarily after a dairy meal. In other words, after taking a drink of milk, or after eating ice cream or soft cheese, one need not wait six hours before having meat. A half hour wait, or even a rinse of the mouth, is all that is necessary. Unless one has had hard cheese, which is not that readily available in today's market, there is no residual impact from the dairy meal, and one may indulge in a meat meal within a reasonable time after the dairy meal.

It is after the meat meal that the waiting period is at issue. Insofar as the basic biblical rule is concerned, the meat–milk prohibition involves a direct mixture of the two types of food. It is rabbinic legislation that extends this, by mandating a significant time separation between meat and dairy products. The separation time varies according to local custom. Many wait six hours, but Jews of German origin wait only three hours, and Dutch Jews, only one hour. Those who would contemplate changing their custom must realize that this is a matter of tradition transmitted from generation to generation. One may move to another country, but one does not thereby renounce one's ancestral tradition.

Upon marriage, the custom of the husband usually prevails, but if the husband comes from a "three-hour" tradition, and the wife from a "six-hour" tradition, they could mutually decide to go for the six-hour tradition.

Misconception: Glass dishes may be used interchangeably for dairy and meat meals.

There is a public perception among many that glass, because of its inherent nature, can never become non-kosher. It is assumed that glass never absorbs, and because of this, it may be used interchangeably for meat and dairy meals.

There is some difference of opinion concerning the glass issue, but generally, this perception is based on isolated circumstances.

A glass that is used for juice, and that one uses at a breakfast dairy meal, may be used later in the evening, if one desires to drink juice for a meat meal.

However, if one places a hot cheese omelette on a glass dish, one may not later place a hot beef steak on the same glass plate.

The glass has become a dairy dish by virtue of the fact that hot food has been placed on it; and it is from then on a dairy dish, and may not be used for a meat meal.

The instances when glass is interchangeable are situations where the glass did not absorb anything, neither dairy nor meat. It is true that glass does not absorb as easily as other substances. Therefore, it is only through intense heat that it will become either a meat or a dairy dish. However, once it has become either meat or dairy, its absorptive powers work in a negative way, in that it is almost impossible to change the glass back to a neutral status.

The same logic would apply for a glass dish that has been used to serve hot cereal. Such a glass dish cannot be used on Passover.

Sephardic practice, by the way, is to use glass interchangeably. But this does not mean that Ashkenazim may do the same.

Misconception: Eating non-kosher meat is wrong. Having it with cheese is a compound felony.

The rule stating that one must separate the eating of dairy products from the eating of meat products refers to meat that is kosher (fit to be eaten), and dairy products that are kosher. These two types of food, permissible when eaten separately after an appropriate time interval, are forbidden when they are joined together in a mixture. Thus, eating non-kosher meat together with kosher dairy products is wrong only because the meat is not kosher, but not because it is a mixture of meat and milk.

Obviously, this is not to be construed as permission to so indulge. The awareness of the legal parameters can serve a useful purpose in the event of emergencies or circumstances in which the mitigating of prohibitions is at issue.

Misconception: All brand-new utensils are kosher and permitted for immediate use.

Certain utensils, including forks, knives, and spoons made of metal, and other types of dishes, must go through an immersion process before being used for eating. They are dipped in a *mikvah*, a specially constructed vessel of water for the *kashering* of dishes. This is not to imply that the dishes are not kosher beforehand. This procedure is to sanctify the utensils, which will be used for the sacred purpose of feeding the body, so that the human being can actualize responsibility energetically.

Misconception: The practice of washing one's hands before eating bread at the beginning of a meal is to clean the hands.

The obligation to wash one's hands prior to a meal applies even to individuals whose hands are immaculately clean. The purpose of the washing is not related to the cleanliness of the hands; it is related to the purity of purpose.

The washing of the hands is an act of sanctification, of realizing that the eating of a meal is a sacred exercise of appreciating God's bounty, and through partaking of God's bounty, having the energy to serve God and to energetically fulfill one's commitments. The eating of the meal is thus a sacred exercise.

The hands are washed to remind the individual who is about to eat that eating is not an exercise in gluttony; instead, it is a holy expression.

Misconception: Having recited the blessing for bread at the start of a meal, one need not recite a blessing for any food eaten in that meal.

The general rule is that once one has washed the hands and recited the blessing for bread (*hamotzi lehem min ha'aretz*) to start the meal, then everything that is normally part of the meal is subordinate to the bread. This means that fish, meat, vegetables, and other components are all covered by the blessing on bread, and no specific blessing is needed for these items.

However, there are exceptions to this rule. Wine is one notable exception. Because of its unique stature, wine requires its own blessing (*boray pri hagafen*), even when consumed in the middle of the meal.

Fruits that are eaten at the end of the meal are also not covered by the blessing over bread, and the blessing *boray pri ha'etz* should be recited for the fruit.

Misconception: There is nothing wrong with sitting on a table.

It depends on the type of table. If it is a table where one reads or writes, it may be permissible to sit on it. However, if it is a table where one usually eats, then sitting on it is not correct.

The table where one eats is the modern-day altar, the place upon which we energize ourselves for sacred service through the eating of God's bounty.

The table is thus a holy place. Because of its sanctity, sitting on a dining table is disrespectful and therefore incorrect.

Misconception: The drinking of wine or liquor to the toast of *L'hayyim* (To life!) at a *Shabbat* meal is a purely cultural expression.

There are certain foods that are potentially dangerous when mixed together. One such mixture that is potentially dangerous is the combination of fish and meat. For whatever reason, this is considered to be harmful to the individual.

The typical *Shabbat* meal includes *gefilte* fish or another type of fish as an appetizer. The fish is followed by a serving of meat.

There is nothing sacrosanct about *gefilte* fish. It is not a must for the *Shabbat* meal; meat is a more basic staple for the *Shabbat* table.

Nevertheless, since this is the usual pattern, there is a problem with eating fish and meat at the same meal. How do we avoid the potentially harmful mixture of fish and meat? One separates the two dishes, not only with chicken soup, but also with a drink of wine or something stronger. The wine acts as a buffer in which the fish "swims."

The exclamatory greeting, *L'hayyim*, literally translates as "to life." Appropriately, since meat and fish do not form a life-enhancing mixture, the wine is intended to dull the impact of the combination. We say "to life," meaning that the meat that follows the fish should not cause any harmful effects on the individuals who are enjoying the meal.

L'hayyim at the *Shabbat* meal is therefore more than just a cultural expression. It is a uniquely Jewish way of addressing a potentially hazardous scenario.

Of course, we say *L'hayyim* on many other occasions, to convey our best wishes in good cheer.

338

Misconception: There is no *mitzvah* to drink wine.

There are certain days in the Jewish religious calendar when one is obliged to celebrate, to rejoice. These are the festivals, most specifically *Pesah, Shavuot, Sukkot,* and *Shmini Atzeret.*

Rejoicing is primarily a mental state, but there are physical inducements that help in attaining a state of joy. One item that is commonly identified with the joy of the festival is the eating of meat. Meat was not a regular item on the menu, and having it on special occasions brought with it special joy.

A second ingredient to engender joy was the drinking of wine. Drinking of wine is a specific fulfillment associated with the obligation to rejoice on *Yom Tov.* Also, wine is the drink over which the *Shabbat* and *Yom Tov Kiddush* is recited. The day is "remembered" over wine.

Yes, it is a *mitzvah* to drink wine. However, it should be noted that in the Jewish scheme of things, the days on which it is a *mitzvah* to drink wine are the same days on which it is forbidden to drive.

Misconception: Only if one eats bread must the full *Birkhat haMazon* be recited.

This is the general assumption based on the reality that one rarely hears the full *Birkhat haMazon* recited for a meal without bread. Many who do not wish to recite the entire Grace carefully avoid eating any bread and thus need not worry about being obligated to recite the full text of *Birkhat haMazon*.

But this is not always the case. If one makes a complete meal of cake made from the basic grains, there is an obligation to recite the entire Grace.

If one eats a piece of pizza, and then decides to have more pizza, making an entire meal of it, the concluding blessing should be the entire Grace after Meals. If one knows in advance that the pizza will be an entire meal, one should wash and recite *Hamotzi* (blessing over bread) for it.

One can have cake and eat it too, but if enough of it is eaten, then it is like eating bread.

Misconception: Concerning eating, the human being takes priority over animals.

In Jewish law, it is prohibited for an individual to eat before having fed the animals. This must be understood in proper perspective.

If it is a matter of saving life, and the choice is between saving the life of an animal or that of a human being, the human being takes priority.

However, in ordinary circumstances, the human being must defer to the animal, who does not have the same willpower and control, and upon whom the effect of hunger is much more serious. Sensitivity for the animal kingdom includes the special care that must be given to the animals in one's charge. The human being can wait. The animal cannot.

There are those who suggest that this priority applies only to eating but not to drinking. The immediate effects of potential dehydration on the human being are quite serious and possibly even life-threatening, so that the human being has priority over animals when the issue under consideration is drinking.

Misconception: Hunting is not forbidden.

According to biblical law human beings are permitted to eat meat, but this does not imply permission to make sport of animals.

The biblically permitted species are those animals that are domesticated rather than wild. These need not be hunted, as they are readily available. The wild animals that are hunted are not of the species that are eligible to be kosher.

Hunting, therefore, refers to the catching of animals that the human being cannot ordinarily approach. Even if one were to hunt an animal that is of the permitted type, shooting it and killing it means that the animal has died in a manner other than by prescribed ritual preparation. Because of this, the animal would be unfit as kosher food.

Hunting as a mere tension release, or for sport, *is* forbidden.

Fishing does not fit into this limitation. Fish do not require ritual preparation, and by merely bringing the fish out of their natural habitat, one can then prepare them for eating. One who fishes engages in a legitimate activity, since it is only through fishing that one can ever catch fish. Ironically, the prohibition against hunting would only apply to Jews. Non-Jews are not required to eat meat that has been ritually prepared and can even eat of animals that have been shot, nor have they any restrictions on which species of animal they may eat. For them, any species is fit for human consumption.

Hunting can then be a legitimate quest for food and is not automatically forbidden to the non-Jew.

Misconception: Since they are not eaten, suits need not be kosher.

This is based on the presumption that the term kosher applies only to food items. In essence, kosher means fit or proper. It can be applied to any situation in which there are standards that must be met. For example, there is such a thing as a kosher *mezuzah*, a kosher *Torah*, a kosher pair of *tefillin*. There is a kosher *etrog* (citron) and a kosher *shofar* (ram's horn). The word kosher, in all these instances, refers to the fact that these items have satisfied the legal requirements and are therefore usable to fulfill a specific *mitzvah*.

With regard to suits, the major issue of contention is whether the suit contains a mixture of wool and linen. According to the *Torah*, such a mixture may not be worn. This is one of the many biblical regulations related to the appreciation of nature and respect for God's creation. Mixing certain diverse species, such as planting wheat with grape seed, or interweaving wool (animal origin) and linen (vegetable origin), are prohibited. Thus, suits or other clothing, whether for men or women, should satisfy the requirements for being kosher. They should not contain any mixture of wool and linen.

Part VI

Past and Present

11

History from
the Beginning

The Bible
Exile
Yearning for Return

Misconception: Eve was created out of Adam's rib.

The biblical story of the creation of Eve describes how Adam was put into a deep sleep, and God then created Eve out of Adam's *tselaw*, which has been translated in most standard texts as "rib." Based on this translation, it is a common misperception that Eve was created out of Adam's rib.

As a result of this misperception, it is assumed that the Bible takes a negative attitude toward women. After all, if the woman is only a rib of a man, and a spare rib at that, the woman is relegated to insignificance.

All this is based on a faulty translation. The word *tselaw* may on occasion mean a "rib," but can also refer to a "side." The Talmud relates that the original human being was created with two forms, a male form and a female form, a male side and a female side.

The surgery performed on that fateful occasion was not the extracting of a spare rib to be fashioned into a woman. The surgery was more akin to separating Siamese twins, separating the female part from the male part, creating two separate entities from the original one.

Man and woman are each half of the totality, equal halves who together make a complete entity.

Eve and all women since Eve are man's equals.

Misconception: The forbidden fruit that Adam ate was an apple.

In rabbinic tradition, there are many suggestions about the exact nature of forbidden fruit eaten by Adam and Eve.

They range from grapes (drunkenness) to wheat. However, in all the speculation, an apple is not one of the possibilities suggested. In other words, one can actually assert with full confidence that the forbidden fruit that Adam ate was something other than an apple.

Misconception: After Adam ate the forbidden fruit, he became wiser.

This would seem to be the conclusion one reaches on reading the biblical account. Adam was told to resist eating the fruit from which he would be able to know about good and evil. Adam ate the fruit and thus became aware of good and evil.

The implication is that prior to this, Adam did not know the difference between good and evil. Therefore, it would seem that by contravening a regulation, Adam gained an advantage.

This seeming incongruity is the subject of a lengthy discussion in Maimonides' classic, *The Guide of the Perplexed.* Maimonides suggests that by eating the fruit, Adam actually lost rather than gained. Previously, Adam had a clear awareness of the distinction between right and wrong. After eating the fruit, he was aware only of the distinction between good and evil.

Beforehand, all truth was objective and tangible reality, but through the rationalization process leading to the eating of that which should not have been eaten, truth and falsehood were brought down to subjective judgment. Adam no longer lived in the pure, objective world of true and false; he now lived in the subjective world of good and bad. He would do things, not because they were true and right, but because they were good. This reduction to utilitarian subjectivity was a significant comedown from the high perch that Adam had previously occupied.

Misconception: Adam and Eve were cursed after eating the forbidden fruit.

At first glance, this would seem to be the case. However, a more careful reading of Scripture reveals that this is not actually so.

Adam was told that he would now earn his bread by the sweat of his brow and that the earth would be cursed. But Scripture adds that the earth would be cursed "on his behalf" for his own sake. Eve was told that she would give birth in pain, in renunciation.

The pain of childbirth and the necessity to work hard in order to eat are not curses. They were a change of reality, which came about through God's acknowledging that living in Paradise, where everything was set and there was little to do, was not advantageous for Adam and Eve.

A human being who lives on welfare feels disconnected from the world. There is no sense that one has achieved, that one is able to persevere and succeed through one's own efforts. Adam and Eve had it too easy in the Garden. The post-Garden experience was designed to assure that they would not live in the same vacuum they had in the Garden. They were told that their achievements would be the result of their own toil and pain. But with this pain would also come fulfillment—fulfillment gained from the knowledge that it was their own efforts that helped make these realities possible.

Misconception: Abraham was the first Jew.

It is difficult to ascertain precisely who was the first Jew. However, it is clear that Abraham was not the first Jew; he was not even Jewish.

This may seem surprising, because it seemingly contradicts one of the more hallowed teachings that are impressed upon Jewish children from their earliest years.

That we trace our ancestral tradition back to *Avraham Avinu* (Abraham our patriarch) and his wife Sarah, our matriarch, is not in question. This remains a fundamental pillar of history, reinforced every day in the prayers referring to God as the God of Abraham, Isaac, and Jacob.

However, Abraham is never referred to in Scripture as a Jew. Throughout the entire Five Books of Moses, the entire *Torah*, the word Jew in its Hebrew form, *Yehudi*, is not to be found.

The people at that time were known as the children of Israel, Israel being the name given to the third of the patriarchs, Jacob. Israel's children bore the names of what later came to be known as the tribes of Israel. All children born to the tribes became known as the descendants of Israel, as the children of Israel (*Bnai Yisrael*), or as Israelites.

Abraham, who lived prior to the birth of Jacob, was not even an Israelite in that sense. He is referred to in the Bible as *Ivri*, commonly translated as Hebrew.

Abraham was alone. He was the first individual to espouse belief in one God, the Creator of the world and God of all humankind. He radically rejected the reigning theology of the day, which was paganistic idolatry. In his belief and in his rejection of the norm, he was alone, or *Ivri*. In the midrashic explanation, all the world was on one side, and Abraham was on the other side (*aiver*). Hence the terminology *Ivri* from *aiver* (side).

In reality, Abraham was a Hebrew; his great-grandchildren were Israelites, and only later on did the terminology of Jew and Judaism come into usage.

Misconception: Moses was not an Egyptian.

Moses (Moshe in Hebrew) had many names, but he is known to us by the name Moshe which was given to him by Batya, the daughter of Pharaoh.

Her name for him reflects the fact that it was through her efforts that Moshe was able to survive the cruel edict requiring that all newborn males be thrown into the river. Batya, Pharaoh's daughter, rescued Moses from certain death and raised him in the royal palace right under her father's nose.

Moses was born in Egypt and was raised there in the royal palace. It is hard to avoid the conclusion that he, in fact, was Egyptian. He was an Egyptian Israelite, or an Israelite born in Egypt and raised in Egyptian surroundings.

Born in Egypt and raised in an Egyptian environment, Moses nevertheless retained his Israelite connection, through the efforts of his family and his protector, Pharaoh's daughter.

When Freud wrote "Moses and Monotheism," he raised a furor because of his claim that Moses was an Egyptian. Freud's motivation for writing this work has been the subject of intense debate. Quite possibly, he was telling the world that had condemned psychoanalysis as a Jewish science, "See Moses was an Egyptian, and I am a German. So do not brand this a Jewish science."

Insofar as the intention may have been to compromise Moshe's Israelite identity, this was a distortion. However, insofar as the actual facts of Moshe's early years are concerned, it was not inaccurate.

Misconception: The only purpose for visiting the Ten Plagues upon the Egyptians was to force them to let the Israelites go.

It is assumed that the Ten Plagues were inflicted upon the Egyptians as a form of punishment and pressure to free the Israelites from the cruel servitude.

If that were the case, God could have inflicted one devastating plague that would have left the Egyptians no choice but to release the Israelites. Why was this seemingly unnecessary punishment meted out?

The plagues escalated in severity. The first ones were not as painful as the latter ones. The Egyptians were given a chance to release the Israelites with a minimum of pain, but they refused.

Another problem chronicled in the *Torah*, is that the Israelites were so overwhelmed by their oppressive burden that they could not contemplate freedom. Had they been given the opportunity to go, it is not clear whether they would have taken it.

With each plague, the Israelites experienced an abatement of the excruciating servitude. They had small doses of freedom, so that by the time of the final plague, they were ready and eager to leave.

Understood in this light, the plagues are not the indiscriminate use of power by God. They are lessons and experiences to effect a desired goal.

Misconception: Moshe hit the rock and therefore was denied entry to the Promised Land.

The famous story of Moshe hitting the rock at Kadesh has been subject to much interpretation. The superficial view is that Moshe hit the rock, instead of speaking to it, and thus was denied entry to the Promised Land.

It is unclear why the hitting of the rock was such a serious breach. In an earlier episode at Refidim, Moshe was, in fact, instructed to hit the rock. He may have simply recalled that experience and reflexively hit the rock.

There are commentaries that suggest that the action of Moses was not a sinful act. If not, why was he denied entry to the Promised Land?

Moses did not have an easy time leading the people. He was continually confronted with rebellion, contentiousness, and strife. But in the episode at Kadesh, the people's request for water was not an act of rebellion. They requested the water because they wanted to live and actualize God's word. Moshe, who had been battered by previous rebellious complaints, saw this in the same light. He reacted with commensurate anger. God asked that Moses only talk to the rock, to signify that God considered the people's request to be legitimate, one that should be made gently, with speech instead of attack.

The fact that Moshe reacted the way he did was ample proof that he had had enough. He could no longer see the actions of the people except in the light of the bitter past experiences. Upon entering into Israel, the people would need a fresh start, unencumbered by the judgments of the past. It was for the sake of Israel that Moshe was told that he would not lead them into the Promised Land. He was a great leader whose cycle of leadership had come to a natural end. Today, we would call this burnout.

Misconception: There is no special obligation to remember the rebellion of our ancestors in the wilderness.

The rebellion of our ancestors in the wilderness, following the redemptive rescue from Egyptian servitude, was a recurring pattern. Perhaps the most serious of the rebellions involved the construction of the Golden Calf, but there were countless others, including the waters of strife, the confrontation following the exploratory expedition of the tribal leaders, and the rebellion of Korah and his cohorts.

These are all episodes we would probably rather forget. They reflect negatively on the people's trust in their most dedicated and committed leader, Moshe. It does not do well for the Jew's self-image to constantly be reminded of these incidents.

In spite of these considerations, the Bible specifically urges that we remember and dare not forget all the provocations of the period in the wilderness, between the time of the Exodus and the entry into Israel. Why is it so important to remember?

Remembering is important because of two major considerations. First, if one erases history, there is no way one can ever learn from history. Second, if past breaches are erased, present breaches are encouraged, with the concomitant assurance that present insubordination will soon be relegated to the forgotten past.

But the past must not be forgotten. For just as one can learn much from proper behavior, one can learn at least as much from aberrant behavior. The object of history is not to create false images of righteousness; it is to project realistic images of the truth, and to grow therefrom.

Misconception: The *schlemiel* is a relatively recent construct of Jewish humor.

In biblical times when the tribes of Israel went to war, the tribe of Shimon invariably suffered the greatest losses compared with the other tribes. This was the case even in battles when Israel was victorious.

The leader of that tribe was a man named Shlumeayl. Hence the word *schlemiel* has come to describe an individual who, no matter what the circumstances, seems to have the unique capacity to rescue failure, or something close to it, from the brink of success.

Schlemiel is thus derived from ancient Israelite history.

Misconception: The outstanding figures of Jewish history were free from sin.

It is almost impossible for an individual to go through life without committing a sin. Such an individual would be almost superhuman.

The models to whom we relate, whom we emulate, are individuals who were not perfect in their lifetime. Moses was not perfect, King David was not perfect, King Solomon was not perfect, nor were the other individuals whom Jewish tradition venerates.

In reality, this is a positive feature. If we are asked to live by the standards of individuals who are so removed from our own condition, we could legitimately contend that we cannot. However, the realization that these individuals were capable of sinning, and actually did sin on occasion, but were still outstanding, makes room for all of us imperfect beings.

Sainthood which is free of sin is unrealistic, and ironically is a faulty model.

Misconception: Herod the Great was a great man.

Herod was an individual who had a great appreciation for art and built some beautiful structures. He is even praised in the Talmud for the beauty of the reconstructed Temple, which he built.

However, to brand him as a great man, to call him Herod the Great, is a travesty of justice. Herod was a murderer, a butcher, who killed his wife, his children, many members of the rabbinical court (*Sanhedrin*), and countless others in cold blood.

The more appropriate title for him would be Herod the Great Scoundrel, or Herod the Great Butcher, or Herod the Great Infidel. Calling him Herod the Great does a disservice to every human value that decent society holds sacred.

Misconception: The *Bet Hamikdash* was burned to the ground on *Tish'ah B'Av*.

The Talmud records the date when the fast we know as *Tish'ah B'Av*, the 9th of Av, should take place. This fast is linked to the destruction of the Temple, but that destruction only began on the 9th of Av. The Temple itself did not burn down competely until the afternoon of the 10th. It was resolved in the Talmud that it is more appropriate to fast and mourn on the day that the destruction began.

Even with this, it is customary when *Tish'ah B'Av* occurs in the middle of the week, to refrain from any joyous activities until the afternoon of the 10th of Av. The activities that are prohibited in the week prior to *Tish'ah B'Av* extend until the afternoon of the 10th, because it was in that time period that the Temple's destruction became final.

Misconception: The Western Wall is a remnant of the Temple.

The Western Wall is not part of an actual wall of the Temple itself. It is, instead, a remnant of the retaining wall around the Temple. The wall has been sanctified by history and venerated for the memories it evokes. But it is important to know its precise origins.

Misconception: Gedaliah was killed on the day after *Rosh Hashanah.*

This assumption is probably related to the fact that the Fast of Gedaliah takes place on the day after *Rosh Hashanah,* except when the day after *Rosh Hashanah* is a *Shabbat,* in which case the Fast of Gedaliah is postponed until Sunday.

Gedaliah's murder signaled the end of Jewish autonomy, however flimsy, within Israel. It firmly established the exile of the Jews from their homeland. We fast on that day to lament this very fact, the loss of any vestige of autonomy in Israel.

Gedaliah was murdered on *Rosh Hashanah,* an obviously contemptible act committed on one of the holiest days of the year. However, we refrain from fasting on *Rosh Hashanah,* the New Year festival, when we must be not only sober and serious, but also optimistic and joyous. Fasting is not conducive to such an atmosphere, and the fasting itself is therefore postponed until the day after *Rosh Hashanah.*

Misconception: The zealots of Masada committed suicide.

This is a commonly held belief, reinforced by a television movie on that topic. The basis for the belief that the zealots committed suicide is primarily the historical report of Josephus.

However, Josephus did not see the events of Masada. He only reported them, based on what he claimed he heard from a few people who said they had escaped and hid in a cave.

One may question whether the zealots would have contemplated murder and suicide. They fought to the very end, and then, we are led to believe they did the unthinkable, namely, kill each other and themselves.

Did the zealots murder and kill themselves, or were they killed by the Romans? Murder and suicide have never been the Jewish way and certainly are contrary to a justifiable theological approach.

One does not really know for sure. The entire account is based on such questionable evidence, from a source of dubious reliability, that one doubts the authenticity of the murder and suicide version.

There may be no definitive answers, but there are enough questions to justify the possibility that the Romans murdered the Jews. If indeed this is what happened, Masada becomes an even greater symbol of Jewish resistance and heroism.

Misconception: Christianity evolved from less traditional Judaism.

The original members of the Christian sect were a group among the Jews who withdrew from the world, who sought salvation from the misery of this world and yearned for a messianic redemption. These individuals, originally numbering just a handful, abstained from the delights of the world, engaged in purification exercises, and manifested other behaviors, that were more extreme than the normative Judaism of the day.

The original group from which Christianity evolved focused in extreme fashion on spiritual matters, to the neglect of earthly concerns. Materialism and pleasure of any sort was renounced, and attention was directed to a future life that would vindicate present agony and suffering. This group proliferated, primarily through an aggressive campaign to attract outsiders.

Misconception: Were it not for belief in Jesus, there would be little difference between Judaism and Christianity.

This calls to mind the famous short rhyme:

> Roses are red
> Violets are bluish.
> If it wasn't for Jesus,
> We all would be Jewish.

However, it is a mistake to think that belief in Jesus is all that differentiates Judaism from Christianity. Even in the earlier stages of the split between Judaism and the Christian sect, there were significant differences between Judaism and Christianity.

Christians placed little emphasis on the sanctity of the Temple, negated the commandments, and withdrew from enjoying the delights of this world. In all these manifestations, they clearly set themselves as separate from the mainstream of Jewish thinking, which placed primacy on the Temple, affirmed the obligations of the *Torah* as explicated by the rabbinic sages, and emphasized the importance of being part of this world and partaking of what God had bestowed upon it. These differences are in addition to the primary theological rupture—namely, Christianity's rejection of the absolute oneness of God.

Additional issues such as vicarious atonement in Christianity, as contrasted with the Jewish insistence that each individual is responsible for his or her own deeds, and through appropriate repentance can gain atonement for any wrongdoing, remain as sharp dividing points. In the retrospect of history, it is obvious how significant these differences were, as Judaism and Christianity separated into very different systems.

On balance, it may be said that it was not Jesus who gave birth to Christianity. Instead, it was Christianity that created the idea of Jesus.

Misconception: Maimonides wrote his famous treatise, the *Mishneh Torah*, for scholars.

The treatise referred to as *Mishneh Torah* is a fourteen-volume codification of the Talmud. This work is a major staple of any talmudic study. After reviewing the basic talmudic text, keen students invariably rush to Maimonides to see how he interprets and adjudicates the talmudic discussion. The work of Maimonides offers profound insight into the meaning of the Talmud.

It will therefore come as a surprise to most that Maimonides' purpose in writing the *Mishneh Torah* was quite different from what has developed. He wrote the work in sympathy for individuals who worked hard all day, who wanted to study but simply did not have the time. He set about to condense the talmudic discourse into its coherent, conclusive, and definitive points, so that students would be able to read his work in the limited time available, and glean the essence of the Talmud.

What started off as a condensation of the Talmud has become a text of its own, with its own array of classical and contemporary commentaries, and with more being added all the time.

Misconception: False messiahs are merely blips in Jewish history.

The messianic yearning, the yearning for redemption, was a natural expression for Jews who lived in cruel exile.

It was only natural that Jewish communities living under the harsh yoke of an oppressive government should desire relief from their plight. The hope for messianic redemption was a reaction to this condition.

Quite often, the conditions were ripe for a messianic figure to promise an end to misery. Thus, even one who today would be considered an obvious fraud would be welcomed by a desperate community.

There have been many false messiahs in Jewish history, some of whom have proposed the most preposterous methodologies for redemption, including Jacob Frank's notion of the holiness of sin. He suggested that redemption would come if the people immersed themselves in sin to such an extreme extent and engaged their lust with such totality that they would not want to sin any more, and so would attain the state of holiness and righteousness. This theology actually found more adherents than one would like to believe.

People who live in a free society are not that desperate for messianic relief, and therefore find it hard to comprehend that such figures as the sixteenth century Shabbatai Zvi and the eighteenth century Jacob Frank could have been considered authentic. But their success is nothing more than an accurate reflection of the desperation of the times.

Misconception: Messianic belief is basic to the Hasidic movement.

The Hasidic movement historically came on the scene as a reaction to the false messianic movement led by Shabbatai Zvi. Messianic movements always had political overtones, and maybe because of this, they likewise had devastating consequences. There has hardly been a messianic movement in Jewish history that did not cause unwarranted and severe tragedy, including significant loss of life. The case of Shabbatai Zvi involved thousands of lives.

In the words of the eminent scholar Gershom Scholem, the Hasidic movement was a "neutralization of Messiah." It is not that the Hasidic movement gave up on the coming of the Messiah; it was that the Hasidic movement emphasized the need of each individual to focus on one's own inner self, on the need for personal redemption. Each individual was obliged to do his or her own redemptive work, and leave the rest to the Messiah.

The Hasidic movement turned the focus inward and thus depoliticized the messianic idea. It is hard to believe that today's Hasidim should be so infused with messianic zeal. This is a historical irony, fraught with some of the dangers that the original Hasidic movement sought to address.

Misconception: The words *Jew* and *Judaism* have described the people and their faith since time immemorial.

The patriarch Jacob was named Israel, and his descendants were known as the children of Israel. Since that time, the people themselves were known as Israelites. The changeover from "Israelite" to "Jew," and from "faith of Israel" to "Judaism," came as the result of an explosive event in history.

Rehoboam became king after the death of his father King Solomon. The people, heavily burdened by the taxes imposed by King Solomon, approached the new king with a request for tax relief. They appreciated the great structures that had been built with tax revenue, but it was becoming too much, and they expressed their concerns to the newly appointed monarch.

The new monarch sought the counsel of his advisers, who gave him conflicting advice. The elders among them suggested that the king agree to the wishes of the populace, and by so doing gain their confidence. The younger advisers suggested that by giving in at such an early stage in his reign, the king would be showing weakness.

Finally, after all these deliberations, Rehoboam announced that he would not lighten their burden, but in fact, would actually increase the taxes.

This lack of sensitivity to the people provoked a spirit of rebellion, which led to the establishment of an alternate kingdom under the leadership of Jeroboam. What had heretofore been one community under the rulership of one king was now split into two kingdoms, the Kingdom of Judah and the Kingdom of Israel, each with its own monarch.

Over the course of the years, this split, which originally was a painful rupture and divorce, became more and more entrenched. The Kingdom of Israel set up a rival alternative to the pilgrimage festivals in Jerusalem. The communities drifted apart, even toward antagonism and actual conflict.

The Kingdom of Israel suffered defeat at the hands of the Assyrians; its people were thrust into exile, and became the so-called ten Lost Tribes of Israel. These tribes have disappeared from the scene.

The Kingdom of Judah, however, persevered for a longer period of time, and even though they suffered defeat, first at the hands of the Babylonians, and later at the hands of the Romans, they managed to survive, to maintain their identity and cohesiveness as a community.

The people from the Kingdom of Judah were called Judeans, or, in its short form, Jews. They practiced Judaism, the religion and life affirmation of the Judeans.

The terms "Jew," to describe the people, and "Judaism," to describe the faith, reflect the tragic split of the Israelite community, and the ensuing loss of the ten tribes. Had that split not occurred, Jews today would still be referred to as Israelites.

The terms Jew and Judaism thus are painful reminders of the internal conflict and rupture within the ancient Israelite community.

Misconception: Jews have always been a unified people.

Looking back over the course of history, it is clear that there were very few times in Jewish history when the Jewish people were united. The Bible relates that just prior to the giving of the *Torah* on Mount Sinai, the people encamped as one. They were united in anticipation of the great event. However, it is safe to say that unfortunately the history of the Jewish people since then has been a history of division. There are for example:

- The episode of the Golden Calf
- The debacle of the spies
- The rebellion of Korah
- The splits in the community in the time of the Judges
- The breakdown of the community in the period following the reign of King Solomon, with the subsequent split into the Kingdom of Judah and the Kingdom of Israel
- The later divisions between the Pharisees and Sadducees
- The Jews and the Judeo-Christian sect
- The Karaites
- The *hasidim–mitnagdim* controversy
- The Orthodox–Conservative–Reform divisions
- The false messianic movements and their impact on the community

These and many other splits, all testify to a long history of conflict, and internal division. Occasionally, civil war erupted among the factions, such as occurred in the period prior to the destruction of the second Temple.

One may theorize that the divisions signify a unique strength of the people. Judaism and Jewish destiny mean so much to so many that we have continually argued about Judaism and its interpretation.

However, it is a gross misperception to think that we have survived because we have been a united people. The Jewish people have essentially survived *in spite of* the many conflicts and the prevailing discord, or perhaps because of it. There are few things that strengthen identity more than actually arguing about it.

Misconception: Falasha is an appropriate term to describe a Jew from Ethiopia.

The word "Falasha" is a derogatory term. It means stranger or alien and was a descriptive word used against the Jews of Ethiopia to indicate that they were strangers and aliens, and therefore did not deserve to be considered the equals of other inhabitants of the country.

It is a denigrating term, intended to isolate and vilify. It is inappropriate for us to give any respectability to this heinous attempt at character defamation by using that word as a standard reference to the Jews of Ethiopia. It is a verbal equivalent of the yellow star.

It is best to refer to these people as Ethiopian Jewry, or simply, the Jews of Ethiopia. This is exactly what they are. Hopefully, those Jews who are still in Ethiopia will soon be described as Jews who were from Ethiopia but who are now at home in Israel.

Misconception: Without the Holocaust, Jewish history is intelligible.

There are many who have wrestled with the question of the meaning of the Holocaust and have attempted to understand Jewish history and Jewish destiny in light of the Holocaust. Because of the great emphasis placed on trying to come to grips with the Holocaust, some may be led to assume that without the Holocaust there is hardly any difficulty understanding the vicissitudes of Jewish history.

It may be safely said that the Holocaust was just a culmination, a bitter, tragic culmination of thousands of years of unrelenting trauma and tragedy. Pogroms, crusades, wanton murders, continual exile, and denial of opportunity were the rule rather than the exception. Why did this happen? No one has definitive answers, any more than there is a definitive answer for "Why the Holocaust?" One is hard-pressed to find a precise, coherent answer. To ask why God did it is presumptuous—as if we can discern the intent of God's actions. Even to assume that it was God who did it is presumptuous, if not blasphemous.

Quite likely, having free will requires that the human being has the capacity for evil and for virtue. It is because one has the capacity for evil but turns away to do good that one's good deeds are meritorious. The downside of this is that some people may opt for the evil expression, as indeed has happened too often in history. Evil may be the unfortunate price that we pay for being human.

Why have the Jewish people gone through so much agony and torture over the generations? There are many theories, but no definitive answers. It may be, as the contemporary thinker George Steiner suggested, that it is in the nature of the Judaic message of monotheism with its higher sense of morality. This elicits a negative response from those who disdain or denigrate such a message. Rather than coming to grips with their own failures, they attack the message or the messenger, or both.

Whatever the case, it is not only the Holocaust, but so much preceding the Holocaust, that defies comprehension. We are also not able to adequately explain the sudden death of an individual in the prime of life, or the sudden death of an infant, or the infant who is born with a permanent defect.

Perhaps the ultimate response to all the perplexities that confront us is to be grateful for the good things, to accentuate the positive, the gift of life, and whatever capacity is granted to enhance it.

The issue of theodicy aside, there is a need and in fact a responsibility to affirm life.

Misconception: The creation of the State of Israel is directly related to the Holocaust.

There is absolutely no causal relationship, from a Judaic perspective, between the Holocaust and the rebirth of the State of Israel.

Jews, ever since the first exile, have prayed for the return to Jerusalem. The link between the Jewish people and the land of Israel goes back to time immemorial. What changed after the Holocaust is that world leaders awoke to the horrendous consequences of Israel's protracted exile; they voted to return to the people of Israel the homeland the Jews had never renounced.

Even then, what was given back was merely a fraction of ancient Israel. A Jewish homeland today is not a concession in recognition of Israel's suffering. It is a rectification of a long-standing travesty of justice.

12

It Is Your Business

Relating to Others
The Work Scene
Truth and Lies
Charity
Interest-ing Loans

Misconception: Other people's mistakes or wrongdoings are none of your business.

We are all part of one big family, interrelated and mutually responsible for each other. To be oblivious to others, even as they do things that demand correction, or that can be harmful to themselves and to others, is to be irresponsible. The definition of friendship includes the responsibility to gently and effectively offer timely and vital corrective advice.

Anything less than this is a dereliction of responsibility, a contravention of the obligation to "surely rebuke your neighbor," a denial of the imperative to be concerned and to delicately and sensitively share insights that can help correct or improve.

Misconception: It is better to contain hatred rather than express it openly.

First, it should be stated without equivocation that Judaism does not countenance the hatred of other individuals. There are instances when a person's actions, inconsistent as they are with primary Judaic values, arouse the enmity of the victims of such behavior.

In such circumstances, the individual who is angered by a friend's behavior is asked not to hide it but to share it with that friend. Harboring enmity allows the sore to fester but does nothing to improve the situation. By sharing it, in an open and sensitive manner with the friend, there is at least a chance that the situation will be corrected.

In situations of understandable enmity, those who feel this emotion should try to correct it by directly approaching the object of one's enmity.

Misconception: We must love everyone in the same way as we love ourselves.

To love others as we love ourselves is an impossibility. It is natural for people to love themselves more than others. Additionally, to love everyone else in the same manner as we love ourselves suggests one must assure that everyone else has clothing before one puts on clothing, or that everyone else has breakfast before one eats breakfast.

Such interpretation of the biblical injunction to "love your neighbor as yourself" would wreak havoc with everyone's existence. Instead, this obligation is interpreted in the Talmud to mean, "That which is hateful unto you, do not unto your neighbor." In other words, we are asked to love and appreciate the dignity and the worth of others, as well as their property, in the same way as we value our own. Just as we would not like trespassers on our property or attacks on our personhood, so should we refrain from such behavior to others.

Additionally, from the Talmud it appears that the primary application of this verse in its literal meaning, is toward one's mate, one's spouse. Since husband and wife are perceived to be as one, united in body and spirit, we are obliged to love our spouse as ourselves. Here one can readily apply the dictum of "love your neighbor" with full meaning. One should make sure that one's partner's needs are taken care of before one takes care of one's own needs. It is only one other and therefore easily manageable. By focusing on the other instead of the self, a pleasant atmosphere of kindness and helpfulness is created, rather than the more narcissistic, self-oriented attitude that destroys rather than builds the marriage.

Misconception: There is no obligation to praise others.

The famous biblical obligation to love others as we love ourselves is more than a pious platitude. As with other biblical injunctions, this imperative has direct application to everyday life.

It is practically impossible to love others as we love ourselves. But it is possible, even obligatory, to extend to others the courtesies and respect we would expect for ourselves.

This includes avoiding insult or injury and, on the active side, speaking words of praise to others. This gives others a good feeling, the feeling that emanates from being appreciated and acknowledged. In this way, we fulfill the obligation to love others as we would like to be loved and valued.

Praising others is a fundamental pillar of Jewish life.

Misconception: Speaking ill of others is permissible if it is true.

Obviously, when the statements about others are untrue, speaking ill is wrong on many counts, not the least of which is that the individual is spreading malicious lies.

However, even statements that are true, but malicious, demeaning, or insulting should not be uttered. The category of speech called *lashon hara* (bad speech) refers to statements that are true, but speak ill of others. This should not be part of any individual's lexicon.

If we do not have good things to say about others, we should say nothing.

Misconception: An employer may make employees work as hard as possible.

A person who employs others does not own these individuals. Human beings are not tools to be used however one desires. Human beings have dignity and must be treated accordingly.

Therefore, placing any demeaning or extraordinary demands on an employee is really a contravention of basic Judaic principle.

Misconception: There is nothing wrong with having two or more jobs.

An individual who seeks employment from someone else has an obligation to take that commitment seriously. If it is understood at the time of the original contractual arrangement that the worker will give full energies to the job, then this obligation must be honored. Even staying up late at night and not being able to work to full capacity the following day, contravenes the essence of the arrangement.

The same would apply if the individual assumes another job, for example, a night job to supplement the wages earned during the day. If such activity makes it impossible for the worker to give full value to the original job, then this is a form of misrepresentation that must be avoided.

In situations where the individual needs extra compensation to make ends meet or even to have a nest egg, the appropriate procedure would be to ask the original employer for permission to assume a second job, to avoid any possibility of breach of responsibility.

Misconception: It is acceptable to open a business in close proximity to a similar one.

In a capitalistic system, one is always looking over his shoulder to keep tabs on the direct competition. It is a generally accepted practice that one may open a business wherever one wants. This is hardly questioned on ethical grounds. One may take the risk of opening up a business right next to another just like it.

There are some enterprising business people who will try to protect themselves with clauses guaranteeing them exclusive rights, first options, and the like; but failing that, hardly anyone seems to consider this direct and challenging competition as ethically questionable.

In Jewish law, however, such practice is absolutely forbidden. One is not allowed to open a business similar to the one next door because in so doing, one may cause the other business to fail, and severe financial loss to the other individual. This is a Judaic ethical imperative that enterprising individuals should take into account when they establish the location of their own enterprises.

Misconception: There is no limit to the profit one may make from the sale of an item.

There are many ways in which one can materially afflict others. The most direct means is by either stealing or robbing. However, there are other ways of cheating that are of concern in Jewish law, including extracting excess profits.

Regarding excess profits, the general rule is that one may not charge more than an additional one-sixth of the basic value of the object when selling it to others. This is forbidden and renders the entire transaction invalid.

There is no problem with making a profit, but there is a great problem with taking advantage of others.

Misconception: There is nothing wrong with window-shopping.

It all depends on which side of the window one does the shopping. Certainly there is nothing wrong with individuals walking down the street or through a mall, gazing through the windows and contemplating whether to buy or not to buy.

However, if one has absolutely no intention of buying an item, and just for curiosity goes into a store and asks the storekeeper the price of an item, this is deception. It is deception if the question is asked when, in fact, there is no intention of buying it.

There is nothing wrong with going into a store and saying that you are not prepared to buy the item just now, but are curious and would like to know the price. The storekeeper then has the option of being kind and stating the price, or saying that since you are not interested in buying, he or she is too busy to chat. Giving false impressions is something that must be avoided.

Misconception: The Ten Commandments prohibit stealing.

The eighth commandment prohibits stealing, but the prohibition refers to kidnapping, not stealing material things.

One should not jump to the conclusion that the Bible permits stealing. Stealing is explicitly prohibited, but the verse which prohibits stealing is found elsewhere in the *Torah*. In the Ten Commandments the prohibition against stealing deals with the devaluation of life by reducing individuals to barter for profit-making purposes. This is considered a crime of capital implications, the transgression of which strikes at the very basis of viable civilization.

Misconception: Gambling is forbidden in Jewish law.

In life, it is very difficult to avoid taking chances. The individual who puts a life's savings into a business is taking a big risk. The individual who buys a piece of real estate in the hope that its value will increase takes a chance. The individual who invests in a stock may lose it all, so may the individual who puts a few dollars on a horse or buys a lottery ticket. These are gambles, but they are not criminal behavior by any stretch of the imagination.

Why, then, is there an impression that Judaism prohibits gambling? There are some types of gambling that are prohibited, because they involve taking money from others under questionable pretenses. Two individuals may bet against each other, each expecting to win the bet. The loser, who never expected to lose, is giving away money reluctantly. The winner is taking away money from an individual who never thought it would come to that point. Such gambling is problematic. Putting money into a pot or on a horse, where it is the individual against an institution is another matter, as is indeed the case with the stock market.

The fact that a gambler is condemned as unfit to testify should not be interpreted as a wholesale condemnation of gambling. It is a talmudic condemnation of an individual who engages in *shady gambling* practices, and/or makes no positive contribution to civilization. If the gambling is of such a nature that it is a continual addiction, and the individual engaging in this habit contributes nothing to the betterment of the world, such an individual is not fit to testify and cannot take a rightful place in normative society.

Misconception: It is worse to rob than to steal.

Before pointing out the error of this statement, it is necessary to explain the difference between robbing and stealing.

Stealing refers to taking something from someone in a stealthy fashion. The one who steals attempts to deprive the rightful owner of an item by catching the owner unaware. On the other hand, robbery is more direct. The robber acts in broad daylight and confronts the victim directly.

At first glance, it would seem as if stealing is not nearly as bad as robbing. The one who steals does not confront the other individual bodily, whereas the robber has no respect for the victim and even causes the victim direct anxiety.

Yet, according to Jewish law, one who steals must pay back more than the amount stolen, in fact double the amount of the theft. On the other hand, the robber must only return the object or its monetary equivalent.

The one who steals is dealt with more harshly. Stealing is considered worse, at least insofar as punitive measures are concerned. Why is this so? The Talmud explains this seemingly illogical proposition in the following manner. The robber has no respect for God, is unafraid of God, and at the same time is not afraid of people either. On the other hand, the one who steals is unafraid of God Who has dictated that stealing is forbidden, but he is afraid of human beings, and therefore can only wrongfully deprive others while the others do not see and are unaware. The thief is thus not only morally corrupt, but also at the same time theologically distorted. The thief needs moral and theological rehabilitation, and must pay back double the amount of the theft.

Misconception: Lying is always prohibited.

The truth about lying is that it is to be avoided, but it is not necessarily prohibited.

Certainly, testifying falsely in court is categorically forbidden. However, there are times when an individual must lie for a higher purpose. For example, if telling a lie can save a life, be it the liar's or someone else's, it would be absurd to say that such lying is prohibited. To insist that telling the truth is such a hallowed principle that even life must give way is to have a distorted set of values.

Even changing the truth in order to maintain peace and tranquility within the home is also permitted, even recommended, when unavoidable. Therefore, the biblical language with regard to lying is that one should "keep far away from lying." One should keep far away from lying, as far as possible, but there may be circumstances when one has no choice but to lie, in order to maintain peace or to save life.

Misconception: The obligation to return an object applies only if it had been lost.

The obligation to return lost objects goes beyond the situation of finding something that was lost.

To illustrate, consider the case of a next-door neighbor who leaves an item out in the yard and then departs from the house. Suddenly, a violent rain storm erupts which threatens to severely damage whatever was left outdoors.

The obligation to return a lost object becomes operative in such an instance. Since leaving it out in the rain would destroy it, it would then be "lost" to the neighbor. The obligation to return a lost object is an imperative; the neighbor should take the object in and protect it from the rain.

Additionally, the Talmud sees the obligation of doctors to heal as a fulfillment of the returning of a lost object, in this instance, health, to individuals.

The Jewish lost-and-found institution is thus an all-embracing ethical norm.

Misconception: Giving charity is laudable, but it is purely voluntary.

The Hebrew word for charity is *tzedakah*. The word comes from the word *tzedek* (righteous or just). This conveys the idea that the giving of charity is not merely something optional; it is just and correct. By implication, the failure to give charity is unjust.

Jewish law on the parameters of charity is quite clear. Every individual is obliged to give 10 percent of one's income to charity. It is a form of income tax, a tax on each individual, obliging all to share the bounty, whether large or small, with others less fortunate.

Individuals may choose which charity they consider most worthwhile, but the fact of giving charity is not optional, it is obligatory.

Misconception: The poor are exempt from giving charity.

Even a person who is sustained by community charity must, in turn, give charity. The giving of charity is a *mitzvah* (commandment), and there is no reason why this should apply only to select individuals. Obviously, if by giving charity, the poor man is deprived of the food necessary for survival, then the giving of charity is set aside. But this is a suspension based on extreme circumstance, and no one should see personal poverty as automatic release from the obligation to be concerned about others.

Misconception: It is better to make an outright gift to a poor person than to grant a loan.

In giving charity to others, one must address two components. One must take cognizance of the individual's pocketbook and of the individual's morale. Giving an outright gift addresses the pocketbook, but it does not address the question of morale. Individuals who are dependent on others often feel a sense of despondency, of futility, of low self-worth, for not being able to make it on their own. Sometimes a gift, even though well intentioned and deeply appreciated, has a devastating effect on the recipient's morale.

Therefore, a loan is preferable. The individual still receives the money, given with no strings attached, but the devastating impact of having to take charity is avoided.

Even greater than the gift, asserts the Talmud, is forming a partnership with the poor. The individual with the money gives it to the poor person to form a partnership, and they split the profits of the venture on an equitable basis. The rich man provides the capital; the poor person provides the effort or labor. In such instances, the poor person does not even suffer the ill effects of receiving a loan. The poor person feels uplifted by the vote of confidence from the benefactor who decides to ally himself with the poor person in a joint venture. This is the ideal form of giving, financially beneficial and psychologically sound.

Misconception: It is ideal to grant a loan with no witnesses or contractual arrangement.

By not insisting on witnesses or even on an I.O.U. note, it would seem as if the creditor is showing ultimate trust in the debtor. Such trust would seem to be an ideal expression of faith in human nature, and, specifically, faith in the debtor.

However ideal as it may seem, this is not a recommended practice. The Talmud indicates that granting a loan in such circumstances can be too enticing a prospect for the debtor, who may conveniently forget later on or may deny that the loan was ever made. The creditor thereby places a pitfall, the proverbial stumbling block before the (blind) unsuspecting debtor.

Granted that there are individuals who under no circumstances would ever contemplate such denial and would go to special lengths to remember the loan and to pay it back in good time. However, there are situations when this may not pertain. In order to prevent such explosive situations, which would disadvantage the creditor and sully the character of the debtor, the Talmud recommends that one should never grant a loan without witnesses, a contract, or receipt of some collateral.

Misconception: If a borrower is willing to pay it, then there is nothing wrong with accepting interest.

The charging of interest, or the payment of interest, is absolutely prohibited. It makes no difference that the borrower is willing to pay the interest. Interest is, by definition, a contravention of the basic principles that must govern human relations. Human beings are here to share, not to capitalize on other people's needs and problems.

If one were to allow the borrower the right to waive this moral principle, then this moral principle would become, for all intents and purposes, nonexistent. Any creditor could justify the interest received with the argument that the debtor wanted to pay it.

No such contention can be countenanced, and one counters such a claim with the legal and moral principle that interest is forbidden, no matter how much the debtor wants to pay it.

Misconception: It is acceptable to be extra friendly to one who grants you a loan.

One of the more serious crimes mentioned in the Bible is the charging of interest to individuals who have been granted a loan. Our material possessions are not ours. They are a blessing from God, which we are asked to share with others. The obligations of charity do not demand that all one's possessions be made available to others. However, at no time should the individual exercise ultimate power and control over the money, as if it really belonged to him or her.

One way in which this power or arrogance would be manifest involves the charging of interest for a loan. Granting someone else the favor of use of money is an act of kindness, but it becomes a potential act of cruelty, if the individual will have to pay back not only the money, but also an extra amount that bites into one's financial stability. To use one's money for a charitable act that at the same time demands the beneficiary to pay the benefactor for the privilege of the loan, is to distort the foundations of human concern and empathy, as well as the true understanding of what being blessed by material possessions should imply. To charge interest is to show disinterest in others.

The sages, deeply concerned about this issue, added to this prohibition even expressions that smack of interest, although they are, strictly and legally speaking, not interest. Thus, saying hello to an individual who has granted you a loan could smack of interest. This would be the case if prior to the loan you had never been friendly with the benefactor, and are now acknowledging that individual because of the favor done for you.

This may sound extreme, but one must understand this in the context of the absolute abhorrence of any extra compensation, whether explicit or implicit, that may directly result from the granting of a loan.

Misconception: The *Bet Din* should favor the poor in monetary litigation.

The Jewish court is governed in all instances by the dictates of justice. In a monetary confrontation between a rich person who could afford to lose the case, and a poor person who cannot, the court must not be swayed by emotional considerations, but by the legitimacy of the claims and the arguments.

However, once the court has decided in favor of the rich individual, it can morally persuade that person to show compassion towards the adversary. But the rich individual would be doing this as an act of kindness and charity, not as an expression of fundamental justice.

Sources

Chapter 1   Special Events

page
5   Dobrinsky, H. C. (1986). *A Treasury of Sephardic Laws and Customs*. Hoboken, N.J.: Ktav and New York: Yeshiva University Press, pp. 3-4, 19-20.

6   *Encyclopedia Judaica* (1971). Vol. 12. Jerusalem: Keter, pp. 803-812.

7   Shulhan Arukh, *Yore De'ah* 262:2,4, 266:8.

8   *Ibid.*, 266:10.

9   *Ibid.*, 262:1.

10   *Ibid.*, 260:1.

11   *Encyclopedia Judaica* (1971). Vol. 14. Jerusalem: Keter, pp. 826-827.

12   Shulhan Arukh, *Yore De'ah* 265:1, 261:1, 263:2-3.

13   *Ibid.*, 305:17-18,24.

14   *Ibid.*, 305:1,3.

15   *Ibid.*, 305:17.

16   Shulhan Arukh, *Hoshen Mishpat* 277:7.

17   Shulhan Arukh, *Orah Hayyim* 53:7; Mishnah Brurah, *ad. loc.*, 53, note 33.

18   Shulhan Arukh, *Orah Hayyim* 617:2.

19   Shulhan Arukh, *Orah Hayyim* 53:10.

20   Encyclopedia Judaica (1971). Vol. 4. Jerusalem: Keter, pp. 244-245.

21   Shulhan Arukh, *Orah Hayyim*, 284:4.

22   *Encyclopedia Judaica* (1971). Vol. 4. Jerusalem: Keter, pp. 243-244.

23   Ezra Chapter 10.

24   Shulhan Arukh, *Yore De'ah* 268:2.

26   *Ibid.*, 268:12. Also, Bulka, R. P. (1983). The Psychology of Conversion. *Midstream* 29:32-35.

27   See, for example, Cohen, S. M. (1986). Vitality and resilience in the American Jewish family. In S. M. Cohen and P. E. Hyman, eds. *The Jewish Family: Myths and Reality*. New York: Holmes & Meier, p. 225.

28   Shulhan Arukh, *Yore De'ah* 268:1-4.

29   *Encyclopedia Judaica* (1971). Vol. 10. Jerusalem: Keter, pp. 54-65.

page
30   Shulhan Arukh, *Yore De'ah* 268:2.
31   Exodus 22:20. See also (1965) *Sefer HaHinukh*. Israel: Eshkol Press. No. 63.

Chapter 2   Special Days

35   Shulhan Arukh, *Orah Hayyim* 263:1.
36   *Ibid.*, 272:9.
37   Bulka, R. P. (1987). *The Jewish Pleasure Principle*. New York: Human Science Press, pp. 88–90.
38   Bulka, R. P. (1973). The Role of the Individual in Jewish Law. *Tradition* 13/14: 129–130.
39   Bulka, R. P. (1987). *The Jewish Pleasure Principle*. New York: Human Sciences Press, pp. 88–90.
40   *Encyclopedia Judaica* (1971). Vol. 13. Jerusalem: Keter, pp. 994–1006. A *Dvar Torah* in the course of *Shabbat* services goes back to ancient times. The controversy surrounding the sermon dealt with the language spoken and the content.
41   *Ibid.*, Vol. 15, p. 1248.
42   Talmud, *Shabbat* 113 a–b.
43   Shulhan Arukh, *Orah Hayyim* Chapter 307.
44   *Ibid.*, 296:1. Maimonides, Mishneh Torah, *Laws of Shabbat* 29:1.
45   *Midrash Rabbah*, Leviticus 29:1.
46   Shulhan Arukh, *Orah Hayyim* 588:1; Talmud, *Rosh Hashanah* 32b.
47   Shulhan Arukh, *Orah Hayyim* 581:1; Leviticus 25:9; Numbers 10:9.
48   Shulhan Arukh, *Orah Hayyim* 583:2.
49   *Siddur Ahavat Shalom* (1987). New York: Mesorah Publications, p. 771.
50   Talmud, *Megillah* 7b.
52   Shulhan Arukh, *Orah Hayyim* Chapter 618.
53   *Ibid.*, 616:2.
54   *Ibid.*, Chapters 613, 614, 615.
55   *Ibid.*, 614:2.
56   The prayer of *Yom Kippur*, as of *Rosh Hashanah*, contains the statement that the evil decree is neutralized through repentance, prayer, and charity.
57   Talmud, *Yoma* 85b.
58   *Encyclopedia Judaica* (1971). Vol. 16. Jerusalem: Keter, p. 846.
59   Shulhan Arukh, *Orah Hayyim* 639:2.
60   *Ibid.*, Chapters 530–548.

page
61   *Ibid.*, 669:1. See Bulka, R. P. (1973). *Torah Therapy: Reflections on the Weekly Sedra and Special Occasions.* New York: Ktav, pp. 165–166.

62   Shulhan Arukh, *Orah Hayyim* Chapter 670.

63   Talmud, *Shabbat* 21b.

64   *Ibid.*, Shulhan Arukh, *Orah Hayyim* 671:2.

65   *Encyclopedia Judaica* (1971). Vol. 7. Jerusalem: Keter, pp. 1280–1288.

66   Esther 9:21–22.

67   Talmud, *Megillah* 15a.

68   *Ibid.*, 2a.

69   *Ibid.*, 4a; *Tosafot, ad. loc.*, at bottom of page, starting with the words "Hayav Adam. . . ."

70   Shulhan Arukh, *Orah Hayyim* 690:17; *Mishnah Brurah, ad. loc.*, notes 59 and 60.

71   Deuteronomy 25:19.

72   Shulhan Arukh, *Orah Hayyim* 695:2.

73   Exodus 12:16; Talmud, *Megillah* 10b.

75   Ganzfried, S. (1974). *Kitzur Shulhan Arukh.* Tel Aviv: Sinai Publishing, 111:8.

76   The contract with the rabbi is called *shtar harsha'ah* (transmission of permission, i.e., power of attorney); the contract with the non-Jew is called a *shtar mekhirah* (contract of sale).

77   Shulhan Arukh, *Orah Hayyim* 448:3.

78   Exodus 12:34,39; Deuteronomy 16:3. See also Sforno, in *Mikraot Gedolot* (1951). New York: Pardes Publishing House.

79   Shulhan Arukh, *Orah Hayyim* Chapters 459 and 462.

80   See for example, Bulka, R. P. (1985). *The Haggadah for Pesach.* Jerusalem: Machon Pri Ha'aretz, p. 70.

81   Shulhan Arukh, *Orah Hayyim* 448:3.

82   *Ibid.*, 550:3, 686:2.

83   Regarding the 10th of Tevet, the word *etzem* (that selfsame day) is used (Ezekiel 24:2), as it is for the Day of Atonement (Leviticus 23:29), thus leading to the view cited that it overrides *Shabbat.* See Talmud, *Rosh Hashanah* 18b.

84   See Talmud, *Shabbat* 119b; *Bava Mezia* 30b.

Chapter 3   Care of the Body

89   Bulka, R. P. (1987). *The Jewish Pleasure Principle.* New York: Human Sciences Press, pp. 31–33.

90   *Ibid.*, pp. 29–30, 77–80.

91   See, for example, Lieberman, L. (1987). Jewish Alcoholism and

page

the Disease Concept. *Journal of Psychology and Judaism*
11:165–180.

92   Bulka, R. P. (1987). *The Jewish Pleasure Principle*. New York:
Human Sciences Press, pp. 36–37.

93   *Midrash Rabbah*, Leviticus 34:3.

94   Bulka, R. P. (1987). *The Jewish Pleasure Principle*. New York:
Human Sciences Press, pp. 35–36. Also, *Siddur Ahavat Shalom*
(1987). New York: Mesorah Publications, pp. 14–15.

95   Talmud, *Makkot* 16b; Shulhan Arukh, *Orah Hayyim* 3:17.

96   See, for example, Rosner, F. (1979). Artificial insemination in
Jewish law. In F. Rosner and J. D. Bleich, eds. *Jewish Bioethics*.
New York: Sanhedrin Press, pp. 105–117.

97   Jakobovits, I. (1979). Jewish views on abortion. In F. Rosner and
J. D. Bleich, eds. *Jewish Bioethics*. New York: Sanhedrin Press,
pp. 118–133. Also, Bleich, J. D. (1979). Abortion in halakhic
literature. In F. Rosner and J. D. Bleich, eds. *Jewish Bioethics*.
New York: Sanhedrin Press, pp. 134–177.

98   Rosner, F. (1979). Autopsy in Jewish law and the Israeli autopsy
controversy. In F. Rosner and J. D. Bleich, eds. *Jewish Bioethics*.
New York: Sanhedrin Press, pp. 331–348.

99   Rabinovitch, N. (1979). What is the halakhah for organ trans-
plants? In F. Rosner and J. D. Bleich, eds. *Jewish Bioethics*.
New York: Sanhedrin Press, pp. 351–357. Also, Rosner, F.
Organ transplantation in Jewish law. In F. Rosner and J. D.
Bleich, eds. *Jewish Bioethics*. New York: Sanhedrin Press,
pp. 358–374.

100   Bulka, R. P. (1976). Setting the Tone: The Psychology–Judaism
Dialogue. *Journal of Psychology and Judaism* 1:3–13. Also,
Bulka, R. P. (1986). *Jewish Marriage: A Halakhic Ethic*. Hoboken, N.J.: Ktav and New York: Yeshiva University Press,
pp. 64–70.

101   Talmud, *Avot*, 2:18.

102   Bulka, R. P. (1987). *The Jewish Pleasure Principle*. New York:
Human Sciences Press, pp. 55–65.

103   Talmud, *Taanit* 22a.

104   Bulka, R. P. (1987). *The Jewish Pleasure Principle*. New York:
Human Sciences Press, pp. 41–54.

105   Kaplan, A. (1985). *Jewish Meditation: A Practical Guide*. New
York: Schocken Books.

106   Rosner, F. (1972). Creation versus evolution. *Studies in Torah
Judaism: Modern Medicine and Jewish Law*. New York: Yeshiva
University Press, pp. 194–216.

page
107   *Ibid.*
108   *Ibid.*
109   Talmud, *Pesahim* 64b; *Taanit* 20b.

Chapter 4   Care of the Soul

113   In the Code of Jewish Law, the section dealing with the laws of the house of prayer is titled "Laws of the Bet haKnesset."
114   Shulhan Arukh, *Orah Hayyim* 94:14.
115   *Ibid.*, 62:2. See also, *Ibid.*, 101:4, regarding the main prayer text being recited in the vernacular.
116   Talmud, Berakhot 26b.
117   Shulhan Arukh, *Orah Hayyim* 117:2, 119:1-2.
118   Talmud, *Berakhot* 21a.
119   Shulhan Arukh, *Orah Hayyim* 101:2.
120   *Ibid.*, 133:1.
121   *Ibid.*, 426:1.
122   *Ibid.*, 128:39.
123   Aviner, S. (1983). *Am K'Lavi.* Jerusalem, p. 39.
124   See the appropriate usage in Shulhan Arukh, *Orah Hayyim* 284.
125   Feinstein, Rabbi M. (1959). *Igros Moshe, Orah Hayyim.* New York: Edison Lithographing. No. 38.
126   Feinstein, Rabbi M. (1959). *Igros Moshe, Orah Hayyim.* New York: Edison Lithographing. No. 1. See also, Aviner, S. (1983). *Am K'Lavi.* Jerusalem, pp. 1-2.
127   Leviticus 19:27. See commentary of S. R. Hirsch to Leviticus 19:27 in Hirsch, S. R. (1962). *The Pentateuch: Translated and Explained*, vol. 3. London: L. Honig & Sons, pp. 551-554.
128   *Leviticus* 19:27.
129   Maimonides, Mishneh Torah, *Laws of Tefillin* 4:25-26.
130   Shulhan Arukh, *Orah Hayyim* 27:9.
131   *Ibid.*, 32:1.
132   *Ibid.*, Chapter 26.
133   *Ibid.*, 38:1.
134   Deuteronomy 6:9, 11:20.
135   Shulhan Arukh, *Yore De'ah* 285:1.
136   *Ibid.*, 289:6.
137   *Ibid.*, 288:3.
138   *Ibid.*, 286:3-4.
139   Shulhan Arukh, *Orah Hayyim* 222:1. See also *Siddur Ahavat Shalom* (1987). New York: Mesorah Publications, p. 230.
140   Shulhan Arukh, *Orah Hayyim* 225:1. For a friend one has not

page
      seen in more than thirty days but in less than a year, the blessing recited is *sheheheyanu*. These blessings, as indicated, are for one you are delighted to see.

141   *Siddur Ahavat Shalom* (1987). New York: Mesorah Publications, pp. 230–231.

142   Shulhan Arukh, *Orah Hayyim* 223:1; see Mishnah Brurah, *ad. loc.*, note 2.

143   Shulhan Arukh, *Orah Hayyim* 226:1, 227:1, Chapter 228, Chapter 229. See also *Siddur Ahavat Shalom* (1987). New York: Mesorah Publications, pp. 228–231.

144   Shulhan Arukh, *Orah Hayyim* 223:5.

Chapter 5   Marriage and Divorce

149   Bulka, R. P. (1986). *Jewish Marriage: A Halakhic Ethic*. Hoboken, N.J.:Ktav and New York: Yeshiva University Press, pp. 7–9, 173–177.

150   Talmud, *Kiddushin* 41a.

151   Shulhan Arukh, *Orah Hayyim* 493:1–3.

152   *Ibid.*, 493:2.

153   Dobrinsky, H. C. (1986). *A Treasury of Sephardic Laws and Customs*. Hoboken, N.J.: Ktav and New York: Yeshiva University Press, pp. 39–63.

154   Shulhan Arukh, *Orah Hayyim* 151:1. See also, Feinstein, Rabbi M. (1973). *Igros Moshe, Orah Hayyim 3*. New York: Balshon. No. 30.

155   Shulhan Arukh, *Even Ha'ezer* Chapter 42.

156   *Ibid.*, 34:1.

157   *Ibid.*, 61:1.

158   Shulhan Arukh, *Even Ha'ezer* Chapter 31. See also, *Sefer HaHinukh* (1965). Israel: Eshkol Press. No. 552.

159   Bulka, R. P. (1986). *Jewish Marriage: A Halakhic Ethic*. Hoboken, N.J.: Ktav and New York: Yeshiva University Press, pp. 24–28.

160   Shulhan Arukh, *Even Ha'ezer* 66:1–5.

161   Shulhan Arukh, *Orah Hayyim* 560:2; Talmud, *Berakhot* 30b–31a, and *Tosafot*, top of 31a, beginning with the words *Eitee Kasa*. . . .

162   Shulhan Arukh, *Even Ha'ezer* 62:6–7.

163   Bulka, R. P. (1986). *Jewish Marriage: A Halakhic Ethic*. Hoboken, N.J.: Ktav and New York: Yeshiva University Press, pp. 104–107.

164   *Ibid.*, pp. 106, 218.

page
165   *Ibid.*, pp. 114–129.
166   *Ibid.*, pp. 110–114.
167   *Ibid.*
168   *Ibid.*, p. 103.
169   Aviner, S. (1983). *Am K'Lavi.* Jerusalem, pp. 286–287.
170   *Midrash Rabbah*, Genesis 22:2; Talmud, *Sanhedrin* 58b.
171   Deuteronomy 21:15; Shulhan Arukh, *Even Ha'ezer* 1:10; *Encyclopedia Judaica* (1971). Vol. 4. Jerusalem: Keter, pp. 985–990.
172   Bulka, R. P. (1986). *Jewish Marriage: A Halakhic Ethic.* Hoboken, N.J.: Ktav and New York: Yeshiva University Press, pp. 156–166.
173   Leviticus 21:7. The explanation for the prohibition of a kohen marrying a divorcee seems almost self-evident, though not mentioned in the commentaries.
175   Deuteronomy 24:1. See also *Sefer HaHinukh* (1965). Israel: Eshkol Press. No. 579.
176   Bulka, R. P. (1986). *Jewish Marriage: A Halakhic Ethic.* Hoboken, N.J.: Ktav and New York: Yeshiva University Press, pp. 28–33.
177   *Ibid.*, pp. 30–33.
178   Shulhan Arukh, *Even Ha'ezer* 13:1,4.
179   Shulhan Arukh, *Yore De'ah* 392:2.
180   Deuteronomy 24:1–4.
181   Bulka, R. P. (1986). *Jewish Marriage: A Halakhic Ethic.* Hoboken, N.J.: Ktav and New York: Yeshiva University Press, pp. 136–141.

Chapter 6   *Illness, Death, and Beyond*

185   Shulhan Arukh, *Yore De'ah* 335:1,4.
186   *Ibid.*, 335:4.
187   Talmud, *Berakhot* 10a.
188   Bulka, R. P. (1979). Rabbinic Attitudes towards Suicide. *Midstream*, 25:43–49.
189   Shulhan Arukh, *Yore De'ah* 343:1.
190   Shulhan Arukh, *Orah Hayyim* 222:2–4.
191   Shulhan Arukh, *Yore De'ah* 340:9–12; Felder, A. (1976). *Yesodai Smochos.* New York, pp. 3–4.
192   Shulhan Arukh, *Yore De'ah* 340:8, 38.
193   *Ibid.*, 340:15; Felder, A. (1976). *Yesodai Smochos.* New York, p. 6.
194   Shulhan Arukh, *Yore De'ah* 389:3, 5. See also, Rabinowicz, H. (1967). *A Guide to Life: Jewish Laws and Customs of Mourning.* New York: Ktav, pp. 97–98.

page
195   See, for example, Felder, A. (1976). *Yesodei Smochos*. New York, p. 35.
196   Shulhan Arukh, *Yoreh De'ah* 363:1.
197   Felder, A. (1976). *Yesodei Smochos*. New York, p. 80.
198   Shulhan Arukh, *Yore De'ah* 387:1. See also, Felder, A., *ibid.*, p. 81, who says that the chair should be no higher than twelve inches.
199   Shulhan Arukh, *Yore De'ah* 395:1.
200   *Ibid.*, 400:1.
201   *Ibid.*, 395:1.
202   Felder, A. (1976). *Yesodei Smochos*. New York, p. 83. He cites the view of Rabbi Moshe Feinstein that for one who desires to join his family for Shabbat, traveling even as early as Friday morning may be allowed, if that is the only way to arrive home in time.
203   Shulhan Arukh, *Yore De'ah* 399:13.
204   This is a case of pure nonsense, of an almost superstitious nature, that has no place in the tradition.
205   Felder, A. (1976). *Yesodei Smochos*. New York, p. 90.
206   See for example, Rabinowicz, H. (1967). *A Guide to Life: Jewish Laws and Customs of Mourning*. New York: Ktav, p. 70. See also, Lamm, M. (1988). *The Jewish Way in Death and Mourning*. New York: Jonathan David, p. 140.
207   The same role applies to the thirty-day period, the *shloshim*. See Shulhan Arukh, *Yore De'ah* 343:10.
208   *Ibid.*, 343, note 9 in ShaKH.
209   Feinstein, Rabbi M. (1973). *Igros Moshe, Yore De'ah* 2. New York: Balshon. No. 169 and No. 171.
210   Shulhan Arukh, *Yore De'ah* 374:6.
211   Felder, A. (1976). *Yesodei Smochos*. New York, p. 37.
212   A profound treatment of this subject is offered by Maurice Lamm. See Lamm, M. (1988). *The Jewish Way in Death and Mourning*. New York: Jonathan David, pp. 150–161.
213   Rabinowicz, H. (1967). *A Guide to Life: Jewish Laws and Customs of Mourning*. New York: Ktav, p. 99.
214   Shulhan Arukh, *Yore De'ah* 402:12.
215   Shulhan Arukh, *Orah Hayyim* 568:7; *Yore De'ah* 402:12.
216   Felder, A. (1976). *Yesodei Smochos*. New York, p. 131.
218   Custom cited, for example, in Rabinowicz, H. (1967). *A Guide to Life: Jewish Laws and Customs of Mourning*. New York: Ktav, p. 110, but disputed by many. See also, Felder, A. (1976). *Yesodei Smochos*. New York, p. 130.
219   Felder, A. (1976). *Yesodei Smochos*. New York, p. 126.

page
220 *Ibid.*
221 Talmud, *Sanhedrin* 91a. See also, Lamm, M. (1988). *The Jewish Way in Death and Mourning.* New York: Jonathan David. pp. 221–238.

Chapter 7   Parents and Teachers

227 *Sefer HaHinukh* (1965). Israel: Eshkol Press. No. 33.
228 Epstein, Y. D. (1972). *Sefer Mitzvos HaBayis,* vol. 2, *Kuntrus HaZivug V'haBayit.* New York: Toras HaAdam, pp. 72–73.
229 *Ibid.,* p. 94.
230 Exodus 21:17; Shulhan Arukh, *Yore De'ah* 241:1.
231 Exodus 21:15, 17; Talmud, *Sanhedrin* 66a, 84b.
232 Shulhan Arukh, *Yore De'ah* 241:3.
233 Talmud, *Kiddushin* 31b; Shulhan Arukh, *Yore De'ah* 240:4.
234 Shulhan Arukh, *Yore De'ah* 240:20. Birkay Yosef cites RITBA that depending on the child's development, hitting may be prohibited even prior to *bar mitzvah* age.
235 Talmud, *Ketuvot* 50a; Shulhan Arukh, *Yore De'ah* 251:3, *Even Ha'ezer* 71:1.
236 See Mishnah Brurah to Shulhan Arukh, *Orah Hayyim* 225, note 7.
237 See, for example, Glatt, M. M. (1973). Alcoholism and drug dependence amongst Jews. In A. Shiloh and I. Cohen Selavan, eds. *Ethnic Groups of America: Their Morbidity, Mortality, and Behavior Disorders, vol. 1, The Jews.* Springfield, Ill.: Charles C Thomas, pp. 265–273.
238 Shulhan Arukh, *Yore De'ah* 240:19–20.
239 Talmud, *Bava Mezia* 33a; Shulhan Arukh, *Yore De'ah* 242:1.
240 Shulhan Arukh, *Yore De'ah* 242:30.
241 Shulhan Arukh, *Yore De'ah* 246:5. See also, Feinstein, Rabbi M. (1981). *Igros Moshe, Yore De'ah* 3. Bnai Brak, Israel: Yeshivas Ohel Yosef. No. 74; (1985). *Igros Moshe, Hoshen Mishpat* 2. Bnai Brak, Israel: Yeshivas Ohel Yosef. No. 59.
242 Talmud, *Berakhot* 62a. See also, Bulka, R. P. (1986). *Jewish Marriage: A Halakhic Ethic.* Hoboken, N.J.: Ktav and New York: Yeshiva University Press, pp. 131–132.
243 Shulhan Arukh, *Yore De'ah* 244:1–3.

Chapter 8   Women and Men

247 Maimonides, M. (1964). *The Guide of the Perplexed.* Chicago: University of Chicago Press, pp. 21–61.

page
248   Genesis 21:9-12, 27:1-40, 38:1-30.
249   Judges 4:4.
250   *Siddur Ahavat Shalom* (1987). New York: Mesorah Publications, pp. 18-19.
251   Exodus 21:7-11; Talmud, *Kiddushin* 20a, 41a. See further, Hirsch, S. R. (1962). *The Pentateuch: Translated and Explained*, vol. 2. London: L. Honig & Sons, pp. 297-303.
252   Numbers 27:1-8; Talmud, *Bava Batra* 139b; Shulhan Arukh, *Even Ha'ezer* 112:11.
253   Bulka, R. P. (1986). *Jewish Marriage: A Halakhic Ethic*. Hoboken, N.J.: Ktav and New York: Yeshiva University Press, pp. 192-193.
254   Talmud, *Yevamot* 65b; Shulhan Arukh, *Even Ha'ezer* 1:13. See also, Bulka, R. P. (1987). *The Jewish Pleasure Principle*. New York: Human Sciences Press, pp. 47-49.
255   Deuteronomy 22:22-27.
256   Shulhan Arukh, *Even Ha'ezer* 119:1, 6.
257   Bulka, R. P. (1979). Woman's Role—Some Ultimate Concerns. *Tradition* 17:27-40.

Chapter 9   Food for Thought

263   Nachmanides, in *Sefer HaMitzvot of Maimonides*. Israel: Pardes Publishers, 1959, Mitzvah 1.
264   Bulka, R. P. (1973). The Role of the Individual in Jewish Law. *Tradition* 13/14:124-136.
265   Talmud, *Sanhedrin*, Chapters 4 and 5.
267   *Ibid.*
268   On the *Shabbat* vs. kosher choice, see Shulhan Arukh, *Orah Hayyim* 328:14, among other sources. With regard to one who is sick, the *Shabbat* vs. kosher matter is a more complex issue.
270   Talmud, *Sanhedrin*, Chapter 5.
272   Talmud, *Sanhedrin*, Chapter 5, *Makkot* 7a.
274   Talmud, *Bava Kamma* 84a.
275   Exodus 21:2-6; Leviticus 25:39-43; Talmud, *Kiddushin* 20a.
276   Talmud, *Kiddushin* 40b; *Avot* 1:17.
277   Talmud, *Yevamot* 79a.
278   Talmud, *Makkot* 23b-24a.
279   Bulka, R. P. (1973). The Role of the Individual in Jewish Law. *Tradition* 13/14:124-136.
281   Bulka, R. P. (1973). *Torah Therapy: Reflections on the Weekly Sedra and Special Occasions*. New York: Ktav, pp. 140-142.

page
282   Bulka, R. P. (1976). Honesty vs. Hypocrisy. *Judaism* 25: 209–216.

283   Bulka, R. P. (1987). *The Jewish Pleasure Principle*. New York: Human Sciences Press, p. 22.

284   *Ibid.*, Chapter 5.

285   *Ibid.*, p. 23.

286   Talmud, *Nedarim* 9a; Shulhan Arukh, *Yore De'ah* 203:1,4 and 257:3,4.

287   Talmud, *Berakhot* 12b.

288   Talmud, *Avot* 2:6.

289   Talmud, *Shabbat* 133b.

290   Exodus 24:7.

291   Weiss-Rosmarin, T. (1984). *Judaism and Christianity: The Differences*. New York: Jonathan David, pp. 109–125.

292   Katsh, A. I. (1980). *Judaism in Islam: Biblical and Talmudic Backgrounds of the Koran and Its Commentaries*. New York: Sepher-Hermon Press.

293   I Chronicles 17:21.

294   Exodus 12:2; Talmud, *Rosh Hashanah* 7a.

295   Talmud, *Sanhedrin* 11a.

296   Talmud, *Shabbat* 156a.

298   Talmud, *Sanhedrin* 65a–b.

299   Talmud, *Sotah* 3a; *Eruvin* 41b.

300   Talmud, *Taanit* 8b.

301   Morris, W., and Morris, M. (1962). *Dictionary of Word and Phrase Origins*. New York: Harper & Row, p. 373.

302   *World Book Encyclopedia* (1986). Chicago: Ascot-Fetzen, p. 458. The number 13 as unlucky traces back to the Last Supper, when there were 13 people present.

303   Bulka, R. P. (1987). *The Jewish Pleasure Principle*. New York: Human Sciences Press, pp. 83–84.

304   Shulhan Arukh, *Orah Hayyim* 560:1.

305   *Encyclopedia Judaica* (1971). Vol. 11. Jerusalem: Keter, pp. 687–697.

306   Talmud, *Shabbat* 10b; *Midrash Rabbah*, Leviticus 9:9.

307   Talmud, *Taanit* 22b.

308   Talmud, *Makkot* 21a.

Chapter 10   Thought for Food

311   Talmud, *Gittin* 70a.

312   Bulka, R. P. (1987). *The Jewish Pleasure Principle*. New York: Human Sciences Press, pp. 98–100.

page
314   *Ibid.*, pp. 97–98.
315   Shulhan Arukh, *Yore De'ah*, Chapters 18–25.
317   *Encyclopedia Judaica* (1971). Vol. 5. Jerusalem: Keter, p. 489.
318   Cohen, A. S. (1981). Vegetarianism from a Jewish Perspective. *The Journal of Halacha and Contemporary Society* 1:38–63.
319   Grunfeld, I. (1972). *The Jewish Dietary Laws, vol. 2, Dietary Laws Regarding Plants and Vegetables with Particular Reference to Produce of the Holy Land.* London: Soncino.
320   Bulka, R. P. (1987). *The Jewish Pleasure Principle.* New York: Human Sciences Press, pp. 96–97.
321   Grunfeld, I. (1972). *The Jewish Dietary Laws, vol. 1, Dietary Laws Regarding Forbidden and Permitted Foods with Particular Reference to Meat and Meat Products.* London: Soncino, pp. 106–107.
322   Leviticus 11:7.
323   Nachmanides, *Commentary on the Torah.* Leviticus 11:10, 13.
324   Rashi on Leviticus 20:26.
325   *Midrash Rabbah*, Genesis 65:1; *Encyclopedia Judaica* (1971). Vol. 13. Jerusalem: Keter, pp. 506–507.
326   Feinstein, Rabbi M. (1959). *Igros Moshe, Yore De'ah.* New York: Gross Brothers, pp. 47–49.
327   Shulhan Arukh, *Yore De'ah* 87:4.
328   Talmud, *Hullin* 113a, 116a; Shulhan Arukh, *Yore De'ah* 87:3.
329   Hirsch, S. R. (1981). *Horeb: A Philosophy of Jewish Laws and Observances.* New York: Soncino, pp. 287–288.
330   Grunfeld, I. (1972). *The Jewish Dietary Laws. vol. 1*, Dietary Laws Regarding Forbidden and Permitted Foods with Particular Reference to Meat and Meat Products. London: Soncino, pp. 123–125.
331   Shulhan Arukh, *Orah Hayyim* 451:26.
332   Shulhan Arukh, *Yore De'ah* 87:3.
333   Shulhan Arukh, *Yore De'ah* Chapter 120.
334   Talmud, *Berakhot* 53b.
335   Shulhan Arukh, *Orah Hayyim* 174:1, 177:2.
336   Aviner, S. (1983). *Am K'Lavi.* Jerusalem, p. 255. A table reserved for Torah study would carry the same prohibition as an eating table.
337   Shulhan Arukh, *Yore De'ah* 116:3.
338   Bulka, R. P. (1987). *The Jewish Pleasure Principle.* New York: Human Sciences Press, pp. 73–77.
339   Shulhan Arukh, *Orah Hayyim* 168:6.
340   Talmud, *Berakhot* 40a; *Magen Avraham* to Shulhan Arukh, *Orah Hayyim* 167:18.

Sources

page
341 Maimonides, M. *Mishneh Torah, Laws of Kings* 6:10. See also *Encyclopedia Judaica* (1971). Vol. 8. Jerusalem: Keter, pp. 1110–1112.
342 Leviticus 19:19; Deuteronomy 22:11.

Chapter 11 History from the Beginning

347 Talmud, *Berakhot* 61a.
348 Talmud, *Sanhedrin* 70a–b.
349 Bulka, R. P. (1983). *Torah Therapy: Reflections on the Weekly Sedra and Special Occasions.* New York: Ktav, pp. 3–5.
350 Hirsch, S. R., (1962). *The Pentateuch: Translated and Explained,* vol. 1. London: L. Honig & Sons, pp. 83–85.
351 Genesis 14:13; *Midrash Rabbah,* Genesis 42:8.
352 Exodus 2:1–10.
353 Bulka, R. P. (1985). *The Haggadah for Pesah.* Jerusalem: Machon Pri Ha'aretz, p. 71.
354 Bulka, R. P. (1983). *Torah Therapy: Reflections on the Weekly Sedra and Special Occasions.* New York: Ktav, pp. 191–205.
355 Deuteronomy 9:7.
356 Morris, W., and Morris, M. (1962). *Dictionary of Word and Phrase Origins.* New York: Harper & Row, p. 306.
357 Ecclesiastes 7:20.
358 Talmud, *Bava Batra* 4a. See also *Encyclopedia Judaica* (1971). Vol. 8. Jerusalem: Keter, pp. 375–387.
359 Talmud, *Taanit* 29a.
360 *Encyclopedia Judaica* (1971). Vol. 16. Jerusalem: Keter, p. 467.
361 See Jeremiah 41:1–2 and commentary of RaDaK to 41:1.
362 Weiss–Rosmarin, T. (1967). Masada, Josephus and Yadin. *Jewish Spectator* 32:2–8, 30–32.
363 *Encyclopedia Judaica* (1971). Vol. 5. Jerusalem: Keter, pp. 505–508.
364 Weiss–Rosmarin, T. (1984). *Judaism and Christianity: The Differences.* New York: Jonathan David.
365 We know this from Maimonides's own introduction to his classic *Mishneh Torah.*
366 *Encyclopedia Judaica* (1971). Vol. 11. Jerusalem: Keter, pp. 1417–1427.
367 Scholem, G. (1954). *Major Trends in Jewish Mysticism.* New York: Schocken Books, pp. 325–350.
368 *Encyclopedia Judaica* (1971). Vol. 10. Jerusalem: Keter, pp. 21–22.
370 Bulka, R. P. (1984). *The Coming Cataclysm: The Orthodox-*

page

Reform Rift and the Future of the Jewish People. Oakville, Ont.: Mosaic Press, pp. 83–92.

372   Rapaport, L. (1983). *The Lost Jews: Last of the Ethiopian Fala-shas.* New York: Stein and Day, p. xv.

373   A good overview of Jewish history is found in *Encyclopedia Judaica* (1971). Vol. 8. Jerusalem: Keter, pp. 569–780.

375   *Ibid.*

Chapter 12   *It Is Your Business*

379   Leviticus 19:17–18; Talmud, *Arakhin* 16b.

380   *Ibid.*

381   Leviticus 19:18. See also, Bulka, R. P. (1986). *Jewish Marriage: A Halakhic Ethic.* Hoboken, N.J.: Ktav and New York: Yeshiva University Press, pp. 90–91.

382   Maimonides, M. *Mishneh Torah, Laws of Tendencies* (De'ot) 6:3.

383   Talmud, *Arakhin* 15b.

384   Leviticus 25:39–43; Talmud, *Bava Mezia* 83a.

385   Talmud, *Bava Mezia* 78a–b; Jerusalem Talmud, *D'mai* 7:3.

386   Deuteronomy 19:14, 27:17; Shulhan Arukh, *Hoshen Mishpat* 156:5.

387   Leviticus 25:14; Shulhan Arukh, *Hoshen Mishpat* 227:1–3.

388   Leviticus 25:17; Shulhan Arukh, *Hoshen Mishpat* 228:4.

389   Exodus 20:13; Talmud, *Sanhedrin* 86a.

390   Talmud, *Sanhedrin* 24b; Shulhan Arukh, *Hoshen Mishpat* 34:16, 370:3.

391   Exodus 22:36; Leviticus 5:23; Talmud, *Bava Kamma* 79b.

392   Exodus 20:13, 23:7; Talmud, *Yevamot* 65b.

393   Exodus 23:4; Deuteronomy 22:1–3; Shulhan Arukh, *Hoshen Mishpat* 259:9, 264:4–7, 267:1.

394   Deuteronomy 15:7–11; Shulhan Arukh, *Yore De'ah* 247:1, 249:1.

395   Shulhan Arukh, *Yoreh De'ah* 248:1.

396   Talmud, *Shabbat* 63a.

397   Talmud, *Bava Mezia* 75b; Shulhan Arukh, *Hoshen Mishpat* 70:1.

398   Shulhan Arukh, *Yore De'ah* 160:4–5.

399   Talmud, *Bava Mezia* 75b; Shulhan Arukh, *Yore De'ah* 160:11.

400   Leviticus 19:15.

Glossary

Ayin Hara: the evil eye

Bar Mitzvah: son of the commandment (attained at age 13)

Bat Mitzvah: daughter of the commandment (attained at age 12)

Bet Din: Jewish court

Bet Hamikdash: Holy Temple

Birkat haMazon: grace after meals

Brit Milah: covenental circumcision

Dvar Torah: word of learning, short explanation

Haftorah: Biblical reading from Prophets that takes place on Shabbat mornings, and is also part of the Bar and Bat Mitzvah ceremonies

Haggadah: text read during Passover seder

Hametz: leavened food products, forbidden on Passover

Hanukah: festival of dedication

Havdalah: Saturday evening ceremony at conclusion of Shabbat

Hol Hamoed: days between first and last days of a holiday week

Hupah: canopy under which weddings take place

Kabbalat Hamitzvot: acceptance of commitment for those wishing to convert to Judaism

Kaddish: prayer of sanctification for the deceased

Kashrut: dietary laws dealing with what is kosher

Ketubah: wedding contract between bride and groom (generally artistic)

Kiddush: prayer of sanctification, usually recited over wine

Kipah: head covering worn by men as a reminder of service to God

Kohen: priest during time of Temple, and people descended from them

Lag B'Omer: The thirty-third day of the forty-nine day mourning period between Pesah and Shavuot

Levi: assistant priest during time of Temple, and people descended from them

Maariv: evening prayer

Matzah: unleavened large wafers eaten during Passover

Megillah: scroll of Esther (read during Purim services)

Menorah: seven- or nine-branched candelabra

Mezuzah: encased parchment containing the Shema prayer, affixed to doors of Jewish homes and establishments

Minhah: afternoon prayer

Mitzvah: commandment

Mohel: one who performs circumcisions

Ner Tamid: eternal light (burns continuously in synagogues)

Pesah: Passover

Pe'yot: sideburns

Pidyon Haben: redemption of the firstborn son

Purim: Feast of Lots

Rosh Hashanah: head or beginning of Hebrew year

Shabbat: Sabbath (from Friday evening to Saturday evening)

Shaharit: morning prayer

Shavuot: Pentecost

Sheheheyanu: prayer of thanks to God (who has enabled us to reach this moment)

Shema: prayer that affirms one's faith

Shivah: mourning period after the death of a relative

Shmini Atzeret: eighth day of Sukkot

Shofar: ram's horn (blown during Rosh Hashanah, Yom Kippur services)

Shtiebel: small congregation (sometimes in a private house or storefront)

Siddur: prayer book

Simhah: celebration

Simhat Torah: annual synagogue celebration at the completion of Torah reading and its immediate resumption

Sukkah: tabernacle or dwelling place open to the air for Sukkot meals

Sukkot: Feast of Tabernacles

Tallit: prayer shawl

Tashlikh: New Year's prayer involving the symbolic casting of sins into a body of water

Tefillin: phylacteries (small leather cases containing Torah excerpts worn by men during certain prayers)

Tishah B'Av: day of mourning commemorating destruction of the Temple

Torah: law, part of Bible

Yahrzeit: anniversary of Hebrew date of death of relative

Yizkor: memorial prayer recited in synagogues during holidays

Yom Tov: festival (literally—good day)

Bibliography

Aviner, S. (1983). *Am K'Lavi*. Jerusalem.

Bulka, R. P. (1973). The role of the individual in jewish law. *Tradition* 13/14:124–136.

—— (1976). Honesty vs. hypocrisy. *Judaism* 25:209–216.

—— (1976). Setting the tone: The psychology-judaism dialogue. *Journal of Psychology and Judaism* 1:3–13.

—— (1979). Woman's role—some ultimate concerns. *Tradition* 17:27–40.

—— (1983). *Torah Therapy: Reflections on the Weekly Sedra and Special Occasions*. New York: Ktav.

—— (1983). The Psychology of Conversion. *Midstream* 29:32–35.

—— (1984). *The Coming Cataclysm: The Orthodox-Reform Rift and the Future of the Jewish People*. Oakville, Ont.: Mosaic Press.

—— (1985). *The Haggadah for Pesah*. Jerusalem: Machon Pri Ha'aretz.

—— (1986). *Jewish Marriage: A Halakhic Ethic*. Hoboken, N.J.: Ktav and New York: Yeshiva University Press.

—— (1987). *The Jewish Pleasure Principle*. New York: Human Sciences Press.

Cohen, A. S. (1981). Vegetarianism from a Jewish perspective. *The Journal of Halacha and Contemporary Society* 1:38–63.

Cohen, S. M., and Hyman, P. E., eds. (1986). *The Jewish Family: Myths and Reality*. New York: Holmes & Meier.

Dobrinsky, H. C. (1986). *A Treasury of Sephardic Laws and Customs*. Hoboken, N.J.: Ktav and New York: Yeshiva University Press.

Encyclopedia Judaica (1971). Jerusalem: Keter.

Epstein, Y. D. (1972). *Sefer Mitzvos HaBayis*. 2 vols. New York: Toras Ha Adam.

Feinstein, M. (1959). *Igros Moshe, Orah Hayyim*. New York: Edison Lithographing.

—— (1959). *Igros Moshe, Yorah De'ah*. New York: Gross Brothers.

—— (1973). *Igros Moshe, Yore De'ah 2*. New York: Balshon.

—— (1973). *Igros Moshe, Orah Hayyim 3*. New York: Balshon.

—— (1981). *Igros Moshe, Yore De'ah 3*. Bnai Brak, Israel: Yeshivas Ohel Yosef.

—— (1985). *Igros Moshe, Hoshen Mishpat 2*. Bnai Brak, Israel: Yeshivas Ohel Yosef.

Felder, A. (1976). *Yesodei Smochos*. New York.

Ganzfried, S. (1974). *Kitzur Shulhan Arukh*. Tel Aviv: Sinai Publishing.

Grunfeld, I. (1972). *The Jewish Dietary Laws*. 2 vols. London: Soncino.

Hirsch, S. R. (1962). *The Pentateuch: Translated and Explained*. 6 vols. London: L. Honig and Sons.

―――― (1981). *Horeb: A Philosophy of Jewish Laws and Observances*. New York: Soncino.

Jerusalem Talmud (5 vols.) (1960). New York: Otzar Hasefarim.

Kaplan, A. (1985). *Jewish Meditation: A Practical Guide*. New York: Schocken Books.

Katsh, A. I. (1980). *Judaism in Islam: Biblical and Talmudic Backgrounds of the Koran and Its Commentaries*. New York: Sepher–Hermon Press.

Lamm, M. (1988). *The Jewish Way in Death and Mourning*. New York: Jonathan David.

Lieberman, L. (1987). Jewish Alcoholism and the Disease Concept. *Journal of Psychology and Judaism* 11:165–180.

Maimonides, M. (1959). *Sefer HaMitzvot*. Israel: Pardes Publishers.

―――― (1962). *Mishneh Torah*. 6 vols. New York: M.P. Press.

―――― (1964). *The Guide of the Perplexed*. Chicago: University of Chicago Press.

Mikraot Gedolot (10 vols.) (1951). New York: Pardes Publishing House.

Mishnah Brurah (6 vols.). Jerusalem: Shonah Halakhot.

Morris, W., and Morris, M. (1962). *Dictionary of Word and Phrase Origins*. New York: Harper and Row.

Rabinowicz, H. (1967). *A Guide to Life: Jewish Laws and Customs of Mourning*. New York: Ktav.

Rapaport, L. (1983). *The Lost Jews: Last of the Ethiopian Falashas*. New York: Stein and Day.

Rosner, F. (1972). Creation versus evolution. *Studies in Torah Judaism: Modern Medicine and Jewish Law*. New York: Yeshiva University Press.

Rosner, F., and Bleich, J. D., eds. (1979). *Jewish Bioethics*. New York: Sanhedrin Press.

Scholem, G. (1954). *Major Trends in Jewish Mysticism*. New York: Schocken Books.

Sefer HaHinukh (1965). Israel: Eshkol Press.

Shiloh, A., and Selavan, I. Cohen, eds. (1973). *Ethnic Groups of America: Their Morbidity, Mortality, and Behavior Disorders, vol. 1, The Jews*. Springfield, Ill.: Charles C Thomas.

Shulhan Arukh (10 vols.) (1965). New York: Otzar Halacha.

Siddur Ahavat Shalom (1987). New York: Mesorah Publications.

The Holy Scriptures (2 vols.) (1955). Philadelphia: Jewish Publication Society.

The Midrash (10 vols.) (1961). Freedman, H., and Simon, M., eds. London: Soncino Press.

The Talmud (18 vols.) (1961). Epstein, I., ed. London: Soncino Press.

The Talmud (20 vols.) (1965). New York: Otzar Hasefarim.

Weiss-Rosmarin, T. (1967). Masada, Josephus and Yadin. *Jewish Spectator* 32:2-8, 30-32.

—— (1984). *Judaism and Christianity: The Differences.* New York: Jonathan David.

World Book Encyclopedia (1986). Chicago: Ascot-Fetzen.

Index